Theories of Imperialism:

WAR, CONQUEST AND CAPITAL

NORMAN ETHERINGTON

CROOM HELM
London & Canberra

BARNES & NOBLE BOOKS
Totowa, New Jersey

for Peggy

Croom Helm Ltd, Provident House, Burrell Row,
Beckenham, Kent BR3 1AT

Croom Helm Australia Pty Ltd, 28 Kembla St.,
Fyshwick, ACT 2609, Australia

British Library Cataloguing in Publication Data

Etherington, Norman
Theories of imperialism: war, conquest and capital
1. Imperialism
I. Title
325'.32 JC359

ISBN 0-7099-0927-6

First published in the USA 1984 by
Barnes and Noble Books
81 Adams Drive
Totowa, New Jersey, 07512

Library of Congress Cataloging in Publication Data

Etherington, Norman.
Theories of imperialism

1. Imperialism-History. I. Title.
JC359.E83 19:4 325'.32 83-21381
ISBN 0-389-20444-7

Printed and bound in Great Britain

CONTENTS

PREFACE AND ACKNOWLEDGMENTS

The best way to explain my purposes and acknowledge my debts is to explain how I came to write this book. It is the result of an unexpected conjuncture of teaching and research interests. As a teacher of British and African history in the early nineteen seventies, I was becoming increasingly dissatisfied with the way the 'classic' theories of imperialism had been applied to the historical study of European colonial empires. Like many of my colleagues, I kept in my filing cabinet a little series of lectures on the Scramble for Africa which never failed to please students. In the first lecture I would expound the theories of imperialism. In the next two lectures I would look at the 'facts' about the partition of Africa. A final lecture pointed up the manifold ways in which the theories 'failed to fit the facts'. To reinforce the lesson, I required the students to read any one of several anthologies of readings on imperialism specially designed for undergraduates. My growing dissatisfaction with this popular section of my courses on Africa and empire stemmed from the preparation I did before lecturing each year. I went beyond the assigned readings and read in their entirety the works which were selectively quoted in the anthologies. The works of Lenin, Hobson and Schumpeter which were emphasised in these books said surprisingly little about the partition of Africa and other important episodes in the expansion of nineteenth-century colonial empires. The germ of the idea that the first theories of imperialism were not intended to account for the growth of those empires began to sprout when I read an elegant article by Eric Stokes which expressed similar doubts.[1]

Stokes limited his attention to the central European and Bolshevik theorists Hilferding, Lenin and Bukharin. He did not explain why or how historians had come to misread the

1. Eric Stokes, Late Nineteenth Century - Colonial Expansion and the Attack on the Theory of Economic Imperialism : A Case of Mistaken Identity? *Historical Journal XII* (1969) 285-301.

socialist theorists. A possible explanation was suggested to me by an apparently unrelated research project I had been carrying on in a desultory fashion for several years. As an undergraduate student I had written a rambling, highly unoriginal honours thesis about British socialists' attitudes to the Boer War. In the course of that work I had come across a few passages in the journal of the Social-Democratic Federation which vaguely anticipated later socialist critiques of colonialism. Eight years later I followed up that lead in later volumes of the journal[2]. By 1902 British socialists were citing 'Comrade Wilshire' in America as the leading expert on the connection between capitalism and imperialism. The name Wilshire was unfamiliar to me except as a boulevard in Los Angeles. I decided to track him down in 1974 on my sabbatical leave in London. I discovered that not only were the originator of the boulevard and the socialist comrade one and the same person, but also that Wilshire had written in 1900 a brief account of "surplus capital" as a factor promoting armed rivalry among nations. His argument was so similar to that put forward by Lenin in 1916, that I suspected some direct connection between them. This research languished, however, after my return to Australia where I pursued my studies of southern Africa. In 1977, my colleague F.S. Zuckerman pushed me into attending a conference I did not wish to attend and giving a paper on Lenin's precursor Wilshire. This moved me to search for the missing link between them. The conclusion of my search was that there was no personal connection. The explanation for the similarity between their theories of imperialism lay elsewhere.

Rereading my copies of *Wilshire's Magazine,* I found that the American socialist had drawn his argument from financial journals published in his own country. Reading the *Notebooks* which Lenin compiled in his research for *Imperialism, the Highest Stage of Capitalism,* revealed that he too made copious use of capitalist sources. Could it be that the precursor of

2. Norman Etherington, 'Hyndman, the Social-Democratic Federation and Imperialism', *Historial Studies XVI* (1974) 89-103.

every socialist theory of imperialism was a capitalist theory expounded in obscure journals of financial and economic opinion? England suggested itself as a test case. Selective reading of the journals which J.A. Hobson knew as a working economist would show whether he was similarly influenced. The test was positive. It also closed the circle of my initial research. There in Hobson's celebrated work, which I had read two or three times before, was a clear reference to Wilshire and his work on imperialism. Every previous researcher had passed it over because Wilshire was unknown and Hobson's footnote unhelpful. By this time, I was ready to present a preliminary public statement of my conclusions, i.e. the reason that it was wrong to apply the classic theories of imperialism to nineteenth-century empire-building was that these theories had their ultimate origin in policy recommendations made by capitalists at the turn of the century. The slogan which seemed to best express my message at the time was, 'theories of imperialism were intended to predict the future, not to explain the past'.

Needing a platform, I sought the help of my first teacher in imperial studies, Robin W. Winks of Yale University who had never let me down before and whom I knew as a man who unfailingly welcomes new ideas. He found me a place on the programme of the American Historical Association Convention in December, 1978 and a marvellously sympathetic Chairman, John S. Galbraith of U.C.L.A., who drew my attention to H.N. Brailsford as a neglected theorist of imperialism. My commentator from the left wing of academic opinion was Martin Sklar from Chicago who, I discovered, had been working for years on the American capitalists who first discovered the 'necessity' of imperialism as an 'outlet for surplus capital'. My other commentator was D. R. Sar Desai of U.C.L.A. who encouraged me to look at Asian aspects of the problem. A.P. Thorton of Toronto offered encouragement and Shula Marks of London University invited me to try my thesis out on an English audience, which I did in March, 1979. All this encouragement seemed to indicate that a book would be a feasible proposition. The book would aim to persuade historians to join me in throwing away our lectures which purported to test theories of imperialism against the 'facts' of nineteenth-century colonialism. It would argue that all the little books of readings on 'the imperialism problem' should be scrapped and not replaced, because they were founded on a misconception. It would show that colonialism, imperialism, and the expansion of capitalism were not synonymous. Doing all these things would require tracing the career of theories of imperialism from their origins in the eighteen nineties down to the present.

Two avenues of research opened before me. Either I could attempt a comprehensive survey of all countries and all fields, or I could proceed as before, following a thread of clues from place to place. The first avenue was unappealing. My object was to clear away undergrowth which impeded progress in the field of research I like best - colonial history. A comprehensive survey would take years, maybe decades, and prevent me from getting on with my own pleasures as a historian. So I took the second avenue and picked up the thread where I had dropped it in 1919. Taking this path meant that the book would light up the terrains I knew best - Africa and the British Empire and Commonwealth. Someone else, starting from a vantage ground in Latin American, Asian or French history would have followed a different set of clues and travelled over other terrains. My hope, however, is that, whatever the starting point, the ultimate destination would be the same. I planned a short book of perhaps 100 pages. That it grew to more than twice that length is partly due to the complexity of the materials I met while following my thread of clues into the inter-war and post-war periods. Partly it is due to encounters with disbelievers. An article expounding my reinterpretation of the original theories of imperialism was sent to three eminent journals of history. One, *History and Theory,* agreed to publish it virtually as submitted. The second, the *American Historical Review,* consulted an astonishing six different readers before a weight of critical opinion settled on the negative side of the balance. The opponents of publication could not accept my assertion that Schumpeter and the other central European theorists of imperialism were not principally concerned with Victorian colonial empires; they demanded more evidence. The critics consulted by the third journal *(The Journal of Modern History)* divided on the merits of the article. One reiterated that Schumpeter had indeed written a tract on the growth of the British Empire. The other felt I had spent too much time on Schumpeter because 'anyone who has read Schumpeter even casually realises that by contrasting German and Austrian "atavistic" imperialism, he does not mean the partition of Africa'. Faced with this and other contradictory advice, I have felt compelled to introduce more supporting quotations and citations than I had at first thought necessary. In the course of this work I developed another slogan to express my conclusions, i.e. theories of imperialism which originated as the policy recommendations of capitalists were turned into accounts of history by later writers who assumed that what capitalists wished to happen did happen.

The book is written with two audiences in mind. On the one hand, it addresses graduate students and academics in the fields of history, economics, sociology and geography. On the other hand it is designed to be read and understood by students and laymen with no previous knowledge of imperialism. (It has been pretested on such an audience. My wife Peggy Brock has read it all, correcting typographical and other errors.) In the later stages of writing I have also benefitted greatly from the critical advice offered by fellow workers in the field of African studies, notably Andrew Roberts, Michael Twaddle, Jeffrey Butler, Deryck Schreuder and Leonard Thompson. To all these, and to my students who suffered through the vicissitudes of my developing opinions about the classic theories, I offer my sincerest thanks.

INTRODUCTION

There is a black stone in Mecca which stands at the centre of the Mohammedan faith, the goal of unnumbered millions of pilgrims. The average pilgrim is not interested in knowing how the stone came to stand there. To see it and to march reverently around it are sacred duties laid down by the Prophet. The best way for an infidel to discover what the stone means to the pilgrims is not to look at the stone. It is to look at the pilgrims at home with their postcards of Mecca or at prayer in the mosque proudly wearing the white cap of the *Haj.*

A tiny fraction of people - religious thinkers and scholars - will be curious to know more about the stone than its present meaning to the faithful of Istambul or Jakarta. According to their individual tastes and fields of study, they will adopt different methods of investigation. A religious mystic might seek the truth by contemplating the stone. A systematic theologian would be more likely to search the *Koran* and commentaries written by holy men. A historian, on the other hand, will aim to understand what the stone has meant to different people in changing social situations over many hundreds of years. This approach leads to the interesting discovery that Muhammad did not put the stone in Mecca. Long before he was born it played a vital part in the ritual observances of a local religion very different from the universal creed proclaimed by the Prophet. The meaning of the stone to that vanished local religion can no more be discovered by questioning modern pilgrims than the original meaning of temperance can be discovered by questioning members of the Women's Christian Temperance Union. Philosophically-minded historians draw a moral from this kind of investigation. Seeing that the social meaning of things - even hard physical things like stones - changes with the passage of time, they conclude that the starting point of any discussion of any phenomenon in history must be a clear understanding of what the phenomenon has meant to particular people at particular times.

The word imperialism, like the black stone in Mecca, has been around long enough for its meaning to have shifted many times. Millions of living persons have heard of imperialism and could probably define it after reflecting for a moment or two. Definitions would vary from person to person but most would probably include in some form or another the idea of rich, powerful developed countries dominating weak, underdeveloped countries. Most people have no need to probe deeper than this ordinary usage. But the curious minority inevitably want to know more and resort to their favorite tools of investigation. Political scientists have classified the forms of domination in a search for useful definitions and regular patterns of behaviour. Economists have studied the economic means and results of domination. Historians have examined the process of domination over time.

Historians who have looked at the definitions given to imperialism in different eras reveal that it has been a very shifty word. For example, one hundred and thirty years ago the word was used in England to describe the dictatorial form of government practised by the emperor Napoleon III of France.[1] In the eighteen nineties the word was sometimes used to refer to the attempt made by Germany to create a closed economic system, self-sufficient in essential raw materials for industry and protected from foreign competition by high tariffs.[2] In 1917 the founder of the Bolshevik revolution in Russia called imperialism 'the highest stage of capitalism'. By the nineteen fifties the word was used almost exclusively to describe the process of getting and keeping colonies. Faced with this bewildering assortment of meanings historians have suggested from time to time that the word

1. W.L. Langer, *The Diplomacy of Imperialism* 2nd ed. (New York, 1951) 67. R. Koebner and H.D. Schmidt, *Imperialism, The Story and Significance of a Political Word 1840-1960* (Cambridge, 1964) 1-26.

2. See for example, W.A.S. Hewins, *The Apologia of an Imperialist* (London, 1929), Chapter One : 'The New Imperialism'.

imperialism be dropped from serious academic discussions. This suggestion was first made about fifty years ago. Almost everybody who has ever heard this advice has ignored it. People will continue to ignore it so long as the word imperialism is commonly used. Banning it from discussions is about as practical as banning ghosts from the dictionary because they don't exist.

Understanding the shifting meanings of imperialism is made doubly difficult by the many theories of imperialism which have been invented in the twentieth century. A theory of imperialism is an attempt to find in the apparent chaos of international relations a regular pattern which arises from one or a few basic causes. In other fields of history attempts like these to find regularities in human behaviour have given extra spice and meaning to research by stimulating debate. The maker of any plausible theory has to offer at least some evidence to support it. Scoffers and sceptics spring up to claim that the evidence is false or inadequate. They may produce counter-evidence of their own. In reaction, the defenders of the theory collect more evidence. The clash of adverse opinions stimulates research into neglected corners of the historical record and ensures that every new piece of evidence, *pro* and *con,* is given a thorough examination. However, all these good things will happen only if the makers and testers of theories agree on the terms of the debate. If they are confused about what they are testing, their debates are likely to be sterile and pointless.

This has been the trouble with most of the historians' debates about imperialism. Confusion has arisen for several reasons. One problem has been the shifty, changing meaning of the word. Another problem is that the first theorists of imperialism in the twentieth century were not historians trying to understand the past. They were economic and political thinkers trying to understand the present in order to predict the future. It was twenty-five years or so before historians first took up imperialism as a concept for explaining the past. A third problem is that much so-called 'debate' about imperialism has been a dialogue between the living and the dead in which the dead cannot answer back. If the early twentieth-century theorists of imperialism could be resurrected to face their latter day critics, they would howl and sneer at many of the things that have been said about them. A fourth problem is the familiar problem of bias in history. What people have written about imperialism reflects their profoundest convictions about man and society, in other words, their ideology. Political purposes, often unstated, have motivated many if not all of the investigators of imperialism. All four of these problems have created confusion in the application and testing of theories of imperialism. In one extreme case historians tried to test a theory devised to explain the coming of the World War I by investigating the reasons why Britain acquired colonies in Africa between 1880 and 1900.

Notwithstanding all the problems and confusion, imperialism is worth the attention of historians. There are still people who are willing to kill and die because of their beliefs about imperialism just as people were once willing to kill and die for possession of the black stone in Mecca. Something worth dying for is worth writing about. It is not an impossible task provided it is approached in the right way, the way historians preach more than they practise. Problems of definition, methodology and ideology are so many explosive mines buried beneath the historical terrain which stretches between us and the first discussions of imperialism in the nineteenth century. A sensible historian named Richard Koebner realised a few decades ago that the proper thing to do was to start in the Victorian era and study how the meaning of the word changed over time.[3] In this way every theoretical mine in the field could be successively charted, labelled and defused or exploded. Unfortunately Koebner died before he had even finished charting all of the eighteen nineties. As a result he was unable to say anything very authoritative about

3. His unfinished work on the subject is brought together in Koebner and Schmidt, *op.cit.* Less than 80 of the book's 341 pages concern the twentieth century.

the meaning ascribed to imperialism by the various theorists of the twentieth century.

This book is an attempt to chart a little bit more of the minefield by looking at theories of imperialism in their original historical context and then looking at their subsequent uses and misuses. The book is not concerned with proving the truth or falsity of any of the theories or with developing an alternative explanation of 'what caused imperialism'. If it succeeds in its purpose it will replace some confused, pointless debates with clear, useful ones which will light up neglected areas of research.

Because of its very nature, this book cannot begin with a definition of imperialism. In the first decade of the twentieth century, the word was commonly used to refer not only to despotic methods of government and empire building, but also to the policy of employing the power of the armed state to secure economic advantages in the world at large. Other definitions emerged in subsequent decades. For the moment it is enough to notice that the common element in almost all the present and past uses of the word is a reference to domination - domination of man over man, country over country, man over threatening circumstances. The subject then is power, a subject as central to historical studies since the Renaissance as the black stone of Mecca is to the Moslem faith. In recent years historians have found new objects of study - daily life, the organisation of cities, the family, sex and the psyche - but much of history continues to be what Edward Gibbon said it was two hundred years ago : 'little more than the register of the crimes, follies and misfortunes of mankind'. In our bloodstained century, dealing with the crimes, follies and misfortunes of nations means dealing with imperialism.

CHAPTER 1
AMERICA'S FIRST CAPITALIST THEORY OF CAPITALIST IMPERIALISM

In his study of what imperialism meant to Englishmen in different historical periods, Richard Koebner got as far as showing that two words, empire and imperialism had different pedigrees. The British Empire had once meant simply the united territories of England, Wales, Scotland and Ireland. As overseas colonies were added to the British isles, the meaning of empire expanded to include them. Imperialism, on the other hand, had a sinister past bound up with strutting dictatorships, contempt for liberty and a lust for military glory. It did not have anything to do with colonies. In the middle years of Queen Victoria's reign, it was perfectly possible for patriotic, freedom-loving Englishmen to love the British Empire while simultaneously hating imperialism and praying that it might never cross the English Channel to threaten their homeland.

By the eighteen nineties, however, the words were beginning to get mixed up. People who opposed any further additions to Britain's colonies were calling the advocates of expansion imperialists. Some expansionists were beginning to accept the name of imperialist and to wear it as a badge of pride instead of shame. Koebner believed that the South African War (1899-1902) swung the balance of meaning sharply back towards the unfavourable connotations of imperialism. He particularly blamed the English economist John A. Hobson for spreading the idea that the South African War with all its horrors — burning civilian farms and putting women and children in stinking concentration camps — came about because of the self-interested manipulations of a little clique of capitalist investors.[1] Koebner also believed that Hobson's idea was taken up by foreign socialists and

1. Hobson, author of *Imperialism a Study* (London, 1902) is made to bear an unfair load of blame. Koebner falsely identifies him as having had 'a close affinity to Marxism' and having 'upheld determinism'.

communists who made it part of their worldwide propaganda against capitalism.

Koebner was partly right and partly wrong. Hobson's study of imperialism has had an enormous impact on later socialists. But Hobson did not invent the idea that capitalists would benefit from imperialism. Capitalists invented that idea. Koebner missed discovering the capitalist inventors of the idea because he did not look into the financial journals which capitalists read and because he failed to look closely enough at the United States.[2] Taking up the trail where Koebner missed it requires leaving England and moving to Boston, Massachusetts in 1898, the year of the Spanish-American War.

In May of that year the Bostonian editor of the weekly newspaper *United States Investor* announced his sudden conversion to the cause of 'imperialism'. The editor makes an ideal source for contemporary American notions about imperialism not only because he suddenly changed his opinions but also because he particularly emphasised that 'imperialism' was a 'word new to our political vocabulary, a word which had lately been on everyone's tongue'.[3] His use of the word was therefore likely to conform to the very latest American usage.

The editor of the *Investor* changed his mind about imperialism when he realised that contrary to almost everyone's expectations the war was good for business. Before the declaration of war the *Investor* along with virtually the whole of the American financial press had hoped for peace.[4] Saving oppressed Cubans from the atrocious rule of the senile Spanish empire did not seem to be a principle worth fighting for. In April, 1898, the editor wrote that the situation was 'humiliating to an extraordinary degree' : fighting 'a nation incapable of coping with us, we fight in the name of

2. Koebner and Schmidt, 236-37 give a confused account of American writing in which key names are misrepresented and sometimes misspelled.

3. *United States Investor* 21 May 1898, 72.

4. Julius Pratt, *Expansionists of 1898*, (Baltimore, 1936).

humanity, and are the occasion of added wretchedness to suffering humanity, and in the end we find ourselves confronted with the problem of what to do with Cuba'.[5] From the commercial point of view the editor expected war to result in 'a paralysis of all kinds of business, in cancellations of orders, in the shortening of time in the mills, in the reduction of earning capacity on the part of the masses'. If, the *Investor* concluded with proper Bostonian prudence, 'we impoverish ourselves, we cannot be of great assistance to downtrodden humanity elsewhere'.

Two weeks later, after Commodore Dewey had captured Spain's Pacific fleet at Manila Bay, the editor confessed to a surge of patriotic pride. Dewey had 'effectively disproved the theory that we are not as efficient in war as in peace'.[6] He added that once 'the mind has habituated itself to the thought that we have at last entered the arena of international politics, the effect is perhaps not altogether unpleasing'. After a further two weeks the *Investor* took up the profit-making aspects of war under the headline : 'The Benefit of the War to Commercial and Financial Interest — How the Thing Will Work'.[7] The most beneficial effect of war would be 'in stimulating financial and commercial confidence among ourselves, and in killing the distrust of venturing in many enterprises, which has been far too prevalent during the last decade'. For most of the eighteen nineties the American economy had been under a cloud. First there had been a panic on the stock exchange followed by a major recession. Then had come worries in 1896 that the radical Populist Party and Free Silver Democrats would succeed in electing William Jennings Bryan as President and bring about a deliberate inflation of the currency which would, in turn, severely reduce the profits made by investors, bankers, and other

5. *U.S. Investor* 28 April 1898, 592.

6. 7 May 1898, 657.

7. 21 May 1898, 707-708, 720-21. See also 'War and the Railroads', 16 July 1898, 1006.

lenders of money. The editor believed that worried investors had sat on their money or sent it to other parts of the world, and that this withdrawal of investment capital had delayed America's economic recovery.

War had come along just at the right time to stimulate the economy by giving large amounts of the taxpayers' money to important industries. The *Investor* could 'safely say that the greater proportion of the money expended by the government comes back to the people': people such as 'the shipyard at Newport News, Va.', which was helping to build the new American navy, 'the great Carnegie and other steel works in Pennsylvania' which made the steel to build the ships, 'ammunition works, ordnance works, cloth factories, clothing makers and other concerns supplying uniforms' to the army, along with food contractors and coal mines. 'Thus we see', the editor concluded, 'that the government in appropriating money for war is really spending most of it in benefiting American industries, and in causing an extraordinary stimulus to business in many branches. The fact is, many imagine a war to be far worse than it really is'. From a commercial point of view that is. Leaving aside the killed, the wounded and the homeless, the *Investor* believed that 'so far as the avowed purpose of the war — the relief of the reconcentrados — is concerned, it has been, and must continue to be, a dismal failure'.

No matter. Whatever the original causes and aims of the war, it had undeniably 'accomplished great things for the country, in removing that depression of spirits which has hung like a pall over the entire American people for the last five years'. In the weeks and months that followed, the *United States Investor* discussed the policy which might help to make prosperity permanent : the policy of 'imperialism'. When, on May 28th the editor weighed up the 'Pros and Cons of "Imperialism"', he identified the pro-imperialists as 'those who favor a broader international policy on the part of the United States'. The *Investor* was vague about the precise details of 'a broader international policy' except to say that 'we should have to maintain a powerful navy and army', and that 'we should have to nominally abandon the Monroe Doctrine'. The reason stated for giving up President Monroe's seventy-six year old warning to Europe that the United States would not tolerate the influence of Old World Powers in New World affairs was that 'we could not trench on what other people consider their preserves, and with decency insist that they should keep out of our "sphere of influence"'. The purpose of building up a big military establishment was partly to counter the hostilities the United States would arouse by its 'participation in the affairs of the other hemisphere' and partly to curb the rambunctious individualism of the average American citizen.

The fact that we should have to maintain a powerful navy and army is not without its compensation. The thought of a big navy and a big army constantly employed in warlike measures would be abhorrent. But such institutions on a peace footing — that is the footing they would practically be on all the time — might be made of immense every-day service to the country. The chief danger to a democracy is a too great freedom from restraint, both of action and of thought. European experience demonstrates that the army and navy are admirably adopted to inculcate orderly habits of thought and action.

In June 1898 the *Investor* amplified and clarified the purposes of this new policy of national discipline and armed swagger in an article on 'The Struggle For Existence'. The editor explained that the reason 'so many of the staid commercial papers of the United States are now advocating "imperialism"' was 'not because the people who conduct these have suddenly become crazyheaded sentimentalists'. It was because 'they have subordinated sentiment to the stern facts of the great world struggle for existence'.[8] The sternest of stern facts was that 'the one great need of the world today is new markets'.

Alexander sighed for new worlds to conquer, but his eagerness was far less intense, because it sprang far less from necessity, than that which now characterises the commercial nations of the globe. If the capital at present in employment throughout the civilised world is to be kept at work, an enlarged field for its product must be discovered.

8. 18 June 1898, 872-73.

This was the first time that the *Investor* had mentioned 'necessity'. Previous discussions of war, armaments and 'a broader international policy on the part of the United States' had presented 'imperialism' as an option with attractive possibilities. Now it was presented as something more compelling than Alexander's hunger for world-wide domination. This key note of 'necessity' with its 'stern facts' and 'musts' grew more pronounced as the paper developed its position on imperialism.

So too did the emphasis on the 'employment of capital'. The *Investor* perceived an intimate connection between investment and markets. The exchange of goods produced profits or capital, part of which was used to produce more goods which in turn had to be sold. In June 1898 the *Investor* believed that a new field needed to be found for both (1) the growing flood of goods produced by 'the great commercial nations of the globe', and (2) the investment of profits made in the course of previous production and trade. The *Investor* stated further that the new 'field lies ready for occupancy. It is to be found among the semi-civilised and barbarian races'. In particular the editor singled out China as the outstanding available field for the realisation of profits from future trade and investment. At the moment 'the great powers of Europe' were 'getting ready to dominate that vast empire under one form or another, and their motive is in each case the extension of trade'. The first task of American 'imperialism' was to see that 'no nation should be allowed to acquire commercial privileges in China which are withheld from us'. One way of going about that business was to build up a big army and navy which 'the great powers' would have to take seriously, and to station part of it in the Philippine Islands.[9]

The editor had come a long way since April when he had worried about 'the problem of what to do with Cuba'. Now he took it for granted that America would keep her recent conquests. 'It may', he wrote, 'be repugnant to us to hold the Philippines and Porto Rico, but we should have thought of

9. 13 Aug. 1898, 1145.

that before we went to war'. The main purpose of holding colonies was to provide strategic points of support for America's new policy of throwing her weight around in the councils of the great. But the *Investor* saw other advantages as well. The colonies themselves could be developed into worthwhile fields of trade. In July 1898 another Massachusetts paper, the *Springfield Republican,* challenged this proposition and forced the *Investor* to clarify its position on colonies. According to the *Republican,* it was not necessary to own a country in order to trade with it. Ownership merely burdened American taxpayers with the administrative expenses of colonial government and increased expenditures for defense. The *Investor* replied that whatever economic theorists might say about ownership and trade, 'the experience of the race for, perhaps ninety centuries, has been in the direction of foreign acquisitions as a means of national prosperity'.[10] Canada, which the Springfield paper had cited as a prime example of the pointlessness of ownership, was turned into a counter-example by the *Investor.* 'Canada', wrote the editor, 'while nominally a British dependency, is practically part of the great American commonwealth'. But even so, her original owners had done very well out of their Canadian connection.

In considering the trade relations of Great Britain with the Dominion, we must not confine them merely to the exports and imports of merchandise commodities. Where England derives her greatest commercial benefit from her Canadian-colony is in her ownership of British North American banks, railroads, steamship companies, trading establishments, etc. Canada contains many men of great wealth and influence, but after all the mechanism of Canadian finance and commerce is largely regulated in back parlors in London, and a very large percentage of the profits accruing therefrom is deposited to the account of English capitalists and investors.

These future returns on investments the *Investor* considered to be as important, or even more important than the strategic and trading benefits of colonies.

No doubt the idea of regulating distant affairs from back parlors and depositing the profits accruing therefrom appealed

10. 9 July 1898, 969-70.

irresistibly to readers of the *Investor*. In weeks to come they heard a great deal more about the ways in which investors could directly profit from 'a broader international policy on the part of the United States'. Some of the anticipated profits were to come — as war profits had come — directly from government contracts. New colonies would require 'improved streets and highways, improved schools, improved dock and terminal facilities, vastly improved railroad facilities, and many other features considered indispensible by the people of this country to the profitable transaction of business'. American 'merchants, and the American owners of mining properties, sugar and tobacco plantations' would 'lose no time in seeing that proper highways, transportation facilities and other conveniences' were provided at government expense.[11] In short, the *Investor* envisioned a threefold profit to be gained from colonies. First would come profit from government contracts let to support the colonial administration itself and to establish the 'infrastructure' required for economic development. Second would come profit from agricultural and mining enterprises. Third, in the distant future, profit would come from trading with the people of developing countries who acquired new wants and purchasing power. Maintaining a permanently enlarged military establishment needing continual modernisation would provide a much larger source of profitable opportunities. And an expanded diplomatic service would literally provide jobs for the boys, that is for the boys of the class to which readers of the *Investor* mostly belonged. It would create 'a new calling for our young men of education and ability. Heretofore there has been no incentive — and in fact no opportunity — for young men of bright parts and good education to enter upon a life career in the diplomatic service of their country'.[12] There is obviously a great deal of pure and simple greed behind the rosy pictures painted by the *Investor*.

11. 10 Dec. 1889, 1750.

12. 13 Aug. 1898, 1130.

The prospects presented of insider deals, government contracts at public expense and class privileges are stated with a disarming candour that surprises twentieth century readers who have come to expect more circumspect language from business publications. But the *Investor* also reiterated with increasing shrillness that imperialism was a 'necessity' (as well as an unexpected but opportune occasion to dip into the public cashbox). The case it made out for necessity deserves to be called a theory of imperialism.

Toward the end of August a new element crept into the discussion of America's sudden eruption into world affairs. The *Springfield Republican* renewed its attack on the *Investor* by accusing its editor of propounding 'the theory that United States has become choked industrially and has attained maturity in respect to industrial growth within the old limits of territory', and that therefore 'the opening of new and outside fields of venture and effort is to be regarded as most opportune and advantageous'.[13] To the *Republican* this conclusion seemed extremely premature considering that only two or three years earlier business had been crying out for more European capital to be invested in American enterprises. It also ran contrary to orthodox economic theory :

> Capital, according to this view, is like water in a cup; the quantity which can be added is absolutely fixed; when some is poured out into another vessel then there is room in the cup for more to be added. It is impossible to discuss such a conception as this; it is only necessary to remind the reader that from the beginning the older portions of our country have been developing the newer, while simultaneously both have furnished fields for the investment of foreign capital.[14]

The *Investor's* first response to this attack was a somewhat lame attempt to prove 'that the capital which we desire to draw from Europe and the capital which we are desirous of sending to Cuba and Porto Rico are, so to speak, two different kinds of capital. From Europe came capital looking for absolutely safe investments even if they offered relatively low

13. *Springfield Republican*, 24 June, 8 and 29 July 1898.

14. *Quoted in U.S. Investor* 20 Aug. 1898.

rates of interest'. In contrast, the 'abundance of capital' which Americans now desired to send abroad was 'speculative capital' looking for high interest rates without much regard to safety. At one time American speculative capital had flowed into the wild west, but boom days out there were now probably gone forever.

Upon further reflection the *Investor* declared that opportunities for investing in American industries were indeed drying up fast, mainly because the capacity of industries to produce goods had outpaced the ability of American consumers to consume goods.

The salient feature of the situation is, that the leading industries of this country have been carried to a point far beyond the needs of our present population, and of that for some time to come.... Many of the best of the remaining opportunities have been seized by large moneyed interests... The long and the short of the matter is, that 'the cream is off' the industries of this country for the average man, for the time being at least. The resources of the United States do not today afford a sufficient outlet for the speculative spirit of our people — for the spirit which longs for bold enterprises and large and immediate profits.

A month later the *Investor* expanded its discussion of relationship between excess capacity for production, the growth of 'large moneyed interests' and the search for new fields of investment. The focal point of the discussion was the increasing tendency for small industries to become absorbed in the big corporations which Americans called trusts. This movement toward the 'combination of capital' the editor called 'the peculiar economic feature of the present time'. It heralded 'a new age' in economic history.

No other age bears any resemblance to this in this particular. It was not possible that any should ... The changes in economic conditions and in the means of satisfying the material wants of mankind have experienced a greater change in the last hundred years than in all the forgoing centuries. .

A congestion of capital is the result. The wealth of the world is now so great that it adds to itself at a phenomenal rate. Hence the problem of finding employment for capital has become one of great magnitude. It is now the greatest of all the economic problems that confronts us.

> The trust is the natural outcome of such a state of affairs. The excess of capital has resulted in an unprofitable competition. To employ Franklin's witticism, the owners of capital are of the opinion they must all hang together or else they will all hang separately.[15]

The aim of the trusts was to monopolise or nearly monopolise a particular industry so they could fix prices at levels which guaranteed at least some profit. As the *Investor* viewed the matter, the trust was not so much the product of capitalist greed as of desperation. The 'trust idea was seized upon as a means of averting the catastrophe which seemed so imminent', the catastrophe of overproduction and ferocious competition leading to a total elimination of profits.

As a solution to the problems of individual hard-pressed industries the trusts appeared to make sense, but they did not solve the world problem of 'the congestion of capital'. By December 1898, the *Investor* was seriously worried that rates of interest would be permanently held down because of the competitive rush of individual investors to find 'outlets' for their excess funds. The editor could 'confidently affirm that the investing public will before long be chafing greatly under the existing low returns on money. The very wealthy and the moderately well-off are alike embarrassed to know where to put their excess funds, in order that they may return them satisfactory results'. He suspected 'that a very large part of the speculation which is inevitable, as a result of the plethora of funds, will be based on projects outside the limits of the United States'.[16]

Linking the rise of trusts and the alleged 'congestion of capital' to 'projects outside the limits of the United States' enabled the *Investor* to make a far stronger case for the 'necessity' of imperialism than the case it had made in June on the basis of 'markets'. The final formulation of the case was published under the headline, 'Economic Necessity'.

> the whole civilised world has become equipped with an excessive machinery of production ... Hence came a larger fund of capital seeking investment

15. 24 Sept. see also 8 Oct. 1898, 1453.

16. 10 Dec. 1898, 1749.

than can find profitable employment. It is not necessary here to dispute with the closest economists whether overproduction is a possibility. It would not be a possibility if production were always directed in proper proportions towards those things which the community still lacked, and if the entire producing power of the community was applied to consumption. Both of these conditions have been lacking during the last half-century because production has increased in many directions faster than consumption has grown up to it, and many members of the community have preferred to put their earnings into permanent form in new investments, instead of applying them to the purchase of articles for immediate consumption. Hence has come the necessity for new permanent investments which has bid up the price of every first-class security on the European and American market, and in consequence forced down to the vanishing point interest on safe investments. How is relief to be found for these conditions in colonial enterprise? Simply by affording new outlets for finished goods and new opportunities for investments .... It is not necessary that the older civilised countries should build up manufacturing rivals in the undeveloped countries. They will undoubtedly do this to some extent, but the logical path to be pursued is that of the development of the natural riches of the tropical countries. These countries are now peopled by races incapable on their own initiative of extracting its full riches from their own soil... What is involved ... [for the present] is not a revolution in the habits and capacities of the people of the tropics, but only their equipment with the best means of rendering their territory productive. This will be attained in some cases by the mere stimulus of government and direction by men of the temperate zones; but it will be attained also by the application of modern machinery and methods of culture to the agricultural and mineral resources of the undeveloped countries.[17]

It is worth lingering over this quotation long enough to absorb its full meaning. The *Investor* is arguing that America — and most of the rest of the economically developed countries of the world — have just entered a new era marked by a surplus of goods produced for sale and a surplus of capital looking for profitable investment opportunities. The *Investor* admits that both surpluses could be reduced either by increasing the power of some people to buy things they want or by increasing the desire of other people to consume instead of invest. But lacking a programme for making either of those things happen, the *Investor* sees the opening up of foreign investment possibilities as the only way of maintaining

17. 19 Jan. 1901, 65-66.

worthwhile interest rates for investors. It does not consider the possibility of heavily investing in other developed countries because undeveloped tropical lands are there for the picking. Finally, the *Investor* recommends conscious planning to ensure that the new fields of investment do not develop, at least in the near future, into industrialised competitors with their own investment needs and urges. This argument encompasses and supercedes all of the editor's previous attempts to show the 'necessity of imperialism'. His original hopes that military spending, new colonies and a policy of thrusting an aggressive jaw towards Europe and Asia would create a sustained economic boom have now grown into a theory about the future. The theory is that in the new economic era marked by 'a congestion of capital' and the rise of trusts, continued economic progress will require the use of the armed might of the state to open and maintain foreign fields of investment.

The *Investor*, while it gloated over America's new conquests, did not specially recommend the acquisition of any more colonies. It specifically deplored any move to partition China. It called for a world-wide 'open door' policy allowing freedom of trade and investment for all countries. But it believed that in the current 'struggle for existence' an awesome military machine, a bigger government and a definite lessening of human freedom in many spheres would be required to sustain America's prosperity. Using military training to instil young Americans with European habits of discipline was only one of several limitations of freedom which the *Investor* was willing to tolerate. America's 'acquired provinces' would 'have to be ruled for some time to come, more or less as military provinces, and a strong and efficient government will thereby be secured'.[18] The paper hoped that 'the conquered districts might hereafter afford us lessons in good government that would make us insist upon having the same sort of rule for ourselves'! While allowing 'that the republican form of government is the best ever devised', the

18. 13 Aug. 1898, 1130.

Investor deplored 'the almost interminable discussion which the solution of every great problem of state invariably calls for'.[19] It was heartening to know that the United States Constitution had given the nation a strong President capable of cutting through democratic obstacles in moments of crisis.

No crowned head in the world, and no cabinet minister — unless it be a servant of the tzar — has so much real authority as the President of the United States. When Rome was under a republic there were times when all power was delegated temporarily to a dictator. The American government is so constituted that in times of war, or other great emergencies, the President, as a matter of course and of prerogative, assumes an almost dictatorial power; which, however, he cannot maintain for more than four years without the consent of the people being obtained.[20]

Many Americans thought that this was a very peculiar view to take of the Constitution. Carl Schurz for example, America's most famous refugee from the 1848 revolution in Germany, believed that autocratic rule in the Philippines would be incompatible with the Constitution's central principle of freely associated, self-governing states. Others held that by retaining any conquered territory the United States would contravene the Constitution because that hallowed document made no provision for aggressive war. The *Investor's* reply to Schurz was that 'no one considers that there is any incongruity in the way in which Alaska, New Mexico, Arizona and the Indian Territory are ruled', and that 'we admit Americanised populations to statehood, but not barbarians'. On the question of war the *Investor* went back to the founding fathers who had given Congress the power 'to declare war'. 'Now the principal idea which the word "war" conveyed to everybody living at the time of our constitution was devised was that of conquest. That is what war had always meant; and if they had stopped to reason about it, the fathers of the republic would probably have said that that was all it ever could mean'. The Constitution was therefore not in conflict with 'the doctrine that war and conquest have their

19. 3 Dec. 1898, 1732.

20. 13 Aug. 1898, 1129.

place in maintaining and developing a nation's trade, and that commercial advantages can after all be sometimes more easily and effectively gained by these means than without them'.[21] In one of its early discussions of imperialism the *Investor* had pointed out that to many people the word meant 'a species of Caesarism' and protested against the use of the word in that sense to describe the new foreign policy it recommended for the United States.[22] However, the more the editor expounded his own doctrines of imperialism, with its dictatorial President, its autocratic rule for 'barbarians', its armaments and wars, the more it sounded like precisely that : a species of Caesarism.

It was, of course, not to be undertaken for its own sake but as a 'necessity' which would enable Americans in general and United States investors in particular to face up to the 'stern facts' of the 'struggle for existence' in the era of trusts and 'a congestion of capital'. Whether embarking upon a career of imperialism would provide a permanent solution to American problems in the twentieth century was a question the *Investor* pondered only occasionally. The paper existed to advise short-term profit seekers, not to plot the course of world history. But it did sometimes worry about the social and political consequences of trusts. If consolidation in basic industries continued at its present rate, the time was fast approaching when the world would face 'a monopoly of all things controlled by a few score of capitalists'. This was an alarming thought, considering 'that the periods when the capital of the world was concentrated in few hands have always been the periods of greatest disaster'. The *Investor* recalled that in the later days of the Roman Empire there had been a drastic 'decline of small proprietorships of all kinds'. What would happen when the United States approached the same state of affairs?

'Trusts make it infinitely harder for every one to assert his influence on

21. 13 Aug. 1898, 1144.

22. 23 July 1898, 1033.

trade, the result being that it is coming to be an accepted doctrine that none except persons of transcendant ability need aspire to more than a subordinate position in life. Human nature is not constituted to bear this patiently'.[23]

There, with the impatient masses squared off against 'a few score of capitalists', the *Investor* dropped its speculations. It was rather like leaving Sherlock Holmes and Professor Moriarity wrestling on the edge of a precipice hundreds of feet above the Reichenbach Falls. The reader demands to know what happens next. The *Investor* did not tell, perhaps because the whole line of thought was uncomfortable for a champion of capitalist enterprise. It was a line of thought that was to recur many times in later studies of imperialism, many of them written by non-capitalists who did not hesitate to write exciting sequels.

Before moving on to consider the first of those non-capitalist studies, there are three points to be made about the *Investor* and the theory of imperialism it developed in the wake of the war with Spain. First, when the *Investor* said that nineteenth-century industrial development had generated surpluses of goods and capital which led to the rise of trusts and made imperialism a 'necessity', the *Investor* meant that imperialism was a necessity *for the future.* It did not pretend that any sort of economic necessity had led to the Spanish-American war. As an early opponent of that war the editor knew very well that a complex mixture of political, diplomatic and humanitarian impulses brought on the conflict. The war was not something America had done because of the economic necessity of imperialism. Imperialism, an economic necessity, was something America could do as a result of a war which gave her colonies, demonstrated her military prowess, and showed her a power to be reckoned with in both the Atlantic and Pacific oceans. Thus, the *Investor's* theory of the necessity of imperialism was a kind of crystal-ball gazing, no more capable of immediate proof than a statement that the world will end next Friday.

23. 12 Nov. 1898, 1652-53.

Only time would tell. There is in fact, something of a millenarian flavour about the *Investor's* whole exposition. With the closing years of the nineteenth century came a feeling that 'a new age' in economic history had dawned which would inaugurate great changes in the behaviour of peoples and governments, maybe even investors.

The second point to be made is that the *Investor* was conscious of the several meanings of imperialism currently in use in 1898. To some people it was a species of Caesarism, an autocratic tendency in government that could be practised at home as well as abroad. (In this sense it is identical with the use of the word Koebner discovered in Britain in earlier decades). To some people it was simply what the United States would be doing if she kept the Spanish territories occupied during the war. (This use of the word is related to the first use inasmuch as everyone knew that Caesar came, saw and conquered, before he made himself Emperor for Life). To other people, including the editor of the *Investor*, imperialism was what the United States would be doing if she deliberately set out to attain great power status in the global community of nations in order to defend and advance her vital economic interests. This sense of the word encompassed the previous two meanings. The editor of the *Investor* admitted that elements of strong, efficient, even autocratic government were part of his programme of imperialism. He looked on colonies as strategic points of support for American participation in the international power game, as well as valuable fields of investment in their own right. But they were only part of imperialism. It is almost impossible to give a succinct definition of what imperialism meant to the *United States Investor* in 1898 that does not somehow include the alleged reason for pursuing the policy. Imperialism was the deliberate use of the power of the state, including its military power, in order to advance alleged national economic interests in the world at large. Something like this meaning of the word informed most discussions of imperialism in most countries between the closing years of the nineteenth century and the end of World War I.

The third point to be made is the obvious one that what a Boston financial paper with a small circulation said about imperialism in 1898 is not the beginning and the end of the story of imperialism in America. In America, as in Great Britain, the word empire had a historical meaning distinct from imperialism. The American historian Richard Van Alstyne has written with great erudition about what Americans meant when they spoke of 'Manifest Destiny' and quoted the tagline 'Westward the course of empire'.[24] Filling up the west with farmers, denuding it of Indians and buffalo, and generally encroaching on the continental neighbours Canada and Mexico were ambitions harboured by many Americans long before 'imperialism' became a fashionable word. Another American historian, Walter La Feber, has shown how the realisation that the continental frontier had closed increasingly turned the eyes of deeper political and economic thinkers towards the larger world beyond the oceans.[25] In the decade immediately preceding the *Investor's* discovery of imperialism, Frederick Jackson Turner had been worrying whether American freedom could long survive without the abundance of free land on which it had been spread and nurtured; Alfred Thayer Mahan had been preaching the historic importance of sea power to national prosperity and international commercial rivalries; Brooks Adams had been writing dark prophecies about the shifting course of world empire.[26] This background profoundly influenced the way the *Investor* looked at the world on the morning after Dewey's victory at Manila Bay.

The most novel element in the *Investor's* discussions was the emphasis on the vast development of productive forces

24. *The Rising American Empire* (New York, 1960).

25. *The New Empire* (Ithaca, 1963).

26. Turner's famous paper of 1893 on '*The Significance of the Frontier in American History*' is collected with later essays in *The Frontier in American History* (New York, 1920). Mahan first expounded his conceptions in *The Influence of Sea Power upon History, 1660-1783* (New York, 1890). Brooks Adams had, by 1900, added an economic component to his prophecies. See 'The New Struggle for Life Among Nations', *Fortnightly Review* LV (1899) 274-83.

which had produced both the trusts and the alleged 'congestion of capital' which made 'imperialism' a necessity. Others besides the editor of the *Investor* seized on this point in the same year, notably the American banking expert Charles A. Conant. In September, 1898, Conant published his first article on 'The Economic Basis of Imperialism' in the *North American Review.* By 1900 he had developed his ideas in a series of further essays which were published under the title *The United States in the Orient.* A worried British reviewer accurately summarised Conant's argument as follows:

1) 'In all advanced countries there has been such excessive saving that no profitable investment for capital remains, and waste and disaster result';
2) 'outlets might be found without the exercise of political and military power, if commercial freedom was the policy of all nations... but it is not, and therefore America must be prepared to use force if necessary';
3) for the impending struggle America has peculiar advantages... the organisation of some of its industries on a large scale in the form of trusts will assist it greatly in the fight for commercial supremacy'.[27]

This tighter, more developed version of what the *Investor* was saying at the same time obviously made a considerable impression on the United States government for Conant was chosen as financial advisor to the new colonial government of the Philippine Islands. All of the points made in this chapter could have been made just as well by using the example of Conant. One reason for using the *Investor* instead, is that some historians have noticed Conant; it is important to show that he was not a lone pioneer of the first theory of economic imperialism.[28] Another reason for using the *Investor* is that one of its readers was the man who liked to be known as 'America's millionaire socialist', H. Gaylord Wilshire of Los Angeles, California. He picked up the new capitalist theory of imperialism, incorporated it in a socialist framework and sent it across the Atlantic where it entered the mainstream of European socialist thought.

27. Review by S.J. Chapman in *The Economic Journal* XI (1901) 78.

28. Langer, *Diplomacy of Imperialism* (New York, 1951) 68, E.M. Winslow, *The Pattern of Imperialism* (New York, 1948) 104-105.

CHAPTER 2
H. GAYLORD WILSHIRE AND THE FIRST SOCIALIST THEORY OF CAPITALIST IMPERIALISM

Starting from the northwest edge of old Los Angeles, Wilshire Boulevard winds a snake-like path towards the sea. Its undulations seem deliberately designed to take in some of the world's most glittering pieces of real estate including Beverley Hills and Hollywood. The boulevard is practically all that now remains to commemorate the name of H. Gaylord Wilshire. He deserves to be better remembered.[1] In his heyday from 1900 to 1914 he was at the heart of the only broadly-based, avowedly socialist movement ever to arise in the historic stronghold of capitalism, a movement which culminated in the Presidential election of 1912 when 897,000 votes were cast for the Socialist candidate Debs. Moreover, Wilshire's career, like the boulevard named after him, took a winding path among many of the bright lights which mark the transition from nineteenth-century modes of thought to twentieth-century ones: Marxism as variously expounded in England, Germany and Russia; English Fabian Socialism as expounded by the Webbs and Bernard Shaw; the new wave in American literature represented by his friends Jack London and Upton Sinclair; psychoanalysis as taught to his wife by C.G. Jung in Zurich; the unorthodox economic theories propounded by J.A. Hobson in London.

Wilshire made his first (and perhaps his only) fortune carving broad barren acres on the outskirts of booming Los Angeles into small, neat, serviced blocks of eminently saleable land connected by the boulevard that bears his name. Profits from this suburban development enable him to travel to England in the early eighteen nineties to fill some of the gaps in his education caused by an adolescent decision to leave

1. Howard H. Quint gives an excellent summary of Wilshire's life and work, 'Wilshire's Magazine', in *American Radical Press* ed., J.R. Conlin, I (Westport, 1974) 72-81. Quint originally set out to write a biography of Wilshire based on his collected papers (now housed in the U.C.L.A. library, Los Angeles, California) but was severely handicapped by the small number of Wilshire's own letters in the collection.

Harvard College after only a year and go west to make a name for himself. Once established as a gentleman of leisure in London, Wilshire also set out to acquaint himself with socialism and socialists. Sometime in the late eighteen eighties he had been seized by the conviction that the days of unfettered competition were passing away forever. In later years he boasted that he had been among the very first to realise that John D. Rockefeller's formation of the Standard Oil Trust in 1888 represented the beginning of a transition from free enterprise to monopoly.[2] In the collected *Fabian Essays* brought out by the English Fabian Society in 1889 Wilshire found the closely related idea that the era of individualism was giving way to the era of collectivism. Fabians saw public ownership of municipal utilities as a first step in a gradual procession leading to state ownership of all basic industries. Wilshire advocated starting at the top rather than the bottom with a state takeover of the trusts. In the late eighteen nineties leading Fabians undertook detailed studies of trusts and other industrial combines with roughly the same goal in mind.[3] By that time, however, Wilshire had moved on to a more revolutionary type of socialism.

His publication of an American edition of the *Fabian Essays* in 1891 marked the height of his interest in gradualist methods. The Fabian approach to social problems — characterised by close study, the collection of voluminous statistics, moral earnestness, and a willingness to wait years and years for socialist ideas to 'permeate' the governing classes — was basically out of tune with Wilshire's mercurial character. His instinct in politics, as in business, was always for the gamble at high stakes, the gimmick, the quick killing. The Revolutionary Marxism preached and practised by the British Social-Democratic Federation (S.D.F.) appealed strongly to this instinct. Marx's explanation of the way in which fierce competition between individual capitalists forced them to cut

2. He frequently cites a letter to the *Los Angeles Evening Express* 21 Sept. 1889.

3. See particularly the works of H.W. Macrosty who was strongly supported by the Webbs.

wages and introduce labour-saving machinery summed up Wilshire's own experience in the business world. The capitalists he had known were not specially bad or greedy specimens of the human race. They struggled to stay alive in a dog-eat-dog world where profits were hard to come by and capitalists had to run fast in order to stay in the same place. If they failed to cut wages to the bone and to adopt the labour-saving devices introduced by competitors, they would stop making profits and go out of business. Marx had predicted that the vicious circle of falling profits, labour-saving inventions and bankruptcies would result in a very small group of surviving capitalists realising that they must combine to stop the destructive struggle by controlling production and fixing prices.[4] In other words, Wilshire saw at once, Marx had predicted the rise of trusts. This single, stunning, practical vindication of Marx's theory was enough to make Wilshire believe in the ultimate vindication of other predictions as well : that the displacement of people by machines would create an army of unemployed workers : that the irony and injustice of a small number of capitalists monopolising industries capable of producing vast numbers of goods which low paid workers and the unemployed could not afford to buy would create an explosive demand for a change in the whole economic system; that capitalists would make every effort to use the government to protect their shrinking profits and to prevent any attempt the workers might make to change the system; and that eventually, the capitalists would run out of schemes for saving their skins and would have to surrender the system to the people. H. Gaylord Wilshire the Los Angeles suburban developer became Comrade Wilshire and in 1895 was selected to stand for election to parliament as a Social-Democratic Federation candidate in Manchester.

It was not necessary for Wilshire to stop being a good capitalist in order to become a good revolutionary socialist. Marx's collaborator Engels had owned a factory and H.M. Hyndman, the head of the British S.D.F., was a well-to-do

4. See Wilshire's first newspaper, *The Challenge* 13 March, 1901.

capitalist from an established family. To Hyndman and Wilshire being good socialists meant understanding the 'scientific reasons' why capitalism was doomed and working energetically to make others understand and hurry up the revolutionary crisis.

It is not surprising that Wilshire, who believed that Marx's predictions were coming true faster in America than anywhere else in the world, returned to Los Angeles before his appeal to English voters could be tested in a general election.[5] In 1900 after he had restored some order and profitability to his neglected business affairs, he launched a socialist magazine (*The Challenge,* later called *Wilshire's Magazine*) with the motto 'Let the Nation Own the Trusts'. Knowing that most Americans associated socialism with poor, probably dangerous European immigrants, Wilshire unashamedly used the methods of bunkum and ballyhoo pioneered by P.T. Barnum to identify socialism with the admired American virtues of education, money, progress and success. He went out of his way to avoid Marxist jargon. When a subscriber asked for more articles on Marxist theory and the history of socialism, Wilshire replied that 'while I out-Herod Herod on Scientific Socialism, I am sick to death of its terminology, and until I recover I have no heart to sicken others. This paper is to be made readable at all costs'.[6] Wilshire realised that in his campaign to make socialism respectable he could be his own best asset. He craftily cultivated the image of 'millionaire socialist' long after he had sold his last tract of Wilshire district real estate. In 1901 when his magazine was still struggling to break even and various other financial difficulties threatened to engulf him, he reprinted without comment the remarks of an eastern newspaper identifying him as 'the owner of a number of cattle ranches', a 'member of the bill board trust, president of a bank', 'otherwise extensively engaged in business' and 'said

5. Quint, op.cit. See also C. Tsuzuki, *Hyndman and British Socialism* (Oxford, 1961) 104.

6. *The Challenge* 19 June, 1901, 7.

to be worth over a million'.[7] He referred often to his education at Harvard without going into the trivial details of years spent there and degrees obtained.

The likelihood is that Wilshire really believed that he would soon be rich again, just as he really believed in the imminence of a socialist revolution in America which would make him famous. After his first marriage broke up, he went through a period of frantic actress chasing. One hapless object of his indefatigable devotion was the dazzling British actress Mrs. Patrick Campbell (who later exchanged witty letters with Bernard Shaw). Wilshire haunted the stage door during the American tour of 1902 and sent big bunches of flowers to her hotel room in the middle of the night with messages such as, 'Ah me! I know now why God made me dislike stimulants — to allow me to be more madly intoxicated by you'. He confessed that he could offer her but little in the way of material comfort at the moment, but promised great and revolutionary changes in over America which would soon give him a guiding role in the nation's affairs.[8] Wilshire's socialism was partly a matter of wanting to be on the winning side. In this he made an apt pupil of Hyndman with whom he maintained a warm correspondence for fifteen years after his departure from England. The Hyndman-Wilshire correspondence is a curiosity in the annals of socialism. Hyndman writes on the stationery of his 'Ashanti Gold Syndicate' to retell old court gossip about Queen Victoria and to complain about the arrogant insularity of the German

7. *The Challenge* 31 July, 1901.

8. Wilshire to Campbell, 8 Aug. 1902, Hotel Manhattan; Wilshire to Campbell, n.d., 6 p.m., Wilshire Papers, folio 1/7, U.C.L.A. Library, Los Angeles, California. The latter communication reads : 'I really am as poor as I pretend.... There is a time coming however when things will be different and when aside from any gold I may have gathered meanwhile the difference [between our fortunes] will be reduced so considerably that it might be unconsidered. To be precise, today you are famous while I am not even infamous. With the approaching of a world revolution and I predict this with the certainty that an astronomer predicts an eclipse, a revolution will start in this country ... which will sweep the world ushering in the Kingdom of God on Earth, I am bound to be a central figure although the matter of that has absolutely nothing to do with inciting me to what I am now doing'.

Social Democrats. Wilshire replies under the letterhead of 'The Los Angeles Billposting Company' with details of his stagedoor romances and his own criticism of the Germans for failing to see that the revolution would happen first in America.

Still there is an important lesson to be read between the lines of these amusing, occasionally hilarious letters. At the turn of the twentieth century, industrial capitalism seemed to many people — including a good many capitalists — to be an exploding star whose continued ascendency in the heavens was doubtful precisely because it had changed its size and colour so often in its short career. The editor of *United States Investor* foresaw 'a monopoly of all things controlled by a few score of capitalists' but preferred not to think about the consequences and hoped that in the meantime imperialism would afford new opportunities for profit. Hyndman and Wilshire read the same prediction of monopoly in Marx, concluded that capitalism could not survive, and staked out their claims on the future by turning socialist.

Wilshire was very conscious of this state of affairs. It had, he told his readers in 1901, always been his 'contention that with the present rapid progress being made by America in the industrial race of nations that a tremendous amount of material for the substantiation of the Socialists' economic position could be obtained from the financial journals'. In proof of this proposition he offered extensive quotations from *The United States Investor.* The coincidence of Marxist theory with the *Investor's* comments on current amalgamations was so nearly exact that Wilshire had to remind readers that 'the Investor is not a Socialist paper and knows not that these consolidations must lead to Socialism'.[9] A knowledge of Marxist theory also enabled Wilshire to see immediately the implications of the *Investor's* claim that a surplus of capital made imperialism a necessity. During Wilshire's stay in London, one of his comrades in the Social Democratic Federation, E. Belfort Bax, had raised and briefly discussed

9. *Challenge* 20 Feb. 1901, 2.

the idea that 'the one hope of prolonging the existence of the present capitalistic system lies in the opening-up of new territories to commercial and industrial enterprise'.[10] In an address to the Economic Club of Los Angeles in January 1900, Wilshire combined the notion of an extended lease of life for capitalism with the theories of economic necessity he had been reading in the *U. S. Investor*.[11] A year later he produced an updated version of his old pamphlet on trusts which turned the capitalist theory of imperialism propounded by the *Investor* and C.A. Conant into a socialist theory of imperialism.[12] This analysis of the 'trust problem' begins by considering the ironic results of America's industrial revolution for the ordinary working man.

I do not think any fair-minded person can but admit that the modern day-laborer on his $1.50 per day, and very uncertain of that, living in a city, wearing shoddy clothes, breathing sewer gas, eating tuberculous beef, drinking typhoid baccilli in his milk and fusel oil in his whisky, and absorbing intellectual garbage from his yellow journal, has had any great augmentation in the pleasures of life through the inventions of the marvelous nineteenth century.... But it may be pertinently asked, 'Where has disappeared this immense stream of products that is the result of the labor of the nation applied to modern industry?'

Wilshire explains what happened to 'the immense stream' using the language a hydraulic engineer might have used to explain the problems involved in supplying water to a new suburb of arid Los Angeles. At the source 'the product of labor as a whole flows into two broad channels', 'one to the capitalists, the holders of wealth, and one to the workers'. Most of the workers get only the barest necessities of life, except for that 'part of the workers, the aristocracy of labor,

10. Bernard Porter, *Critics of Empire* (London, 1968) 100-01. For a later formulation, influenced by Wilshire, see *Justices, the Organ of the Social Democracy* 16 April, 1904, 2. A summary of Bax's life and work appears in S. Pierson, 'E. Belfort Bax 1854-1925, The Encounter of Marxism and Late Victorian Culture', *Journal of British Studies* XII (1972) 39-60.

11. *The Problem of the Trust* (Los Angeles, 1900).

12. 'The Trust Problem', *Challenge* April 1901. A later version was published as 'The Significance of the Trust' in *Wilshire's Magazine* Nov. 1901, 16-26 and July 1902, 56-68.

the trade unionists and skilled labor generally, who sell their brains rather than their hands'. The situation is very different for the rich whose delectable pleasures and unique perils Wilshire describes from his privileged position on the inside.

> The stream of wealth flowing into the coffers of the rich is itself again divided into two streams, one of which goes to satisfy what they are pleased to regard as their necessities of existence, a wonderful conglomerate of beefsteaks, truffles, champagne, automobiles, private [railroad] cars, steam yachts, golf balls, picture galleries, food and clothing for their servants, etc., all classified under the general head of consumables and denominated by the general term of 'spent' money.
>
> The other divison of the stream of wealth flowing to the rich is what is termed 'saved' money, and goes into the building of new machinery of production, new railroads, canals, iron furnaces, mills, etc. It is this last channel for the 'saved' money that has been the great sluice-way for carrying off the surplus product of labor and so avoiding the constant menace of a money plethora in our industrial system.

Because the rich are small in number they can only devote part of their 'stream' to the pleasures of their 'consumables'. However gross their appetites, they must eventually gag because they are, for all their wealth, mere mortals.[13] 'No man cares for two dinners, and when Mr. Rockefeller with his $100,000,000 a year income "spends" over a thousand dollars a day on himself and his household he finds it probably both pleasanter and easier to "save" the remainder than to lay awake nights devising bizarre ways to "spend" it'. But in order to use his savings, Rockefeller must have industries to invest in. Here he gets into difficulties. Once he had been able to invest all savings in his own oil business which grew and grew. His competitors did the same until 'finally the capacity for refining oil becaume greater than the market demanded'. 'Each refiner was bound to get rid of his surplus product at any price, and the price of the surplus determined the price of the whole. Ruin stared them in the face. Over-production must be curtailed. The Standard Oil

13. Wilshire appears to have been unaware of his contemporary Thorstein Veblen's ingenious solution of this difficulty through the concept of 'conspicuous consumption'. See his *Theory of the Leisure Class* (New York, 1899), Chapter 4.

Trust was born.' Wilshire sees the Standard Oil story repeated in one industry after another. He ridicules the politicians who try to stop the inevitable progression towards monopoly by passing 'anti-trust' legislation; they are seeking 'to overturn the laws of nature and make water run up hill'.

The proliferation of trusts, however, cannot continue indefinitely. Each time a new trust is formed, the owners solve their immediate problem of overproduction but they can no longer invest their saved profits in their own industry. They must look for other fields of investment. The available fields grow smaller and smaller as one industry after another is organised into a monopolistic trust. At this point Wilshire introduces a fundamental axiom of his argument, the proposition that new industries cannot go on springing up so long as the power of most people to buy goods is limited by their low wages. The 'plethora of capital' — which first caused the rich to save as well as spend, and next caused the owners of trusts to invest in other industries at this point becomes a nation-wide affair.

Always anxious to extend a helping hand to his fellow millionaires, Wilshire casts a 'broad sympathetic look over the surface of the United States, with the perplexed eye of a man with a million dollars or more looking for a promising and safe investment'. The astonishing truth appears to be that there is not 'one single industry which he could find that is of a sufficiently large capital that is not palpably overdone'. The relentless progression from cut-throat competition to monopoly has dammed up every possible channel of investment and created 'the present immense flood of surplus capital in the United States'. At last the flood bursts through the dikes of the North American continent and rushes abroad.

> For the first time in history American money is entering into the world's markets as a buyer of bonds of foreign nations. When England had to borrow $50,000,000 to defray expenditures on account of the Boer War, America took half of the loan and would have taken it all if she had been allowed. The American gold now building railways in China would never be there, if there were opportunities for home investment....

American capitalists are today more in need of foreign fields for investment of their capital than are European capitalists. Within the last two years the international financial market has reversed itself, and America is now the creditor instead of the debtor nation.

Now Wilshire introduces imperialism.

This explains the sudden craze for 'imperialism' and its advocacy by the Republican Party, which is the political expression of the organised wealth of the country. The 'trusts' are a dam built to prevent the swamping of domestic industries by the rising flood of surplus capital. The 'trusts', however, do not prevent the rising of this flood.

'Imperialism' is a means of diverting to foreign shores this threatening deluge of domestic 'savings'.

He hastens to add that imperialism can only be of help to the capitalists as a delaying tactic. Even on a global scale the process of 'trustification' progresses inexorably towards the same end. 'The workers now engaged in producing new machinery of production will join the unemployed army in regiments'. In the face of this angry and desperate army the handful of remaining capitalists will be helpless. They must peaceably hand the trusts to the people or have them seized in a bloody revolution. Aside from imperialism only a very few expedients remain to delay the final crisis.

The capitalists may possibly see the danger first and make a turn that will give them a short and precarious lease of life in their present position. An eight-hour law, old age pensions, etc., all such reforms might possibly extend the capitalist system. The best of all, however, to bolster up the capitalist system is a rattling good war between the great powers followed by a prolonged civil war with great destruction of life and property....

However, wars cannot last forever. The capitalists are sooner or later forced to face the problem of finding work for men when there is absolutely no work to be found.

In his summing up Wilshire makes it clear that imperialism, however it may be expressed in foreign and colonial policy, is in essence autocratic government with warlike tendencies. The trust employs autocratic methods in industry; imperialism employs autocratic methods in government.

> The trust is here and here to stay as long as our competitive system of industry endures. Democracy has been ousted from industry by autocracy, and, as our political institutions are but a reflection of our industrial institions, we should not pretend that anything but a sham democratic political state remains. When we see imperialism, which is simply political autocracy, expressing itself in the Philippines or in the bullpen for the [striking] Idaho miners, we should not stultify ourselves by striving to prevent a result without first attacking the cause.

The workers should reject all short-sighted reformist policies. Anti-trust and anti-tariff campaigns were of no more ultimate use than the eight-hour day or 'free silver'.

> Democracy must be established in industry and re-established in politics. There is really no first step to nationalization of industry; that time has passed. A half-way policy is impossible industrially, unrighteous ethically, and unsound politically. Revolution and not reform must be our battle cry. The main plank, and in fact the only necessary plank, in our political platform should be: We demand, The Nationalization of Industry.

Even allowing for its shortness and its folksy language Wilshire's article is an impressive piece of work. Without appealing to the name of Karl Marx or the jargon then in vogue among revolutionary socialists (except perhaps his reference to 'the aristocracy of labor') he manages to reach a revolutionary conclusion of unimpeachable Marxist orthodoxy. He also made an important contribution to the heated debate among Marxists caused by the 'revisionist' ideas propounded by Edward Bernstein in Germany. Bernstein had argued in his book *Evolutionary Socialism* (1898) that many of Marx's predictions were evidently not coming true. This indicated to Bernstein that 'revisions' should be made in Marxist theory and practice; it was possible to achieve socialism gradually by using established institutions of representative government. Bernstein had also shown a willingness to develop a socialist policy on Germany's colonies that was more 'constructive' than simply opposing their existence. In England H.M. Hyndman's Social-Democratic Federation scorned the Fabian Society as the equivalent of Bernstein and pointed to leading Fabians who condoned Britain's war against the Boer republics in

South Africa as proof of the parallel. But neither Hyndman nor the principal S.D.F. theoretician, E. Belfort Bax, offered anything like Wilshire's cogent reply to the revisionist challenge. Wilshire believed that the reformist trade union leaders of the United States strongly resembled the revisionists of Europe (even though most of them had never heard of Marx and had no idea that they were revising anything). Wilshire's reply to them was that: 1) the rise of the trust was the most spectacular vindication of Marx's prophetic powers that anyone could wish for short of the revolution itself; and 2) that both imperialism and the 'reformist' programmes of the revisionists were nothing more than means for temporarily postponing capitalism's demise. The obvious weakness in Wilshire's argument is that he does not discuss how long — years? decades? centuries? — these devices for postponing the revolution might prove effective. Whereas the editor of *United States Investor* tried to avoid thinking about the dangerous future which appeared to loom beyond the present opportunities provided by trusts and imperialism, Wilshire wished so fervently for the advent of the future that he preferred not to think much about the period of half-hearted reforms, imperialism and war that separated him from the revolution. He is nevertheless an important figure in the history of socialism because he was the first socialist to conjecture that capitalists threatened by overproduction and a 'surplus of capital' would resort to foreign investment, armaments and and a bellicose foreign policy in order to delay the collapse of their system.

Marx gave Wilshire the theoretical framework he needed to fit the American debate over imperialism into the overall scheme of world economic history, but it is possible to wonder whether he would have reached the conclusions he did if he had not had the *Investor* and other capitalist publications to show him the way. Everywhere he looked in the early months of 1901 he found capitalist sources who supported his theory.[14] Professor Jenks of Cornell University

14. *Challenge* 13 Feb. 1901, 1; 20 Feb. 1901, 11; 6 March 1901, 1, 6; 13 March 1901, 3.

confirmed his assertion that the growth of monopoly was a world-wide trend rather than a passing American fad. The elder statesman and railroad magnate Chauncey Depew believed 'that we have here in the United States a surplus of two billion a year', admitted 'that there is no room for it in the United States', and proposed 'that now we have battered in the gates of Peking', 'we can invest it in China'. The well-known journalist Ray Stannard Baker agreed with Wilshire's observation that the Spanish-American War signaled the beginning of a general American invasion of overseas markets. In the writings of J.P. Foley and Brooks Adams, Wilshire found predictions that the decay of the old colonial powers France and England would be followed by a struggle for the redivision of the globe which might well generate a world war.

Wilshire's socialist theory of capitalist imperialism is in fact the capitalist theory of capitalist imperialism with an added twist. Like the editor of the *Investor,* Wilshire's understanding of imperialism includes the old notion of autocracy or Caesarism. Wilshire too sees the acquisition of colonies as a part of a policy of imperialism but again agrees with the *Investor* that ramifications of imperialism extend far beyond colonies. Wilshire would probably have accepted as a reasonable definition of imperialism, 'the deliberate use of the power of the state, including its military power in order to advance alleged national economic interest in the world at large'. However, Wilshire scorned the idea that the real interests of the American people made imperialism 'a necessity'. Imperialism was a necessity for nobody but the capitalists who must find 'outlets' abroad for their 'plethora' of capital or face a revolution at home. Wilshire's explanation of imperialism is, if anything, even more future-oriented than the *Investor's.* While Wilshire as a Marxist had expected over-production, monopolies and a 'plethora of capital', he was not at all concerned to explain why any nation had made war, acquired colonies or invested abroad in the past. Believing America to be in the revolutionary vanguard of industrial nations, he regarded her trusts and her imperialism as unprecedented phenomena. The vital difference between the *Investor's* theory and Wilshire's theory is that what the financial journal presented as a policy recommendation to the government (it should practise imperialism to save the economic system), Wilshire presented as fact (without imperialism, capitalism would collapse).

Wilshire lived on for twenty-six years after writing his article on trusts and imperialism. He reprinted it occasionally but never expanded or developed its ideas. It is typical of his life and work, sparkling with wit and verve and promise but not designed to last. Precisely because he had borrowed most of the analysis from capitalist sources it did not occur to him to claim originality as a socialist theorist.

For the remainder of his life he chased ideas, causes, and moneymaking schemes as he had once chased actresses. Up until about 1906 he could maintain a reasonable claim to be an orthodox Marxist. In that year the Russian writer Maxim Gorky came to America to raise money for V.I. Lenin's Bolshevik faction of the Russian Social Democrats. When the press discovered that Gorky's actress companion was not his wife, the big Russian was thrown out of his hotel and ran to Wilshire for shelter. Not long afterwards Wilshire bought a gold mine and concocted a scheme for selling shares to socialist readers of his magazine. The profits were to be used to advance the cause. Not much gold ever came out of the mine and some people openly accused him of fraud. About the same time he became a supporter of Big Bill Haywood and the 'syndicalist' programme for organising all workers into 'one big union' which would then call a general strike which was supposed to bring the capitalists to their knees. His old friend Hyndman and others who considered themselves to be faithful followers of Marx looked on syndicalism as the fool's gold of socialist theory. After the first World War, Wilshire seemed to lose interest in socialism altogether and was critical of Lenin's Bolshevik revolution in Russia. Wilshire's last years were taken up with a ludicrous company for selling a radioactive radium beauty cream to Hollywood stars of the Valentino era. There is no evidence that he ever knew that Lenin — in the darkest days of his exile in Switzerland during the first world war — carefully copied some paragraphs from Wilshire's article on 'The Trust Problem' into the notebooks he used in writing a book on imperialism. Lenin came across Wilshire's words in J.A. Hobson's famous book, *Imperialism, A Study* first published in London in 1902.

CHAPTER 3
J.A. HOBSON AND THE ECONOMIC TAPROOT OF IMPERIALISM

The next time Wilshire published his article he called it 'The Significance of the Trust'. J.A. Hobson came across it under this title sometime early in 1902. He wrote to Wilshire to say that 'your article, "Significance of the Trust" which I have just read, is the straightest, strongest, most convincing, and most scientifically accurate account of the relation between capital and imperialism that has yet appeared'. He then sat down to compliment Wilshire with a sincerer form of flattery than imitation. In August an article by Hobson which borrowed Wilshire's words as well as his ideas appeared in the English *Contemporary Review.*

Hobson's article, entitled 'The Economic Taproot of Imperialism', begins by quoting the contemporary argument of British businessmen that the need to develop future markets and provide an outlet for surplus capital made imperialism 'not a choice, but a necessity'. Hobson proposes to illustrate 'the practical force of this economic argument' by considering 'the recent history of the United States'.

> Here is a country which suddenly breaks through a conservative policy, strongly held by both political parties, bound up with very popular instinct and tradition, and flings itself upon a rapid imperial career for which it possesses neither the material nor the moral equipment, risking the principles and practices of liberty and equality by the establishment of militarism and the forcible subjugation of peoples which it cannot safely admit to the condition of American citizenship.

His explanation for the transformation of America into an aggressive world power goes right down the line with Wilshire, as can be seen by setting Hobson's sequential argument along side Wilshire's.

Hobson	**Wilshire**
'during the last two decades... the United States... has developed the best equipped and most productive manufacturing economy the world has yet seen'.	'there is no country in which the industrial machinery is not only so completed, but actually over-completed... as in the United States'.

Hobson	Wilshire
'An era of cut-throat competition followed by a rapid process of amalgamation has thrown an enormous quantity of wealth into the hands of a small number of captains of industry.	'The trust arose from the desire of the manufacturers to protect themselves from over-production and the consequent mad and suicidal struggle to dispose of their surplus stock'. 'The trusts will afford . . . a temporary breastwork for our captains of industry'.
'No luxury of living to which this class could attain kept pace with its rise of income, and a process of automatic saving set in upon an unprecedented scale'.	'Not withstanding ... the prodigality of the American rich in unbounded luxury ..., still the percentage of the very rich is so small that all efforts in lavish "spending" have had little effect economically compared with the wealth they have been forced to "save" owing to lack of ingenuity in discovering modes for "spending"'.
'It is quite evident that a trust which is motivated by cut-throat competition, due to an excess of capital, cannot normally find inside the "trusted" industry employment for that portion of the profits which the trust-makers desire to save and invest'.	'Rockefeller, with his enormous surplus income, which he is bound to "save" and cannot from the very nature of things find room to invest in his own oil business, is constantly forced to seek out new industrial fields to conquer'.
'the manufacturing power of a country like the United States does grow so fast as to exceed the demands of the home market.. Her manufactures are saturated with capital and can absorb no more'.	'We are saturated with capital and can absorb no more'.

Hobson	Wilshire
'It is this sudden demand for foreign markets for manufacturers and for investments which is avowedly responsible for the adoption of imperialism as a political policy and practice by the Republican party to which the great industrial and financial chiefs belong, and which belongs to them'.	'This explains the sudden craze for "imperialism" and its advocacy by the Republican Party, which is the political expression of the organised wealth of the country'.

The point of setting the words of Hobson and Wilshire side by side is not to convict Hobson of plagiarism. It is simply to show that what historians later came to call the 'Hobson thesis' was not Hobson's alone. It was made in America by American capitalists at the time of the Spanish-American war, noticed by the Marxist Wilshire, who gave it a socialist twist, and then taken up by Hobson who was so pleased with his 1902 article for the *Contemporary Review* that he used it, virtually unchanged, as a chapter in a big rambling book he was currently writing on imperialism.

For his part, Wilshire was anything but upset by Hobson's borrowing of his ideas (Hobson, had in fact acknowledged Wilshire in a footnote when he directly quoted him). When Hobson travelled to the United States on a lecture tour in 1903 Wilshire reprinted his own article with Hobson's congratulatory letter attached. He also sent a friend in New York to interview the famous English economist and featured the interview in the April issue of his magazine.[1] The interviewer made a point of asking how Hobson could endorse Wilshire's ideas and yet not declare himself a socialist. Hobson allegedly replied that in the first place new enterprises were springing up as fast as old ones were incorporated in trusts, and in the second place most people in America and Great Britain did not seem to care much for socialism. Whether or not that was the sum total of Hobson's

1. J. Spargo, 'Talk with Hobson, the English economist', *Wilshire's Magazine* (April 1903) 45-48.

answer, he did not return to England with the feeling that the rampant growth of trusts was about to turn Americans to socialism. He wrote, referring to Wilshire, that 'there is indeed a sort of socialist party, broken into many groups, which takes as one of its mottoes, "Let the nation own the trusts", but doubted that 'this definitely socialist sentiment and policy were 'a serious factor in the situation'.[2]

Hobson's unwillingness to trust to the 'inevitable' events of the future to right the wrongs of the present was the fundamental reason for his lack of interest in Wilshire's programme of combatting imperialism by preaching socialism in the form of an all-or-nothing demand for the nationalisation of industry. If the future was inevitable it would take care of itself. In the meantime Hobson preferred reforms that could be made now to revolutionary changes that might not come for decades or perhaps might never come at all. This led him to diverge from Wilshire in the concluding pages of his article on the 'Economic Taproot of Imperialism'. The editor of the *United States Investor* had perceived a glut of manufactured goods and capital seeking outlets, had decided that imperialism was inevitable without a basic change in the economic system and had thrown himself enthusiastically into the campaign to make imperialism the keynote of American foreign policy. Wilshire accepted the capitalists' word that a glut of goods and capital existed and predicted a nasty era of autocracy at home and abroad that would continue till the nation owned the trusts. Hobson also accepted that the glut existed: 'The process we may be told is inevitable, and so it seems upon a superficial inspection. Everywhere appear excessive powers of production, excessive capital in search of investment'. But it did not seem logical to Hobson to conclude from this that the only way to attack imperialism was to make a sudden, sweeping change in the whole economic and political system. Anything that could be done to provide alternative, home-based 'outlets' for goods and capital would to some extent relieve the pressure behind the aggressive

2. The American Trust', *Economic Review* XIV (Jan. 1904) 1-22.

foreign policies of nations. Hobson's remedy was social reform, the remedy Wilshire had dismissed as merely a temporary expedient which capitalists might use to put off their day of final reckoning with the masses. As Hobson saw it, any action which either 1) raised the consuming power of the poorer part of the population or 2) spent government funds on projects to benefit the people at large such as public housing, education, new towns, the beautification of cities, etc., would create new outlets for goods and capital, thus removing the pressure to seek outlets overseas. A little reform would relieve some of the pressure; a lot of reform would relieve a lot of the pressure. The contrasting conclusions of Wilshire and Hobson show up their basic differences. Wilshire wrote 'When we see imperialism, which is simply political autocracy ... we should not stultify ourselves by striving to prevent a result without first attacking the cause. Revolution and not reform must be our battle cry'. Hobson agreed that 'it is idle to attack imperialism or militarism as expedients or policies unless the axe is laid at the economic root of the tree', but concluded that since 'imperialism is the fruit' of a 'false economy, Social Reform is its remedy'.

At the same time it must be said that Hobson was very far from being a mild or wishy-washy reformist. He stated bluntly and firmly that 'the only safety of nations lies in removing the unearned increments of income from the possessing classes and adding them to the wage-income of the working classes or to the public income, in order that they may be spent in raising the standard of consumption'. That was an enormous demand to make in 1902. Many people denounced it as socialism. Many still do.

The British background to Hobson's ***Imperialism***

Hobson was already well along in his study of imperialism when he read Wilshire's article. He did not need an American to tell him that special interests benefitted greatly from armaments, territorial aggrandisement and a generally belligerent foreign policy. Hobson's tour of duty as a special correspondent in South Africa during the Boer War had confirmed his long-standing suspicion that such was the case. Nor did Hobson need an American to convince him that at a certain stage of capitalist development production will outpace consumption unless the state intervenes to boost consumption. Hobson as a theoretical economist had been writing about underconsumption since 1888.[3]

In August 1898 at the very time the *U.S. Investor* was discovering the virtues of imperialism, Hobson wrote an article on 'Free Trade and Foreign Policy' for the *Contemporary Review* which includes a couple of sentences which vaguely suggest the argument he would later make in the 'Taproot' essay. Although the article was essentially an argument against using force to 'open' markets, it contains the statement that 'our surplus products, which the working classes cannot buy and the wealthier classes do not wish to buy, must find customers among foreign nations, and, since those who sell them do not even desire to consume their equivalent in existing foreign goods, they must lie in foreign countries as loans or other permanent investments'. Thus, 'in the first resort, it is the excessive purchasing power of the well-to-do classes which, by requiring foreign investments, forces the opening up of foreign markets, and uses the public purse for the purposes of private profit-making'. Inasmuch as this short passage ignores trusts and cartels and mentions foreign investment only as an incidental by-product of the struggle for foreign markets, it cannot be regarded as a preliminary statement of the case he would make in 1902. It does, however, show that his mind was already working on lines parallel to Wilshire's.

Wilshire's particular contributions were, first, to relate a 'glut' of capital to industrial amalgamations designed to cope with excess capacity for production, and second, to show how investors were advocating the use of the state, armaments, colonial development and other forms of overseas activity to employ excess funds. At the time Hobson wrote his article Germans were talking for the first time about a glut of capital.

3. J. A. Hobson, *Confessions of an Economic Heretic* (London, 1938) 29-37.

He immediately applied Wilshire's argument to them. 'Germany is at the present time suffering severely from what is called a glut of capital and of manufacturing power: she must have new markets, her Consuls all over the world are "hustling" for trade, trading settlements are forced upon Asia Minor; in East and West Africa, in China and elsewhere the German Empire is impelled to a policy of colonisation and protectorates as outlets for German commercial energy'. As a man of peace Hobson was naturally alarmed that America, Germany and other countries were adopting increasingly warlike foreign policies. But of more immediate concern to him were the people in his own country who were saying that imperialism was not a choice but a necessity. The arguments for the 'necessity of imperialism' which Hobson put at the beginning of his article did not have to be borrowed from Wilshire or America. They were arguments being made in Britain at the turn of the century in the financial and economic journals which Hobson knew as a working economist and in journals like the *Contemporary Review* to which he contributed. These arguments, made mostly by unashamed capitalists, were to Hobson what the *United States Investor* was to Wilshire. They were the source of the idea that the necessity to develop future fields for investment required a policy of imperialism; they also represented the enemy which Hobson strove to defeat.

In Britain, as in America, there was a tendency to see the end of the nineteenth century as the end of an era in economic history. The age of competition was dead or dying. An age of monopolies and imperialism had dawned bringing with it social and political consequences for Europe which were bound to be momentous. In the nineteenth century Great Britain had flourished under the doctrines of free competition, free trade, and minimal government which had been expounded by Adam Smith in economic theory and by Richard Cobden in parliament. Many economic and financial writers doubted whether Britain would be able to dominate the new age as she had dominated the old one unless she fell into line with her rising economic competitors Germany and America whose industries were being organised into larger units and who used high protective tariffs to keep merchandise produced in other countries from competing with locally made goods. The respected economist A. C. Pigou pronounced in 1902 that 'whatever title it may choose or be compelled to take — Trust, Voting Trust, Consolidation, Combine — there can be no doubt at all that it has come to stay'.[4] The *Financial Times* asked for a reasoned discussion of a protectionist policy for Britain on the ground that 'we live now in an era of trusts and tariffs which Mr. Cobden in his wildest dreams could scarcely have imagined'.[5] An article in the *Fortnightly Review* entitled 'Face to Face with the Trusts' saw in the formation of the United States Steel Corporation a sign that the twentieth century would be 'the age of combination and monopoly'. The author believed that without protective tariffs British industry would be unable to withstand competition from the foreign giants.[6]

A crucial element in the American theory of imperialism was the supposed existence of surplus capital. In America trusts arose before anyone noticed surplus capital seeking outlets. The *U.S. Investor* and Wilshire were therefore able to attribute the glut to the progressive development of trusts. In Britain the situation was reversed. Hobson noticed that as early as 1885 a parliamentary report had drawn attention to 'the competition of the capital which is being steadily accumulated in the country'.[7] Monopolistic combinations were much slower to develop. This gave a different character to the British discussion of what the Americans called a 'plethora' of capital and what the English called a 'glut' of capital. A glut of capital was assumed to exist when interest

4. Review of J.B. Clark, *The Control of Trusts,* in *Economic Journal* XII (1902) 63.

5. 17 Jan. 1903, 2.

6. H.W. Wilson, 'Face to Face with the Trusts', *Fortnightly Review* LXXVI (July, 1901) 76-87.

7. 'The Economic Taproot of Imperialism', *Contemporary Review* LXXII (1902) 224.

rates on borrowed money were very low. This was often a merely temporary phenomenon which could be satisfactorily explained by current conditions. During a recession or a period of international tension, uncertainty in the business world could narrow the range of promising investment opportunities. For example, in 1895 the editor of *Bankers' Magazine* welcomed a boom in South African mining shares as an 'outlet for idle money' without for a moment thinking that there was a permanent glut.[8] For extended periods unhappy investors might prefer low rates of interest offered by British enterprises to high rates of interest offered abroad if foreign circumstances appeared to be exceptionally threatening. The influential financial weekly *The Statist* believed this had been the case throughout most of the eighteen nineties and hoped in 1900 that a British takeover of the Transvaal Republic along with an improvement in relations between the great powers would revive prospects for foreign investment.[9]

The situation which required most explaining and which aroused fears of a permanent surplus was one in which, during a boom period for domestic industries, interest rates stayed low and capital flowed abroad in search of investment opportunities. This was the American situation in 1900 which the *Statist* found 'remarkable' and which raised in the minds of other financial editors the possibility of a coming world-wide glut. The *Investor's Chronicle* perceived 'in the distance an era of superabundance of capital — a glut'. There would be no more 'new countries yearning for it, and ready to take, for a consideration, the surplus of the "creditor" nations. But that prospect appeared to the editor to be a 'problem for our grandchildren'. In the meantime there were possibilities in the undeveloped world.

The world is fast growing rich, and by degrees the profitable lending out of capital becomes more difficult and less remunerative. Countries which

8. *Bankers', Insurance Managers' and Agents' Magazine* LIX (1895) 61, 62, 187-88, 329-39, 609-11.

9. 30 June 1900, 985-86. The paper, subsidised by South African interests, had been advocating British intervention long before the outbreak of war.

> twenty years ago lacked the money to fully develop their own resources, and consequently had to borrow it abroad, have by this time accumulated such a vast store of wealth that they seek an outlet for part of it....The yield of capital goes down, and the difficulty of combining a good return with safety leads people into speculative ventures and loss. This compels us to remain on the lookout for unexplored fields for investment — China for instance; and the person who offers a really good first-class 4 per cent investment finds an eager market ready to absorb to almost any amount.[10]

By the time Hobson began his study of imperialism, talk of overproduction, a general glut, and the need for overseas outlets permeated the financial community. So lowly a person as 'an English Savings Bank Manager' fretted that 'at the present time the English nation is suffering from a plethora of gold, and that to such an extent that it is becoming acquainted with the multi-millionaire's difficulty, how to dispose of his ever-accumulating savings'.[11]

Some people believed that government action to deal with these problems in an increasingly dangerous world was not only desirable but 'inevitable'. At the turn of the century the idea of economic determinism took hold of economists in much the same way that Darwin's theory of evolution had gripped biologists of the previous generation and Freud's theory of the primacy of the subconscious would grip psychologists of the next generation. In a paper read before the Economic Section of the British Association in September, 1898 Ethel Faraday used the theory of economic determinism to account for the sudden enthusiasm for imperial expansion among advanced industrial nations.[12] 'In most cases', she explained, 'the rage for Empire is not a symptom of national insanity, but a natural result of the interdependence of economics and politics. History affords

10. *Investor's Chronicle* I (1900) 114; III (1902) 197.

11. 'The Problem of Our National Savings', *Economic Journal* IX (1899) 569. The surplus named was literally the deposits of the savings banks, not the whole sum of national investment capital. It is cited as an example of language current among financial writers.

12. 'Some Economic Aspects of the Imperial Idea', *Fortnightly Review* LXX (1898) 961-67.

sufficient proof that a change in economic principles or conditions is usually accompanied by a corresponding change in political institutions and theories'. In her own era, Faraday believed that the expansion of empires was the political expression of changed economic conditions and 'the imperial idea' was the expression of those same conditions in the world of theory.

Faraday gave a very special meaning to 'the imperial idea'. It was not something that the vast British Empire had adopted in the past; it was something she expected the British to embrace in the near future. That is, it was 'the German conception of Empire' which had come 'into sudden prominence' in the year 1871: an empire conceived as a group of united territories self-sufficient in all the raw materials required for economic growth and protected by high tariffs against trading goods manufactured outside the empire. If Britain were to adopt the 'imperial idea' as a national policy she would have to abandon free trade and erect tariff walls around the empire. She would also have to adopt a rational plan of economic development to meet future contingencies.

This feeling, that other countries were ahead of Britain in adopting development plans appropriate to changing economic conditions, was heightened by what foreigners themselves were saying about imperial policy. In the *Economic Journal*, England's most prestigious and intellectual journal of economic opinion, there were full, frequent and disquieting reviews of foreign publications. An article on 'Germany's Commercial Progress' traced the origins of the prevalent, slightly absurd idea of a German Ambassador as 'a sort of superior commercial agent' to the fact that 'German diplomatic representatives abroad are very properly alive to the close connection of national trade and national prosperity'.[13] A review of George Adler's book on *The Future of the Social Question (Die Zukunft der Sozialen Fragen)* called attention to his contention that the welfare of the German

13. W.H. Dawson, 'Germany's Commercial Progress', *Economic Journal* XI (1901) 573.

middle and working classes depended above all on 'the growth of capitalistic production which necessitates national expansion'.[14] The reviewer of a book on *The German Empire of Today* thought that what the Germans were currently saying about colonies was harmless ('at present little more than expensive toys') but what they understood by 'colonial policy' — a big army and navy in pursuit of world power — was 'pregnant with possibilities of dangerous, costly conflict'.[15]

By the time Hobson brought out his study of imperialism, readers of the *Economic Journal* were also reasonably familiar with the new American theory of capitalist imperialism, not only through notices of Conant's work, but also through reviews of the latest writings of Brooks Adams. In 1899 another journal, the *Fortnightly Review* treated readers to a concentrated dose of Adams by reprinting his essay on "The New Struggle for Life Among Nations'.[16] Like Ethel Faraday, Adams believed that the rise of 'an entirely new economic system' in Germany in 1870 inaugurated a new 'phase of civilization'. At about the same time Britain and France had begun spectacular and probably irreversible slides towards insignificance in global politics. Everywhere there was a movement away from individualism towards collectivism, a movement which was best exemplified by the rise of 'those huge agglomerations called trusts', by 'the centralisation of Germany' and by 'the organisation of Russia'. As Adams envisioned the future, central and eastern Europe were destined to coalesce into a power bloc governed by a grey, bureaucratised state socialism. The only conceivable rival to this eastern bloc would be the United States. Both the Americans and their adversaries had developed to the point where a 'glut' was imminent unless they developed overseas outlets. Because 'the most tempting regions of the earth' had been seized by the decaying powers of western Europe in their

14. Review by M. Beer, *Economic Journal* XI (1901) 392.

15. Review by L.L. Price, *Economic Journal* XII (1902) 383-84.

16. *Fortnightly Review* LXV (1899) 274-83.

bygone era of imperial expansion, the focus of the bipolar struggle for world power had narrowed to east Asia. Either America would succeed in staking out a permanent field for goods and capital in that far quarter of the globe or she herself would be forced to adopt the stultifying 'system of State socialism'. Success or failure would depend on the Americans' ability to abandon the more inefficient aspects of 'Anglo-Saxon individualism' and 'to organise so as to be able to strike quickly and sharply in war' in order to 'terrify their adversary, or crush him if he attacks'.

S.J. Chapman who reviewed Adams' book on *America's Economic Supremacy* for the *Economic Journal* was less than terrified by the prospects of a precipitous British decline into obscurity.[17] He poked fun at Adams' solemn attempt to prove 'the decay of England' by 'her preference for Dickens to Sir Walter Scott'. According to Chapman, Sir Robert Giffen of the Royal Statistical Society could produce unchallengeable facts and figures to refute every item of the statistical case Adams tried to make out for Britain's decline. Giffen did indeed claim to have such figures but he was far from optimistic about the future. In fact, he was quite as concerned as Brooks Adams about the growing militarised powers of continental Europe. 'The three great military governments' are, he wrote in 1900,

> taking a novel interest in the affairs of distant countries which are important to us as countries with which we have a great deal of trade, which makes their action dangerous to peace among themselves and to peace with this country. No concession we can make will permanently satisfy them, not even the partition of our Colonial possessions amongst them.[18]

One way of meeting the threat was to build up Britain's military forces to such an extent that even a coalition of hostile powers would fear to confront her.

A separate fear was that without a resort to brute force the monopolistic trusts and cartels growing up in America would destroy British industry bit by bit through the process

17. *Economic Journal* X (1900) 522-23.

18. 'Our Trade Prosperity and the Outlook', *Economic Journal* X (1900) 299-305.

known as 'dumping'. Dumping depends on the existence of protective tariffs. The idea is that by amalgamation or a gentlemen's agreement the producers in a particular industry acquire the power to fix prices in their own country at levels which guarantee them a good profit. Goods produced in other countries are prevented from underselling them by the customs duties which the government charges on foreign made goods. If the monopolists produce more goods than consumers in their own country are willing or able to buy, the goods are 'dumped' in other countries. That is, they are sold at prices at or below the cost of production. The monopolistic profits made in the home market offset the losses made on foreign sales. Unless the foreign producers invent cheaper techniques for manufacturing their own products or persuade their governments to impose tariffs high enough to keep out 'dumped' goods, they will be unable to compete and will go out of business. In 1901 the newly formed United States Steel Corporation appeared to be set to give the world an object lesson in the theory and practice of dumping.[19]

To some British economic and financial writers it appeared that the best way to meet the triple threat of domestic surplus capital, foreign militarism and foreign trusts capable of wiping out British industry by dumping was to take up the 'imperial idea' — that is, to throw a wall of protective tariffs around the British empire and weld its diverse peoples and territories into a self-sufficient economic system with enormous military strength. By the end of the eighteen nineties this conception of the world divided into heavily armed, competing systems which aspired to self-sufficient future growth was what most British economists meant when they used the phrase 'the new imperialism'. Because Germany had pioneered this approach, it was usual to date the rise of 'the new imperialism' (as Ethel Faraday and Brooks Adams did) to either 1870 when Germany triumphed in the Franco-Prussian war or 1871 when Wilhelm, King of Prussia,

19. Wilson, 'Face to Face with the Trusts', 76, 85-87.

was proclaimed Emperor of Germany.[20] Thus, when Ethel Faraday spoke to the British Association in 1898 on 'Economic Aspects of the Imperial Idea' she did not speak of imperialism as something Britain had been doing during the past few decades; she talked about something Britain might do in the future in order to meet her rivals on equal or better than equal terms. From this point of view Britain's overseas territories, however vast they might be, would not become an empire in the modern German sense until they were surrounded by a wall of tariffs. Without protection they were, as another economist wrote a few years later, no more than 'a set of second rate States' linked by history and sentiment alone.[21] Joseph Chamberlain, who as British Colonial Secretary had proposed in 1897 to copy the Germans by creating an 'Imperial Zollverein' (customs union) and who resigned his ministry in 1903 to campaign for protective tariffs, had this special meaning in mind when he spoke of the need to create 'an Empire such as the world had never seen' by cementing 'the union of the States beyond the seas, to consolidate the British race to meet the clash of competition and strife'.

In this conception of empire colonies were more important as future fields for trade and investment and as sources of essential raw materials than as present assets. Few if any economists imagined that Britain's old colonies had been acquired with these particular aims in mind. Indeed, most would have agreed with the historian J.R. Seeley who said they had been acquired in a 'fit of absence of mind'.[22] However, what had been acquired for no reasons or for 'strategic' reasons could be turned to worthwhile economic purposes. This discriminating functional approach to colonial questions is fairly well exemplified by the attitudes taken by the financial paper, the *Statist*.

20. In 1871 the German Empire was economically still only a customs union. Protection was adopted in the late 1870s and was by no means universally approved. See Edward Bernstein, 'German Professors and Protectionism', *Contemporary Review* (1904) 18-31.

21. W.J. Ashley, 'The Argument for Preference', *Economic Journal* XIV (1904) 1-8.

22. J.R. Seeley, *The Expansion of England,* (London, 1883) 10.

Lloyd, the editor, believed that foreign trade was less important to Britain than domestic trade and he was distinctly hostile to the notion of grabbing territory for trading purposes. In 1898 he advocated letting France take what she wanted in West Africa. 'The whole of West Africa', he claimed, was 'not worth the powder that would be fired away in a single great naval engagement'. To quarrel with France over 'West African swamps' or with Germany over Samoa would be 'absurd'. India was worth keeping but was handicapped as a field for investment by the bureaucratic British administration which breathed the spirit of eighteenth-century monopoly rather than modern capitalism. On the subject of China the *Statist* took issue with other capitalist papers who believed in a great potential for trade. Official involvement in China, apart from supporting the principle of the 'open door' for traders of all nations, would risk war merely 'for the sake of putting money into the pockets of adventurous institutions, syndicates and merchants'. However, where great investment opportunities and real strategic interests did exist — in south, central and east Africa for example — the *Statist* believed in imperial development with no holds barred. In Lloyd's opinion the continued revival of the entire world economy in the late eighteen nineties depended on expanding gold production. He believed that the antiquated government of the Transvaal Republic in South Africa must be reformed or removed before the great gold fields of the Witwatersrand could develop their full potential. To the north, Rhodesia appeared to be a promising field for future investments. Egypt had to remain in British hands because of the strategic importance of the Suez Canal route to India. And 'it would be madness to allow the headwaters of the Nile to fall into the hands of any Power, no matter what, able to divert the river from Egypt'. For the consolidation and development of all these African interests, Lloyd believed that a Cape-to-Cairo railway should be constructed as soon as possible. War in defense of such vital interests would be entirely justifiable. Recognising that in twentieth-century conditions Britain would need an even more powerful army and navy, Lloyd recommended the wholesale recruitment of non-white soldiers from the more warlike peoples of the British empire.[23]

The very idea of employing black or yellow soldiers in European wars horrified a great many of Lloyd's contemporaries, but there was nearly universal support in economic and financial journals for expanded armaments. Some protectionists proposed to use revenue from the collection of customs and duties to pay for a bigger army and a more awe-inspiring navy.[24] Some believed that an equally good case could be made out in favour of government subsidies to strategic interests such as the shipping industry which would be of vital importance in the event of a major European war.[25] Sir Robert Giffen wrote in 1902 that

> On all sides it is felt that British shipping is now exposed to competition of a far graver character than any it has yet experienced, while the connected questions of the bounties or subsidies given by foreign Governments to promote a particular business, and of the effect of the huge combinations or trusts which have obtained so much vogue in America, acquires a new importance.[26]

This generalised worry was given a specific focus by the takeover of Britain's Leyland Shipping line by the American J.P. Morgan syndicate in 1901. Shipbuilding had long been recognised as an essential market for British steel. The ability of orders received from the Royal Navy to expand employment of skilled and unskilled labour had occasionally been a godsend to the economy at large. Thus, in 1902 when Hobson was compiling his study of imperialism there was

23. *Statist.* 26 Feb., 9 and 16 April, 14 and 21 May, 13 Aug., 10 and 17 Sept., 1 and 15 Oct. 1898, pp. 333, 600-602, 638-39, 801, 840, 243, 379-81, 416, 495, 575; 7 and 21 Jan., 8, 15 and 16 April, 9 Sept., 1899, pp. 18-19, 85, 535-36, 580, 637, 399.24. *Economic Journal* XIV (1904) 496.

24. G. W. Gough, 'Constructive Economics', *Economic Journal* XIV (1904) 496.

25. Benjamin Taylor, 'The Commercial Sovereignty of the Seas', *Fortnightly Review* LXV (1899) 284-99.

26. 'City Notes', *Economic Journal* XII (1902) 282.

widespread talk of government intervention to safeguard this highly beneficial and strategic industry.[27]

The 'new imperialism' with its comprehensive programme of consolidating, developing, defending and subsidising the empire would obviously entail massive government participation in the economy as well as curbs on individual freedom. Some British capitalists took the position adopted by the *U.S. Investor* in America, that the abandonment of *laissez faire* economics and limitations on freedom were the prices which had to be paid for continued capitalist development in the twentieth century. Faraday's consideration of the 'Economic Aspects of the Imperial Idea' attempted to face facts calmly. Great Britain along with other developed countries, was looking for a guaranteed future 'outlet for capital'. Faraday believed that the Empire could provide that outlet if it were united and protected by a customs union. Assured of future markets, the 'Mother Country' could continue to expand her production of finished goods. The colonies would be equally assured of a future market for their raw materials and would therefore not be 'exposed to the danger of an excessive development of manufacturing industry'. Colonies with populations 'in different stages of progress, belonging to different races and sometimes to different types of civilisation' offered some exciting opportunities for profit.

> New colonies often reproduce the conditions of earlier periods of social growth, such as the medieval phenomena of high rates of interest, labour rents and the importance of the municipality. In such cases, the economic conception of Empire requires that the application of the latest conclusions of economic science should be postponed. The Imperial idea allows the existence of Bagehot's 'provisional institutions'. An economist, without denying that slavery is an unsocial institution and free contract the best stimulus to exertion, may yet hold that in certain parts of South Africa a system of forced native labour is capable of becoming economically beneficial to both colonists and aborigines.

27. B. Taylor, 'The Martime Expansion of America', *Fortnightly Review* LXXVI (1901) 61-75; J. Quail, 'British Investors and American combines', *Investor's Chronicle* IV (1902) 239-42; *Statist*, 16 April 1898, 646 and 28 Jan. 1899, 133.

She foresaw that politicians might raise humanitarian and democratic objections to these hard-nosed doctrines, but warned against 'a traditional and exaggerated respect for Parliament'.'Modern thought', she continued,

> assigns to constitutional history a place subordinate to economic and military history, and suggests that the possibilities of representative Government are not infinite, and that the living interests of the future will be economic rather than political. What is certain is that the fate of the Imperial idea, for years to come, remains with the economist....[28]

Medieval rates of interest, forced labour, and authoritarian rule by experts — in its own cool, reserved British way, Faraday's prospectus for the 'new imperialism' is as unsettling as the firebreathing American oratory of Brooks Adams or the self-righteous cupidity of the *United States Investor.* None of these economic prophets exulted in the illiberal future that lay ahead; they claimed that they were simply bowing to 'stern facts' of the age.

When British economic and financial writers looked beyond current 'necessities' and asked themselves 'where will it all end?', they were capable of conjuring up some nasty, even nightmarish scenarios. Some believed that without the adoption of protective tariffs and an imperial development plan the eventual effect of business as usual in foreign investment would be the rise of new economic monsters who would turn upon and perhaps ruin their creators. The United States was a prime example of a one-time field of investment grown into a threatening giant. The super-industrious Chinese might turn the tables on Europe in much the same way.[29] Another potential danger was European war, possibly fought on a global scale by mercenary coloured armies.[30] Alternatively, advanced nations might settle their differences and undertake what the German Socialist Karl Kautsky would

28. 'Economic Aspects', 964-67.

29. *Statist* 12 Feb. 1898; *Financial Times* 10 Oct. 1903, 2.

30. *Statist* 24 Nov. 1900, 839. This idea was partly inspired by the experience of migratory labour in different parts of the Empire; see *Economic Journal* XIII (1903) 140-41.

later call 'ultra-imperialism': that is, the systematic exploitation of the underdeveloped world could be undertaken either by a consortium of European nations or by 'the whole English-speaking world', 'combined for certain great purposes in vast parts of the world'.[31]

In the longer run, there were signs that the era of trusts and imperialism would force the pace of social change, perhaps even to the point of revolution. Giffen foresaw 'a possible change in the national character resulting from the very magnitude of the accumulation of capital'; an increasing section of the British population was 'living upon its capital, and not taking part in the actual everyday work of the world'.[32] At the opposite end of the scale from this burgeoning 'rentier' class were the unemployed and the wretched poor. It did not require a great deal of imagination to see the irony of a 'demand for expansion of trade abroad... based upon the idea that we manufacture more than we consume, when there are so many of our people who are workless, ahungered and ragged'.[33] Even a stoutly capitalist paper like the *Statist* could, when it suited its purposes, discourage rich 'City friends' from investing money in high risk areas such as China when there was so much human suffering in western Ireland, in the Scottish highlands, and in 'the slums and alleys of our great cities'.[34] Another writer prophesied great problems if British manufacturers had to stand up to competition from American trusts and German cartels free to 'dump' excess production at low prices. The competition could only be met by introducing labour saving machines on an unprecendented scale, but

Capital dare not and cannot force labour to accept these appliances because

31. *Economic Journal* XII (1902) 279-80; *Statist* 14 May 1898, 809.

32. *Economic Journal* XII (1902) 279-82.

33. J. G. Brooks, 'Organised Labour in the United States', *Economic Journal* IX (1899) 90.

34. *Statist* 15 Jan. 1898. Investment in South Africa gold mines was, of course, quite a different matter.

of the grave social problems which the situation of the dislodged workers would present .... Sir R. Giffen has spoken of the growth of 'social wreckage' in our industrial system, and Mr. J.A. Hobson thinks that of the working classes 'nearly two millions are liable at any time to figure as surplus labour'. Before such terrifying facts the attitudes of both unions and employers become intelligible. The one class dreads the sacrifice of its members; the other class dreads the social result of that sacrifice.[35]

He thought the only way to stave off social upheaval was to 'put up a tariff wall round our islands, and round the Empire'. To the right of him were capitalists who feared that even protective tariffs were a form of state intervention in the economy which might lead towards socialism.[36] To the left were Wilshire's old associates, the Fabian economists who saw in every aspect of economic life — in trusts, protection and imperialism — an inevitable, though gradual progress towards the same end.[37] And of course farther still to the left were Wilshire's revolutionary comrades who saw that the trusts could 'be made to fit so well into the Marxian doctrine' and predicted that 'if capitalism bursts up in America, it will burst up in Europe'.[38]

It can now be seen that when Hobson set out to write his book on imperialism in 1902 he was entering into a lively discussion among capitalists and economists in his own country as well as in America. On all sides there were writers who believed in economic determinism and proclaimed the 'necessity' or 'inevitability' of imperialism. Hobson hated imperialism and all the anti-democratic tendencies that were associated with it. He set out to disprove the thesis of economic determinism by convincing the British people that it was open to them to choose a different, more humane foreign policy. Capitalists put forward the thesis that a surplus of

35. Wilson, 'Face to Face with the Trusts', 83-84.

36. *Financial Times*, 28 Nov. 1903, 5.

37. See, for example A.W. Flux's review of J.W. Macrosty's *Trusts and the State*, *Economic Journal* XI (1901) 213. The best treatment of the Fabian attitudes is still Bernard Semmel, *Imperialism* and *Social Reform* (Harvard, 1960).

38. H.W. Macrosty, review of P. Lagargue, *Les Trusts Americains*, *Economic Journal* XIV (1904) 73.

capital made imperialism inevitable. Hobson replied with the counter-thesis that if investors were stripped of their surplus funds and those funds were applied to worthwhile social purposes such as higher wages and public works, there would be no irresistible economic pressure on Britain to practise imperialism.

Hobson's method of argument

Hobson's article on 'the Economic Taproot of Imperialism' became the sixth of the fourteen chapters in his book on imperialism. It has been necessary to consider it at length in order to bring out two points. The first is that it was the discussion in America and Britain concerning the imperial implications of surplus investment capital and industrial amalgamations that inspired the article. The second is that in the 'Taproot' article Hobson displays his favourite technique of argumentation — one that is used in almost every chapter of his book. First he sets out the argument of his opponents, in this case that surplus capital and productive capacity make imperialism a necessity. He goes out of his way to state the opposing case as fairly and convincingly as possible. (Sometimes he does this so well that readers fall into the mistake of taking the opposing arguments to be Hobson's own beliefs). His next step is to show up errors of fact and logic in the opposing argument; in the case of imperialism, the mistake is to think that an aggressive foreign policy is the only means of coping with excess goods and capital. The third step is to point out that supporters of the opposing case are often self-interested individuals and groups who try to identify their own selfish aims with the national interest. In the 'taproot' article, it is worried investors who claim that their own enrichment through the development of special overseas fields of investment is essential to Britain's progress and prosperity. Finally, Hobson offers his own policy for promoting the general good.

CHAPTER 4
HOBSON'S STUDY OF IMPERIALISM

Hobson's famous book, *Imperialism A Study* has an episodic, disjointed character. This is partly due to his argumentative technique. By introducing each chapter with the arguments of unidentified opponents, he destroys the continuity of his own case. Another reason for the episodic character of the book is that other chapters besides the 'Taproot' chapter were originally written and published as self-contained articles. But the most basic reason for the disjointed nature of Hobson's book is that in his day imperialism as a doctrine was a many-headed monster. The advocates of protection, colonial expansion and militarism had other arguments to make besides the argument based upon surplus investment capital. They said the continuation of Britain's expansion would provide an outlet for surplus population, that it would open new opportunities for trade, that it would bring moral and material benefits to 'lower races', that the unification of freedom-loving English-speaking peoples was a noble aim, and that in any case struggle for growth and life was as important to the progress of nations as Darwin had shown it to be in the evolution of species. Hobson decided that it was wiser to attack the heads of the monster one by one rather than to take them all on at once. The chapters of his book are therefore single combats which can be read in almost any order. His arguments have been distorted and caricatured so often that it is worthwhile summarising those chapters and spelling out his own alternative programmes for world economic development.

It is a moral stance rather that a single thesis or developing argument which gives a sense of overall unity to Hobson's study. He perpetuated in his generation the values of the old Victorian school of political economy whose watchwords were peace and freedom. Back in the days when imperialism meant only autocratic government and militarism, Richard Cobden had worked to purge the British empire of all its illiberal practices. He and his parliamentary allies were close enough to the eighteenth century to detect the stink of class privilege and corruption in almost every corner of the empire. They had learned from Adam Smith that the whole eighteenth-century imperial system with its tariffs, monopolistic royal charters and navigation laws enriched the favoured few while it actually hampered the progress of the rest of the nation whose interests it was alleged to protect. In the generation before Cobden, James Mill had called the empire 'a vast system of outdoor relief for the upper classes'. By eliminating the last protective tariffs, advocating representative government for the colonies, transfering the government of India from the East India Company to the Crown, and opposing the use of the army and navy for any but defensive purposes, the Cobdenites of the eighteen fifties hoped to liberate the empire from any hint of imperialism. They expected that international free trade, minimal government, representative institutions, and the development of unfettered competitive capitalism would eventually spread peace, prosperity and freedom everywhere.

Hobson had seen enough of unfettered capitalism to doubt the inevitability of any of these happy developments and he challenged the economic theory that first generated those predictions. But he clung passionately to the ideals of peace, freedom and a better material life for all. Though he abandoned laissez faire capitalism, he remained as suspicious of tariffs as Adam Smith, as cynical about imperial office holders as James Mill. The new doctrines of outlets for investment and imperial consolidation gave a sense of urgency to Hobson's critique of imperialism. He set out to link the dangerous doctrines of the present to the abuses of the past, to provide humane alternatives for imperial development, and to portray some of the nightmarish future developments which might occur if his good advice were ignored.[1] Hobson's views may, therefore, be conveniently

1. The place of Hobson's work in the British radical tradition has been explored by Bernard Porter, *Critics of Empire* (London, 1968) and P.J. Cain, 'J.A. Hobson, Cobdenism, and the Radical Theory of Economic Imperialism, 1898-1914', *Economic History Review*, 2nd series, XXII (1978) 565-84.

summarised under three headings; first, Hobson's updating of the Cobdenite critique of illiberal empire; second, Hobson's preferred alternatives for world developments; and third, Hobson's dark prophecies of the future.

Hobson the Cobdenite

Hobson did not follow Faraday, Adams and most economists in tracing the origins of 'the new imperialism' to the appearance of the 'German system of empire' in 1870. Instead he began his book with a brief look at what Britain had been doing for the last thirty years. He aimed to show:

1) that the colonial territories most recently added to the Empire were unsuitable for the programme of consolidation, development and future trade which the imperial enthusiasts proposed.

2) that Britain's aggressive foreign policy and military build-up had endangered rather than promoted peace.

3) that the only people who gained any tangible benefit from these policies were a privileged minority of vested interests.

4) that further imperialism would spread autocracy abroad, endanger liberty at home, and make the many pay for the enrichment of the few.

Though the statistics he used to make out his case were as up-to-date as the latest issue of the Journal of the Royal Statistical Society, the arguments he used were old hat.

Orthodox free trade theory held that it was not necessary to own a country to trade with it and that the best way to promote profitable trading was to let traders deal with whomever they wished. The orthodox conclusion drawn from this theory was that acquiring colonies did nothing to improve trade. However, there had long been a vocal minority who believed that whatever ivory-tower theorists might say, 'trade did follow the flag'.[2] At the time Hobson wrote, this old dissenting view seemed to be making headway because it linked up with the new argument that in a world of trusts and tariffs British traders would need the protection of the flag. Hobson's way of refuting the proposition was to look at the part played by the most recently acquired colonies in the over-all pattern of British trade. With the help of some devastatingly effective statistics Hobson easily succeeded in reaffirming the faith of Cobden : trade did not follow the flag. 'The greatest increase of our foreign trade was with that group of industrial nations whom we regard as our industrial enemies, and whose political enmity we are in danger of arousing by our policy of expansion – France, Germany, Russia, and the United States .... of the trade with British possessions the tropical trade, and in particular the trade with the new tropical possessions is the smallest, least progressive, and most fluctuating in quantity, while it is lowest in the character of the goods which it embraces'.[3] In the next chapter Hobson scored an equally easy victory over those who said that an empire materially benefited the British people by giving them an outlet for surplus population. The free movement of people was as much an article of faith with the old free traders as the free movement of goods. Hobson again used statistics to show that lately the rate of emigration from Britain had been declining and that those who did emigrate showed a marked preference for settling outside the newer parts of the Empire.

Who then had gained anything real from British imperial expansion? Hobson gave the answer James Mill had given

2. Attempts to prove that trade followed the flag almost always failed for want of evidence. See: Lord Farer, 'Does Trade Follow the Flag?', *Contemporary Review* LXXIV (1898) 810-35; Lord Masham, 'Does Trade Follow the Flag? A Reply', *Contemporary Review* LXXV (1899) 218-22; A.W. Flux, 'The Flag and Trade', *Journal of the Royal Statistical Society* LXII (1899) 489-533.

3. *Imperialism, A Study* (London, 1902) 38, 44. Subsequent quotations are taken from the first edition except when a later edition is indicated by a footnote.

decades earlier : a very small number of privileged, self-interested people. In chapter IV he identified these 'economic parasites of imperialism'. The agents of imperialism which he singles out in this chapter are very similar to those identified in America by Wilshire and the *United States Investor.* They include the army, the navy, and the diplomatic service as well as the administrators of overseas territories. Since the British government was not in the business of making its own guns, ships, uniforms, railways, office buildings, etc., it had to purchase them from private suppliers. Hobson believed that there was a self-interested alliance between the ambitious officials who ran the empire and the private businesses who supplied them. A lesser group of self-interested allies of the public agencies of imperialism were the pioneering settlers of new territories who looked to the government to promote their prosperity. When a foreign government in a backward country fell under the influence or inspiration of Britain, borrowed money by selling bonds to British investors, and spent it to employ British rail manufacturers, engineers or military advisors, similar advantages accrued to the same privileged classes.

There was nothing in this account of Britain's foreign and colonial policy that Cobden could not have written had he lived longer, but it does nonetheless offer an interesting hypothesis about the growth of the British empire in the nineteenth century. Hobson presented expansion as a continuous and ongoing process which fed on itself. Old institutions once dominated by the aristocracy adapted to new circumstances by forming profitable alliances with some upper middle class business interests. Bureaucratic inertia, tradition and unquestioned assumptions about the nation's commercial and strategic interests made the empire grow like a weed except when other more powerful interests might be hurt by the expansion. Hobson was not an historian, so he did not bother accumulating documentary evidence to prove his case. For reasons that will be suggested later, no historian since Hobson's day has tried to test the thesis by examining the class origins of the men who ran the empire and the men who supplied it. Instead most imperial historians have concentrated on proving Hobson's other assertions: that nineteenth-century imperial expansion was motivated neither by prospects of trade nor by the economic interests of most businessmen.

Hobson was concerned with the future rather than the past and realised that the arguments of Cobden's day were not quite enough to defeat the 'new imperialists' of the twentieth century. In Britain and America the enthusiasts of aggressive imperialism were not arguing that expansion *had been* necessary to provide outlets for investment and trade *in the past.* They were arguing that those outlets *would be necessary in the future* and that without them the whole British economy would be gradually ruined by competition from foreign rivals sheltering under 'the German conception of empire'. To bring Cobden fully up to date Hobson needed to show that lurking behind this new appeal to the national interest there was also the greed of a vested interest. It is at this point that Hobson brings in Wilshire's explanation of investment imperialism. Wilshire claimed that the investors with surplus capital were anything but representative of the whole American people. They were an insignificant fraction of the super-rich who had gagged on their own inability to spend their money and whose opportunities for investment were being cut off by the progressive organisation of industries into trusts with excess capacity for production. This was the very thing Hobson needed to close the ring of his argument. The possessors of surplus capital demanding outlets for investment were also a self-interested clique pushing the government into bellicose policies that harmed the nation at large.

Wilshire's argument as incorporated in Hobson's article on 'The Economic Taproot of Imperialism' became Chapter VI of his book. Hobson laid the groundword for the introduction of the argument by adding two sections to his chapter IV on the 'Economic Parasites of Imperialism'. The first of these sections concerned investors and investments in general. He pointed out that 'the period of energetic Imperialism' after 1884 'coincided with a remarkable growth in the income from foreign investments' received by people in Great Britain. (p. 57) He regarded this burgeoning of investment income as prima facia evidence that a 'glut' or 'plethora' of capital existed. Seeing that British investments were going to every corner of the globe (he neither said nor implied that they were going mostly to present or prospective colonies), Hobson believed that investors would use every influence they possessed to ensure that British foreign policy enhanced the value of their speculations. He stated the proposition broadly and baldly: 'It is not too much to say that the modern foreign policy of Great Britain is primarily a struggle for profitable markets of investment'. This may seem exaggerated and oversimplified to modern readers but it merely repeated a commonplace idea held by Hobson's contemporaries. A few months before the publication of *Imperialism, A Study*, one enthusiastic imperialist wrote 'Ambassadors and consuls, the complex machinery which they keep going, and even war itself, owe their existence, in the last analysis, to a nation's resolve to hold the old outlets for its industry or to win new ones'.[4]

The second section Hobson added to Chapter IV concerned 'the special interest of the financier, the general dealer in investments'. In Hobson's view, the 'financier' made money by fluctuations in the market place rather than by sinking capital in long-term investments which aimed to create wealth. Whereas the capitalist whose entire fortune was staked on the success of Australian mining would alternatively gasp with despair and chuckle with glee as the market value of his shares rose and fell, the financier shifted funds from industry to industry and from country to country

4. Ogniben, 'The United States of Imperial Britain', *Contemporary Review* LXXXI (1902) 305-26. Compare also *U.S. Investor* 23 April 1898, 593: 'Wars, treaties, colonization schemes, and all the intricacies of diplomacy are really, on a final analysis, but means to one great end — the extension of trade, and the enlargement of the means of acquiring wealth'.

with blithe unconcern. The financier had special techniques which enabled him to make money as fast in a falling share market as in a rising one. The ultimate fate of particular nations mattered as little to him as the fate of particular companies or industries. If the value of French francs was falling and the value of German marks was rising, the financier sold francs and bought marks. Hobson argued that imperialism, understood ·in the broadest sense as the aggressive use of the armed state power abroad, was good for the financier because it created continual uncertainties and fluctuations in the market place. 'A policy which arouses fears of aggression in Asiatic states, and which fans the rivalry of commercial nations in Europe, evokes vast expenditure on armaments, and ever-accumulating public debts, while the doubts and risks accruing from this policy promote that constant oscillation of values, of securities which is so profitable to the skilled financier. There is not a war, a revolution, and anarchist assassination, or any other public shock, which is not gainful to these men; they are harpies who suck their gains from every new forced expenditure and every sudden disturbance of public credit'. He stops just short of accusing them of deliberately stirring up war. 'The policy of these men, it is true, does not make for war; where war would bring about too great and too permanent a damage to the substantial fabric of industry, which is the ultimate and essential basis of speculation, their influence is cast for peace....' (pp. 64-66)

It would seem far-fetched in the extreme to accuse financiers who operated on such a gigantic scale of taking a close interest in individual pieces of gun-boat diplomacy or territorial annexations. Hobson wisely refrains from doing so. He says that 'the motor-power of imperialism' was supplied by the 'politicians, soldiers, philanthropists' and other narrow interests he listed earlier in the chapter. 'Finance' is 'the governor of the imperial engine, directing the energy and determining its work'. Through their influence with politicians and their control of the press, financiers are generally able to exacerbate the processes of armament, expansion and international rivalry.

This was a view of world affairs which differed considerably from the theories of the *U.S. Investor*, C.A. Conant, Gaylord Wilshire, and Hobson's British contemporaries. In addition to saying that investors with surplus capital tried to interest governments in maintaining aggressive foreign policies, Hobson said that a little group of particular individuals was so clever and knowledgeable as to know in advance how to profit from the fluctuations in share and currency values caused by international tensions. Hobson underlined the point with an unsubstantiated accusation that was unworthy of his intelligence and his generally high moral principles. He said there was an international conspiracy of Jewish financiers. 'These great businesses — banking, broking, bill discounting, loan floating, company promoting — form the central ganglion of international capitalism. United by the strongest bonds of organisation, always in closest and quickest touch with one another, situated in the very heart of every state, controlled, so far as Europe is concerned, chiefly by men of a single and peculiar race, who have behind them many centuries of financial experience, they are in a unique position to manipulate the policy of nations'. (p. 64) The argument stands alone in the book, and is not repeated in Chapter VI on 'The Economic Taproot'. It does not fit very well with the rest of Hobson's argument, since the British establishment which Hobson blamed as much as government contractors and colonial adventurers for the previous growth of the British empire — was not famous for its partiality to Jewish financiers. In fact, the whole section on financiers is so irrelevant to Hobson's other economic arguments that one wonders why he included it in the book. The alarming reason seems to be that he really believed it.

Hobson's closing arguments in Part I of his book were much more in the Cobdenite tradition. Chapter III on 'Imperialist Finance' predicted that the privileged minority who benefitted from colonial expansion, militarism and an aggressive foreign policy would make the whole burden of paying for imperialism fall on the mass of the population rather than on themselves. Hobson said that the high cost of armaments in the twentieth century would not be met by raising the income taxes imposed on the upper classes. It would be met by increasing the national debt and by raising revenue through the imposition of protective tariffs. Since the national debt consisted mainly in money borrowed from British investors who had to be repaid with interest, the effect of raising the national debt was to raise the amount of money which the nation as a whole had to give to the small, privileged section of the population which had money to invest. Raising revenue through the imposition of tariffs would raise the prices British consumers had to pay for imported goods. Since the poor spent a much greater proportion of their income on consumption than the rich, they would bear most of the burden. Hobson also predicted that shipping companies and other businesses who could claim to be of strategic or military value to the nation would ask for subsidies to protect them from foreign competition. Finally, Hobson predicted that a wall of protective tariffs for the empire would be demanded on the ground that 'a military nation surrounded by hostile empires must have within her boundaries adequate supplies of the sinews of war, efficient recruits, and a large food supply'. It required very little imagination on Hobson's part to make any of these predictions because, as we have seen, such measures were being widely advocated in the journals which Hobson read and which published his own articles.

The first chapter of Part II ('The Politics of Imperialism') rounds off Hobson's updating of Cobden's critique of empire. This chapter, entitled 'The Political Significance of Imperialism', is built around a quotation. 'Cobden, writing in 1860 of our Indian Empire, put this pithy question : "Is it not just possible that we may be corrupted at home by the reaction of arbitrary political maxims in the East upon our domestic politics, just as Greece and Rome were demoralised by their contact with Asia?'" (p. 150) Hobson's short answer to that rhetorical question was yes. Unlike the editor of the *United States Investor*, who thought it would be a damn good thing if Americans learned something about firm efficient government through the autocratic administration of their new colonies, Hobson dreaded the recoil of autocracy upon liberal England. He believed that the 'old colonial hands' constituted a vipers' nest in the body politic.

> As the despotic portion of our Empire has grown in area, a larger and larger number of men, trained in the temper and methods of autocracy as soldiers and civil officials in our Crown colonies, protectorates, and Indian Empire, reinforced by number of merchants, planters, engineers, and overseers, whose lives have been those of a superior caste living an artificial life removed from all the healthy restraints of ordinary European society, have returned to this country, bringing back the characters, sentiments, and ideas imposed by this foreign environment. The South and South-West of England is richly sprinkled with these men, many of them wealthy, most of them endowed with leisure, men openly contemptuous of democracy, devoted to material luxury, social display, and the shallower arts of intellectual life. The wealthier among them discover political ambitions, introducing into our Houses of Parliament the coarsest and most selfish spirit of 'Imperialism', using their imperial experience and connections to push profitable companies and concessions for their private benefits, and posing as authorities so as to keep the yoke of Imperialism firmly fixed upon the shoulders of the 'nigger' .... everywhere they stand for coercion and for resistance to reform. (p. 159)

Hobson claimed that the only way to stop the rot at home was to stop it at its source overseas.

Hobson's alternative programme for world development

Hobson has often been misrepresented as an uncompromising opponent of European rule of the undeveloped world. This is very far from the truth. His chapter on 'The Scientific Defence of Imperialism' (Chapter II of Part II) begins in characteristic Hobsonian style with the statement of an opposing case. In this instance it is the argument that the progress of humanity depends on constant struggle among races and nations; without struggle the unfit will survive and perpetuate their unfitness; the armed contest between European nations for economic supremacy and the struggle between 'the white race' and the 'backward races' are therefore both instruments of human progress. Any educated modern reader would dismiss immediately the argument as pseudo-scientific rubbish based on gross misconceptions about race, evolutionary theory and 'progress'. Hobson, however, took it very seriously and agreed on a number of points with Karl Pearson, the most illustrious exponent of the argument in England at the turn of the century. Hobson agreed that 'Professor Pearson justly recognises and boldly admits the danger which attends the humanitarianism that has in huge measure suspended the 'struggle for life' among individuals. 'Professor Pearson', he continued, 'rightly urges that truly enlightened national government will insist on mending the slow, painful, and irregular elimination of bad stock which goes on through progressive degeneracy by substituting some rational control of parentage, at least to the extent of preventing through public education, or if necessary by law, the propagation of certain surely recognised unfitness'. He admitted that what was necessary on the individual level might also be necessary on the racial level.

> As lower individuals within a society perish by contact with a civilization to which they cannot properly assimilate themselves, so 'lower races' in some instances disappear by similar contact with higher races whose diseases and physical vices prove too strong for them. A rational stirpiculture [i.e., weeding out or selective extermination] in the wide social interest might... require a repression of the spread of degenerate or unprogressive races, corresponding to the check which a nation might place upon the propagation from bad individual stock.

To put it bluntly, Hobson believed in state action to prevent the spread or breeding 'of the physically and morally unfit, the least effective portion of the population'. (pp. 172, 183, 190, 202).

Believing that there were races too degenerate and 'unprogressive' to be permitted to multiply without control, Hobson was equally ready to admit there were peoples who should not be permitted to govern themselves — at least not for the moment. In his chapter on 'Imperialism and the Lower Races' (Chapter IV of Part II) he readily fell into the prevailing habit of treating certain people (mostly Africans) as children. 'The real issue' he wrote, 'is whether, and under what circumstances, it is justifiable for Western nations to use compulsory government for the control and education in the arts of industrial and political civilization of the inhabitants of tropical countries and other so-called lower races....The analogy furnished by the education of a child is prima facie a sound one, and is not invalidated by the dangerous abuses to which it is exposed in practice'. (pp. 240-41). He absolutely rejected the notion of giving up European direction of the government of those peoples.

If organised Governments of civilized Powers refused the task, they would let loose a horde of private adventurers, slavers, piratical traders, treasure hunters, concession mongers, who, animated by mere greed of gold or power, would set about the work of exploitation under no public control and with no regard to the future; playing havoc with the political, economic, and moral institutions of the peoples....it opens grave dangers in the future, from the political or military ambitions of native or imported rulers, who, playing upon the religious fanaticism or the combative instincts of great hordes of semi-savages, may impose upon them so effective a military discipline as to give terrible significance to some black or yellow 'peril'. (pp. 242-44).

If thinking that 'backward peoples' needed to be weeded out and governed by 'progressive' white men makes a person an imperialist, then Hobson was an imperialist — just as much as the great Victorian liberal John Stuart Mill had been when he wrote that 'despotism is the best form of government for barbarians'.[5] But Hobson absolved himself from self-contradiction by laying down very strict conditions for European administration of peoples incapable of governing themselves. Strict precautions were needed to keep the government out of the hands of selfish cliques. It could not be left to individual governments to decide for themselves whom they should govern; the world needed 'some organization representative of international interests, which shall sanction the undertaking of a trust by the nation exercising such control'. In the second place, it was necessary

5. *On Liberty* (London, 1874) 23. F. Madden was the first to call attention to this aspect of Hobson's thought, *Cambridge History of the British Empire* III 350, 383.

for the governing power to prove that its administration contributed tangible benefits not only to itself but also to the people ruled and to the world at large. In this way Hobson hoped to avoid the militarism, international rivalries and exploitation in the interest of tiny minorities which had hitherto accompanied the extension of European administrations into tropical regions. (p. 280).

Hobson also contributed his own thoughts on what constituted good and bad administrative practice. A really benevolent and efficient administrator would begin 'by studying the religious, political and other social institutions and habits of the people'. By 'endeavouring to penetrate into their present mind and capacities, by learning their language and their history' the good administrator would determine their position on the evolutionary ladder of peoples ('to place them in the natural history of man'). A programme for economic development would take account of the total environment 'and not just its agricultural and mining resources alone'. Private companies and adventurers would be prevented from 'prematurely' exploiting the country for their own benefit. The administrator would try to avoid the appearance of force even if it were necessary to keep 'force in the background as a last resort'. This would enable administrators to appear more in 'the position of advisers' to the people's own real authorities than as lordly and alien rulers. The object of the administration could be summed up as 'natural growth and industry along tropical lines'.

Anyone familiar with the history of British colonial administration in Africa will recognise this programme as the system of 'indirect rule' popularised by Frederick Lugard.[6] The difference between Hobson and Lugard is in fact no more than a sheet of paper. Lugard believed that the goal of 'national growth and industry along tropical lines' could be achieved by British administrators on their own initiative. Hobson believed that a system of international supervision was needed to keep administrators honest and selfish

6. See especially Lugard's *Dual Mandate in Tropical Africa* (Edinburgh, 1922).

exploiters out. He would accept no substitutes, not even agreement among the colonising nations, because the way would still be open for exploitation by 'economic parasites'. Until and unless European rule was subjected to disinterested international control, he would distrust all talk of 'the white man's burden' and 'trusts undertaken for civilization' as empty words. There were, he thought, some fine men in the British colonial and Indian services who were doing good work in isolated corners of the world, but their efficiency was undermined everywhere by the predominant influence of vested interests.

Hobson's programme for the development of the undeveloped world thus resembled his programme for the betterment of England. Government action was needed to promote the objects of peace, progress and prosperity which the mid-Victorian apostles of free trade and laissez faire had promised but had not delivered. He rejected the notion that the elimination of 'unfit people' or the evolutionary progress of mankind could be achieved sooner by an uncontrolled struggle than by rational planning. However, because he largely accepted the pseudo-scientific evolutionary and racial theories of his time, and because he doubted the ability of 'backward' peoples to cope successfully with the initial penetration of capitalism, he was prepared to put up with a degree of force and undemocratic government in undeveloped countries that he would never have accepted in England. He lived long enough to see his programme for tropical development become official orthodoxy in the British Colonial Service and his idea of an international commission to oversee European colonial administrations partially translated into action as the 'mandates' system of the League of Nations.

Hobson the gloomy prophet

In 1902 Hobson was not very hopeful that his ideas would influence anyone. In the face of what he recognised as 'the most powerful movement in the current politics of the Western World' he did not dare to do more than address his book 'to the intelligence of the minority'. He thought the worst consequences of imperialism were yet to come and challenged 'the statement, often made, that the work of expansion is virtually complete ... this in most instances marks rather the beginning of a process of imperialization than a definite attainment of empire'. (p. 235) Part of his worry was, as we have seen, that the popular new theories of investment imperialism and protection were leading Britain down the road previously travelled by the militaristic nations of continental Europe.

> ...Protection is the natural ally of Imperialism.. War, militarism, and a 'spirited foreign policy' are the necessary means to this end.....Imperialism with its wars and its armaments is undeniably responsible for the growing debts of the continental nations and while the unparalleled industrial prosperity of Great Britain and the isolation of the United States have enabled these great nations to escape this ruinous competition during recent decades, the period of their immunity is over; both, committed as they seem to an Imperialism without limit, will succumb more and more to the money lending classes dressed as imperialists and patriots. (pp. 112-14)

His most immediate worry was that the imperial rivalries of European powers in east Asia would accelerate the arms race, establish ominous new forms of domination, and possibly push western civilisation into an irrevocable decline.

In line with the racialist theories of his day, Hobson put Indian and Chinese people on a higher evolutionary plane than Africans. He subscribed in general terms to the myth of the inscrutable, mysterious East. 'The few', he wrote, 'who have made some serious attempt to penetrate into the Indian mind admit their failure to grasp with any adequacy even the rudiments of a human nature which differs, in its fundamental valuations and its methods of conduct, so radically from our own as to present for its chief interest a series of baffling psychological puzzles'. The 'psychology of the Chinese' was likewise '*terra incognita*'. (pp. 323, 343) It followed that the development programme he recommended for Africa was inappropriate for east Asia because European administrators could not understand the 'eastern mind' well enough to give it an intelligent push in the direction of 'natural growth and industry'. Reviewing the history of the British in India, Hobson concluded that 'the one real and indisputable success of our rule' was 'the maintenance of order upon a large scale, the prevention of internecine war, riot, or organised violence'. (p. 317) But it was above all 'in China that the spirit and methods of Western Imperialism' were 'likely to find their most crucial test'. It was, Hobson thought, likely to be a very different show from the 'amicable' partition of Africa. For one thing there were a number of important new participants in the game. 'The entrance of Germany and America upon a manufacturing career, and the occidentation of Japan, enhances the mercantile competition, and the struggle for the Far Eastern markets becomes a more definite object of national industrial policy'. (p. 327) He then projected five different scenarios for the progress of imperialism in China. In scenario number one China reacts to the invasion of profiteers from different countries by 'setting her enemies to fight among themselves', thereby delaying the modernisation of the country for a long time to come. (p. 331) In scenario number two Japan gets the better of European and American competitors in a mainly peaceful 'open-door' penetration of China because of her geographical position and because of 'the associations of race, language, religion, literature [and] modes of life' between the two countries.[7] In scenario number three 'there is closing of doors, ear-marking, and further political absorption of chosen areas by the Western powers':

> Japan will be driven to enter this sort of competition, and with her better understanding of the conditions of success, and her superior faculty for managing the Chinese, is likely to get the better of her European and American competitors.
>
> Should European nations resent the growing industrial or perhaps political, supremacy of Japan in China and adopt some concerted action to defend their 'spheres of influence' or their extorted 'concessions', it is not wholly improbable that Japan may organise a great military and naval power in

7. 1905 ed., 278-79.

which she will utilise the latent force of China to drive Western nations out of the China seas.[8]

In scenario number four European investment interests behave like modern multi-national companies. They force their capital into China and use it to unleash an industrial revolution. Part of the profits from this development go to a rising capitalist group in China itself, who 'following Western lines, would ally themselves with imperialist politics in order to protect their vested interests. Capitalism, centralised government, militarism, protection, and a whole chain of public regulations to preserve the new order against the rising of old conservative traditional forces — such would be the inevitable outcome'. (p. 343) The fifth and last of Hobson's scenarios deliberately invokes the menace of 'the yellow peril'. Again the multi-national process of investment launches an industrial revolution but this time Chinese leadership is too weak to resist European domination. Masses of super-industrious yellow men are employed to make profits for parasitic investors overseas. This Chinese competition weakens the ability of European workers to stand up for higher wages: 'the pressure of working class movements in politics and industry in the West can be met by a flood of China goods, so as to keep down wages and compel industry, or, where the power of the imperialist obligarchy is well set, by menaces of yellow workmen or of yellow mercenary troops, while collaboration in this huge Eastern development may involve an understanding between the groups of business politicians in the Western States close enough and strong enough to secure international peace in Europe and some relaxation of militarism'. (pp. 334-35) Europe would then resemble Rome in the later stages of her imperial career. A degenerate parasitic obligarchy would bask in luxurious idleness while impoverished masses slipped into virtual serfdom. Mercenary armies recruited from the distant lands would keep the structure intact until they realised that they might seize power for themselves. Or the 'barbarians'

8. Ibid.

might revolt. Or 'Asia and Africa may furnish huge cockpits for the struggles of black and yellow armies representing the imperialist rivalries of Christendom. The present tendencies of imperialism plainly make in this direction, involving in their recoil a graduation of Western States and a possible debacle of Western civilization'.

These dark forebodings strike an authentic twentieth-century note and mark the distance Hobson travelled beyond mid-Victorian critiques of empire. Progress for mankind seems a vague possibility rather than a sure thing; civilization is a brittle crust threatened by bubbling subterranean forces of darkness and barbarism. Compared with the rising forms of imperialism Hobson discovered in China, the cosy upper-class business of building the nineteenth-century British empire seeems almost benign. And in fact the Cobdenite explanation Hobson offered for previous imperial expansion is not enough to account for the hellish possibilities of the future. They depend on the willingness of states to use force to stake out or protect fields of investment. When many states rather than just one or two are involved in the struggle, and when the process of investment itself can create new states with similar aims, the game becomes desperate and tends towards world war. The thesis Hobson uses to explain this dangerous new game is the thesis he borrowed from Wilshire and which Wilshire read in the *U.S. Investor*: the thesis that a perceived need to expand investment opportunities was causing nation after nation to arm itself to the teeth and to adopt an aggressive foreign policy.

It should be recalled at this point that nightmarish as Hobson's visions of the futue may have been, they were little more than highly coloured versions of what contemporary British capitalists and economists had been saying about the future. The critical difference between Hobson and those capitalist theorists of imperialism is that he presented as attractive alternative what appeared to the capitalists as yet another nightmare: a sweeping change in the distribution of wealth.

Hobson's definitions and theses of imperialism

An infuriating feature of Hobson's book on imperialism is that although he begins by stating that 'this study of modern imperialism is designed to give more precision to a term which is on everbody's lips', he does not actually provide a straightforward definition of imperialism. He makes a number of statements which appear to be definitions but which differ among themselves and create uncertainties by including suggested causes for the phenomena they describe. At one point Hobson says imperialism 'is a debasement of...genuine nationalism, by attempts to overflow its natural banks and absorb the near or distant territory of reluctant and unassimilable peoples'. At another point he says 'imperialism is a depraved choice of national life, imposed by selfseeking interests which appeal to the lusts of quantitative acquisitiveness and of forceful domination surviving in a nation from early centuries of animal struggle for existence'. At yet another point he says that imperialism represents the 'growing tendency' of the 'wealthy classes' to 'use their politicial power as citizens of this state to interfere with the political conditions of those States where they have an industrial stake'. Hobson usually finds it difficult to write of imperialism without simultaneously referring to 'its natural supports, militarism, oligarchy, bureaucracy, protection, concentration of capital, and violent trade fluctuations'. (pp. 4, 379, 381, 389) Sometimes he writes of imperialism as virtually the same thing as the drive to acquire and retain colonies. But just as often — for example in his discussion of the Far East and his reference to employing the political power of one state to interfere with 'the political conditions' of other states — he writes as though imperialism as a policy could be practiced without any territorial acquisitions.

The key to sorting out the apparent discrepencies among Hobson's definitions is recognising that he employs not one, but two theses. One is derived from the Cobdenite critique of empire and the other, from the new American theory of investment-powered imperialism. Hobson uses the Cobdenite argument to explain the past behaviour of British empire builders; he uses the American theory to explain the ominous forces behind the aggressive foreign policies of nations at the time he wrote in 1902 and to predict the future consequences of these policies. There is, however, a definition of imperialism which will embrace all of Hobson's various uses of the word. It is the same definition used before to epitomise what imperialism meant to Wilshire and the editor of the *United States Investor*: imperialism is the deliberate use of the power of the state, including its military power, in order to advance alleged national economic interests in the world at large. This includes not only grabbing colonies but a great deal of other aggressive and coercive activity.

Hobson contributed two new theses to the theoretical discussion of imperialism. One thesis concerned the past growth of the British empire — a subject of no concern to the American theorists. It was that the growth of Britain's huge empire and war machine served the interlocking class and institutional interests of a tiny minority of the population, and that these interests had been able to subvert the real welfare of the rest of the nation through clever appeals to the general good and 'aggressive instincts' surviving from an earlier era in human evolution. Hobson's second new thesis concerned the future. In contrast to the editor of the *United States Investor* and others who said that surplus investment capital made imperialism a present and future necessity, Hobson offered his thesis that a redistribution of income and a diversion of more money to worthwhile state projects at home would relieve most of the pressure for aggressive foreign policies. He added virtually nothing of his own to the American theory of capitalist imperialism except to produce a few tables showing that foreign investments had been growing and to imply that some investor pressures had existed even before the current talk of surplus capital. But when all was said and done, Hobson was quite as future-oriented as the American theorists. His concentration in the later sections of his book on the prospects for armaments, war and a possible 'debacle' of western civilisation foreshadowed the direction most discussions of imperialism would take during the next two decades.

CHAPTER 5
BRITISH DISCUSSION OF IMPERIALISM AND WAR ON THE EVE OF WORLD WAR I - NORMAN ANGEL AND H.N. BRAILSFORD

It is perhaps a good idea at this point to review the ground that has been covered so far, because the account of developing theories of imperialism given in chapters two through five differs considerably from Richard Koebner's. Here is Koebner's conjectural account of what happened to the meaning of imperialism immediately after the period he studied (1830-1900):

> In 1901 there was as yet no elaborate general theory of imperialism in existence. Imperialism and anti-imperialism were still sentiments and beliefs of vague and varying content in the British Isles. There and in America a minority of alert minds had set into motion an anti-imperialist campaign and created a pattern of ideas and a terminology which formed the fertile soil for such a theory to emerge. The Boer War was, indeed, more than a local clash of two nations and opposing political and economical interests. It was more than a chapter in the history of the industrialization of Africa. In the career of imperialism it was an essential turning point. It made the word an international slogan in Europe, just as the Spanish War had made it a slogan in America. It also gave rise to the world-wide misinterpretation of the Boer War as a capitalist plot. That misinterpretation became the basis of all subsequent theories of imperialism. Imperialism as a political and economic theory first emerged during and immediately after the Boer War [i.e. in Hobson's work]. It originated in England.[1]

A more accurate account would run along the following lines. Despite the growing popularity of imperialism as a proud political slogan in Britain during the eighteen nineties, the word was never entirely divested of its old associations with 'Caesarism', militarism and autocratic methods of government. (Indeed most enthusiasts for the consolidation and expansion of the British Empire during this period made no pretence of dispensing with either force or autocratic government in their dealings with non-white peoples). Advocates of expansion often attempted to argue that their programmes would promote the material as well as the spiritual welfare of the British people. Cecil Rhodes and

1. Koebner and Schmidt, 248-49.

Joseph Chamberlain in particular emphasised the need to stake out tropical estates to preserve the prosperity of coming generations. But until the very end of the nineteenth century, these economic arguments made little headway against the orthodox theory of free trade. The concurrence of three new factors — the apparent success of protectionist policies in Germany and America, the rise of trusts, and the notion of 'surplus' investment capital — called into question the most fundamental premises of the old school of economists whose watchwords had been free competition, free trade and minimal government. More and more writers on economic affairs came to accept that an era in world economic history and had closed and that monopolistic organisation in basic industries and struggles for fields of profitable investment between militarised competing protectionist empires would be the dominant features of economic life in the twentieth century. This, the so-called German conception of empire, was what increasing numbers of writers meant when they used the work imperialism. The first full-blown theory that a 'plethora' of capital made this sort of imperialism a necessity was developed by American capitalists in the course of the year 1898, but the rudiments of that theory can be found in capitalist literature of the same period in Britain and on the continent of Europe. On both sides of Atlantic the idea was commonly expressed that unless imperialism were adopted as a deliberate policy, there might be irresistable pressure for fundamental changes in the economic system.

In America the socialist Gaylord Wilshire accepted the statements of capitalists that surplus investment capital made imperialism a necessity under the prevailing economic system, but argued that Americans should make a socialist revolution rather than accept passively the imposition of 'economic autocracy' in the form of trusts and 'political autocracy' in the form of imperialism. In England J.A. Hobson chose a different method of combating the idea that imperialism was an economic necessity. He took up Wilshire's point that the only people who really needed imperialism were the tiny minority with surplus capital to invest, and linked this to the old Cobdenite argument that wherever the British Empire was not subject to democratic control it served only a minority of vested interests. He challenged the capitalist theory of 'inevitable' imperialism with his counter-theory that stripping investors of their surplus and putting that money to work implementing social reform in Britain would remove the supposed necessity for an aggressive foreign policy. In reply to the 'altruistic' arguments made in favour of imperialism on the grounds that it promoted social evolution, material progress for backward countries and good government for 'lower races', Hobson claimed that all these worthy ends would be achieved better by international cooperation with democratic safeguards than by an anarchic struggle for power among competing empires.

Thus, in the course of the economic discussion about imperialism at the turn of the century, most writers had come to give a more specific meaning to the word imperialism that can be summed up as 'the deliberate use of the power of the state, including its military power in order to advance alleged national economic interests in the world at large'. The later portions of Hobson's book emphasised that this policy was being practised by several nations in the Far East without the territorial annexations characteristic of older forms of imperialism but with much greater danger to world peace. Hobson also gave concise expression to the spreading fear that the present competition for supremacy in armaments and economic strength might lead to a cataclysymic world war which could bring about the end of 'Western civilization'.

Norman Angell's pacifist challenge to the theory of economic imperialism

Though Koebner was wrong in thinking that anti-imperialists invented the idea that imperialism served the needs of investors, he rightly drew attention to a precipitate decline in the popularity of imperialism as a political slogan in the first decade of the twentieth century. In America the final death-knell of imperialism as a rallying cry was not definitely sounded until 1912 when Theodore Roosevelt's Bull Moose splinter group of the Republican Party was decisively smashed at the polls. In England the end came sooner, in the General Election of 1905 when the Liberals won a huge majority and ended Joseph Chamberlain's career. As one unrepentent imperialist summed up the situation in 1906.

> With the fall of the Government... there came one of those waves of reaction which now and then break in upon our national steadfastness. The name of 'Empire' stank in the nostrils of the electorate. Those who used it fell like ninepins; in the huge majority which the new Ministry acquired there were many who openly blasphemed it; and the few who still cherished the faith thought it wise to don temporarily the garb of indifference.[2]

But, if imperialism were permanently tarnished as a vote-winning slogan in English-speaking countries, the belief lived on that the armed force of the state must be employed to maintain the national prosperity and to protect foreign outlets for surplus investment capital. Spending on armaments increased with every passing year and the international competition for concessions and 'spheres of influence' in the far corners of the globe continued undiminished.

In 1910, a then unknown British writer named Norman Angell appealed to the Great Powers in the name of reason to stop their insane arms race.[3] He had no hesitation in identifying the cause of the arms race as 'the universally accepted theory that military and political power give a nation commercial and social advantage'. That theory was, he claimed, 'the Great Illusion'. That Angell could state unequivocally that the theory was 'universally accepted' and that Angell himself believed that Britain needed 'to create markets and find a field for the employment of her capital', shows how little impact Hobson's book had made upon

2. John Buchan, *A Lodge in the Wilderness* (London, 1906), 1-2.

3. Norman Angell was the adopted name of Ralph Norman Angell Lane (1874-1967). While serving as continental editor of Lord Northcliffe's *Daily Mail* in 1909, he wrote *Europe's Optical Illusion* which was eventually published as *The Great Illusion* (London, 1910). See his autobiography, *After All* (London, 1951), 138-51.

educated opinion.[4] Angell used different tactics in his attempt to stop the arms race. Perhaps because he hoped to influence powerful people, he steered well clear of Hobson's argument that a little clique of them made money out of armaments and imperialism. Angell spoke only of the broad national interest and took at face value the assertion that the British government was arming itself to the teeth for the sole purpose of deterring other similarly armed nations from attacking her.

Angell correctly observed that the government spokesmen for all the other nations in the arms race said exactly the same thing. Assuming that the Great Powers were mostly led by honest, intelligent, civilised men, Angell pointed out that their fear of attack must be based on the belief that a successful aggressor would reap a material reward from a war of conquest. He set out to demonstrate that under modern conditions the conquest of territory was a profitless business. The capitalist system of private ownership and exchange for profit, which was established in all advanced countries, ensured that no conqueror would seize the property of conquered peoples or impose any form of tribute. Angell therefore held that 'the only possible policy in our day for a conqueror to pursue is to leave the wealth of a territory in the complete possession of the individuals inhabiting that territory'. It was, he went on, 'a logical fallacy and an optical illusion in Europe to regard a nation as increasing its wealth when it increases its territory, because when a province or State is annexed, the population, who are the real and only owners of wealth therein, are also annexed, and the conqueror gets nothing. The facts of modern history abundantly illustrate this. When Germany annexed Schleswig-Holstein and Alsatia not a single ordinary German citizen was one pfenning the richer'. (p. 31) It followed that if Germany conquered Britain she would have to leave British property, business and finance intact; she could not impose heavy taxes or tribute on the British people without lessening

4. p. 228. The full quotation is 'Rome did not have to create markets and find a field for the employment of her capital. We do'. This and subsequent quotations are taken from Heinemann's edition of 1911.

their ability to buy German goods. The situation would be exactly the same if Britain conquered Germany, or France conquered Spain or Belgium conquered Holland. In every case the military expenditure involved in conquering a piece of territory would be immense, the profit accruing to the conqueror would be nothing.

Angell offered the Boer War as another example of the pointlessness of conquest. He recalled that 'alike in England and on the Continent it was generally assumed that Great Britain was 'after the gold mines'. Well, he asked, now that the Transvaal had been conquered 'how many shares in the goldmines does the British Government hold?' The answer was of course none. Nor could it be said that Britain had oppressed its defeated enemies. 'The present Government of the Transvaal is in the hands of the Boer party. England has achieved the union of South Africa in which the Boer element is predominant, Britain has enforced against the British Indian in the Transvaal and Natal, the same Boer regulations which were one of our grievances before the war, and the Houses of Parliament have just ratified an Act of Union in which the Boer attitude with reference to the native [i.e. the black African] is codified and made permanent'. Angell also denied that Britain made money out of her other colonies, or that the loss of those colonies would in any way imperil her own prosperity. 'Economically, England would gain by their formal separation, since she would be relieved of the cost of their defence. Their loss, involving, therefore, no change in economic fact (beyond saving the Mother Country), could not involve the ruin of the Empire and the starvation of the Mother Country, as those who commonly treat of such a contingency are apt to aver'. The standard answer to this argument was that a conqueror might throw a wall of protective tariffs around his conquests and cut them off from British traders. Angell dismissed that argument on the ground that tariffs were not nearly as effective as most people supposed. Swiss watch and instrument makers had displaced British manufacturers as suppliers to the protected Canadian market. 'Protectionist Germany' was 'one of the best markets that we have in Europe'. (pp. 31, 117) Angell believed that in the long run quality and efficiency would find a way through any tariff wall, no matter how high it might built.

On the other hand, he admitted that advanced economies generated surplus capital that must find outlets and looked on colonies as legitimate fields for investment. He even admitted that there was a worthwhile purpose to be served by conquering disordered areas of the world where the advent of European rule brought the law and order which made economic progress possible. In these cases Angell preferred to call the European aggressor a 'policeman' rather than a conqueror.

> Order was just as well maintained in Alsace-Lorraine before the German conquest as after, and for that reason Germany has not benefitted by the Conquest. But order was not maintained in California [before 1848] and would not have been as well maintained under Mexican as under American rule, and for that reason America has benefitted by the conquest of California. France has benefitted by the conquest of Algeria, England by that of India, because in each case the arms were employed not, properly speaking, for conquest at all, but for police purposes, for the establishment and maintenance of order; and, so far as they filled that role, their role was a useful one. (p. 115)

What Angell objected to was the widespread belief that the advantages of policing backward countries accrued mostly to the colonial powers who did the policing. Nothing prevented French or German investors and traders from operating in British India, just as nothing stood in the way of Englishmen wishing to put money into French Algeria. At the time Angell wrote German capitalists were very active in Turkey; he saw no reason for Britain to be alarmed by this activity even if it led to German rule.

> German industry is coming to have a dominating situation in the Near East, and as those interests — her markets and investments — increase, the necessity for better order in, and the better organisation of, such territories increases in corresponding degree. Germany may need to police Asia Minor.
>
> What interest have we in attempting to prevent her?... If a second Germany were created in the Near East, if Turkey had a population, with the German

purchasing power and the German tariff, the markets would be worth forty to fifty millions instead of some ten to fifteen. Why should we try to prevent Germany increasing our trade?

This may seem a very odd position for a pacifist to take. Any German attempt 'to police Asia Minor' was likely to be forcibly resisted by the present rulers of the place. But to Angell the looming evil of a war between great powers far outweighed the lesser evil of a little war between Germans and Turks. The best of all methods of 'policing' backward countries, Angell thought, was to convince the peoples of those places to do the job themselves. The next best method would be for the Great Powers to reach a friendly agreement about who should police what. (pp. 115, 120) The first step towards such an agreement would be for all statesmen to understand that ownership of territory brought no special economic advantages.

Angell dealt quickly with the argument that military power enabled countries to throw their weight around in the world, thus winning economic advantages without ever going to war or grabbing territory (this was the argument that had most entranced the editor of *United States Investor* in 1898). Plain, incontrovertible facts showed the falsity of that doctrine. Had Swiss or Belgian capitalists fared worse in trade or investment because their countries had no battleships or big battalions? Obviously not. (p. 60) Thus it seemed to Norman Angell that every reasonable politician in every reasonable country should immediately set about dismantling the huge armies and navies which imperilled the peace of Europe and the very existence of Western Civilisation. He realised, however, that one final obstacle must be overcome before a general process of disarmament could begin, namely, the widespread belief that human beings are not reasonable animals — that deplorable as it might seem to the mild-mannered, bespectacled pacifist, the urge to struggle and kill is as natural to man as swimming is to fish. Believers in the instinctual urge to fight held that even if there were no real economic advantages to be won from aggressive behaviour, politicans would find other excuses to arm and conquer. Even Hobson had recognised 'lusts of quantitative acquisitiveness and of forceful domination' surviving 'from early centuries of animal struggle'. Angell devoted more than half of his book to proving that 'man's disposition to fight, far from being unchanged, is becoming rapidly enfeebled'. In one glorious passage Angell uses the example of a bloodthirsty American general to show that even the most devout believers in the killer instinct had to admit that the instinct was being gradually snuffed out by economic progress.

> A large part of General Lea's book [on war] is a sort of Carlylean girding at what he terms 'protoplasmic gourmandising and retching' (otherwise the busy American industrial and social life of his countrymen). He declares that when a country makes wealth production and industries its sole aim, it becomes 'a glutton among nations, vulgar, swinish, arrogant'; 'commercialism, having seized hold of the American people, overshadows it, and tends to destroy not only the aspirations and world-wide career open to the nation, but the Republic itself'. 'Patriotism in the true sense' (i.e., the desire to go and kill other people) General Lea declares almost dead in the United States. (p. 167)

All in all, Angell's book was a *tour de force* of reasoned argument that made a huge sensation when it was published. Enthusiastic reviewers seemed to forget that arguments against the irrationality of war had a very long pedigree in England and that much of what Angell had to say had been heard before. What made the message so arresting now was the verve with which it was written at a time when some great war was almost daily expected. One journalist ranked Angell 'with Cobden, among the greatest of our pamphleteers, perhaps the greatest since Swift'. The *Daily News* noted that 'the critics have failed to find a serious flaw in Norman Angell's logical, coherent, masterly analysis'. Best of all, the *Daily Mail* congratulated him 'upon a very clever work... which is being widely discussed at the present moment in political circles both here and on the Continent'. But the arms race went on much as before and a few years later the world went to war.

The importance of Angell to the theoretical discussion of

imperialism lies in his contention that the *idea* of using the armed power of the state to advance alleged national economic interests had itself become the major reason for international rivalries. If Angell was correct, the theory of the necessity of imperialism first voiced in America in the late eighteen nineties had become an accepted axiom of foreign policy makers in the most powerful nations on earth. It may or may not have been a rational belief but the fact that important people believed it was more significant than its theoretical validity. The rest of Angell's comments on imperialism were completely unoriginal; they merely echoed Hobson's argument that imperialism did not serve the real economic interests of the overwhelming majority of the people, including most capitalists.

H.N. Brailsford and the armed peace.

It is easy to think of plausible reasons why Angell's book did nothing at all to slow down the European arms race. The people whose decisions concerning armaments and strategy matter most do not generally take their cues from pacifist pamphleteers. If they were as intelligent and reasonable as Angell supposed them to be, the economic futility of war and conquest must already have been apparent to them. By 1911, the atmosphere of international relations was so poisoned with mutual distrust that it was difficult to imagine any nation laying down its arms until all of its potential adversaries had first laid down theirs. In London, hard-headed men reacted to Angell's book by saying, in effect, very good, Mr. Angell, we are convinced and will certainly disarm just as soon as we see the success of your preaching in Berlin and Vienna. This reaction is the perennial obstacle to the achievement of world peace through pacifist propaganda.

Of course, those people who regarded arming and fighting as the inevitable expression of an irrational human instinct could point then — as like-minded people point now — to the perpetual failure of reasoned argument to stop wars as proof of their theory of aggression. But there is another method of accounting for Angell's failure that appealed strongly to intellectuals of the Edwardian era. The essence of this method is to show that the persistence of any seemingly irrational human behaviour can be explained by a hidden rationality. Sir James Frazer's pioneering work on anthropology used this method to explain the apparently pointless activities of 'primitive peoples'. Sigmund Freud's theory of psychoanalysis purported to demonstrate in similar fashion that there were hidden reasons for the antics of madmen. The American economist Thorstein Veblen purported to show in *The Theory of the Leisure Class* that the seemingly crazy expenditures of the super-rich could be explained as the ritual behaviour of social animals. Hobson had tried to do something similar by showing how the rational pursuit of self-interest by a privileged class had plunged the nation into the otherwise irrational policy of imperialism. In 1914 the British socialist Henry Noel Brailsford sharpened and extended Hobson's critique of imperialism in order to prove the futility of Norman Angell's attempt to prevail against the sword with his pen.

Brailsford called his book *The War of Steel and Gold*, a phrase he used to describe the phenomenon others were calling 'the armed peace'. Without ever actually going to war, the great powers built their military machines up and up. Every power was involved in 'a conscious struggle to achieve by expenditure and science, by diplomacy and alliances, a balance of power which always eludes us, and because it is always variable and unstable condemns us to a bloodless battle, a dry warfare of steel and gold'.[5] Brailsford accused Angell of failing to see that 'the governing class' of every country in the arms race plainly benefitted from armaments which the mass of the people were forced to pay for. The purpose of the armaments was not to make war, but to enrich the members of the governing class in winning profitable investment opportunities abroad. By concentrating on the profits of trade and the ownership of territory, Angell had, in Brailford's opinion, missed the whole point. Here is how

5. *The War of Steel and Gold* (London, 1914).

Brailsford refuted the main contentions of Angell's case.

First, Angell said that conquering territory brought neither trade nor wealth nor tribute to the conqueror. Brailsford agreed: 'conquest indeed in this barbaric sense of the word is obsolete, and belongs to the agricultural stage of civilisation'. (p. 162) In biblical times (Brailsford was a clergyman's son) Ahab coveted and seized Naboth's vineyard. Not so in modern times:

> Our Ahabs do not take Naboth's vineyard; they invest money in it. The struggle for a balance of power means today a struggle for liberty and opportunity to use 'places in the sun' across the seas. For the modern world a place in the sun is not a smiling valley, or a rich plain in which a victorious army will settle, and build homes and found families. It is a territory to 'exploit', and the active agents in the process are now the bankers and investors who float loans, and secure concessions. Even where conquest is incidentally necessary, as in Morocco, there is no migration to the new territory and the conquering Power rarely troubles to annex it. It 'occupies' it only because without occupation it cannot safely employ its capital in building railways or sinking mines. Land hunger is not the malady of the modern world. (p. 32)

If investors and governments alike were reluctant annexationists, what then was the point of armaments? The Great Powers maintained big military machines and extensive diplomatic corps, Brailsford explained, primarily for the purpose of bullying. He used Angell's example of Turkey to make his point. Germany had no intention of annexing Asia Minor or excluding British traders from doing business there. Germany's aim in parading her military powers before the Turks and in sending her diplomats to scheme and connive in the back rooms of Istambul was to win loans, concessions, and contracts for German firms. Germans were there to tell the Sultan's ministers they they needed bridges and railroads which Germans were very good at building. If the Sultan was short of money to spend on railways or bridges, German banks were on hand to lend money. If the Sultan feared that other powers would resent this favouritism, Germany could offer a defensive alliance backed up by her formidable war machine. As proof of the success of this policy Brailsford offered the example of a railway line he had seen in Turkey.

> It seemed as though the line had laid itself across the countryside in the track of some writhing serpent. It curled in sinuous folds, it described enormous arcs, it bent and doubled so that a passing train resembled nothing so much as a kitten in pursuit of its own tail. Yet the country was a vast level plain. There were neither mountains nor rivers to avoid....And oddly enough the railway did not seem to serve any visible town, indeed, a plausible theory of its gyrations might have been that it was desperately trying to dodge the towns . . . . The explanation was simple enough when one heard it. The railway had indeed been constructed by a private company, and was owned by this company. But the concession included what is called a kilometric guarantee. In order to induce the European financiers — who all the while were bribing and competing to obtain the favour — to perform the onerous work of 'opening up Turkey', the Government agreed to guarantee to the fortunate company an assured profit, reckoned at so much on every mile or kilometre of rails which it laid down. Hence the astounding performances of the line....Every unnecessary curve means so many miles added to the total length of the line, and so many hundreds or thousands of pounds to its annual guaranteed profits. (pp. 83-84)

Brailsford denied his readers the pleasure of laughing too much at this and other follies by pointing out that it was the poor peasantry which provided the taxes which enabled the Sultan to pay his annual debt to German capitalists. It was not, however, the exploitation of the peasants, or the unequal bargain struck between the contractors and the Sultan, or the profits sent back to German investors that made the example of the serpentine railway a clear case of imperialism in Brailsford's eyes. It was the participation of the German government in the process. Brailsford doubted very much whether such unholy deals would have been struck in the first place without German consuls to introduce contractors to Turkish ministers, military attaches to keep the idea of German power and prestige constantly before the eyes of the Sultan, and the German fleet to threaten the coastline in case the Turks failed to meet their annual debt. Here then was a rational purpose served by aggressive foreign policy which Angell had failed to see.

Brailsford refuted the second of Angell's contentions — that no country could profit from possessing its own colonies or grabbing someone else's colonies — by reiterating the Cobdenite argument Hobson had used to identify the beneficiaries of Britain's expanding empire. Even if the proper justification of European government of backward peoples was, as Angell said, providing efficient 'police' it had to be admitted that colonies provided plenty of jobs for policeman. In the case of India the policemen's jobs went almost entirely to members of the British upper and upper-middle classes. Brailsford estimated there must be 'tens of thousands of families, all relatively wealthy, influential and well educated, to whom the sudden ending of the Empire would mean financial ruin and social extinction'. To those people the colonies had 'a real meaning — they are the places where a son, a brother, or at the least a cousin, is "doing well"'. If Indian soldiers, he asked, were as brave, loyal and efficient as they were said to be, why were they prohibited from holding any commission in the Indian army 'above subaltern rank'. The self-evident answer was 'that the closing of these posts to the young men of the English upper and middle classes would not be tolerated by public opinion at home'. Citing statistics which reckoned the total funds annually sent from India to Britain in the form of interest on investments, pensions paid to retired civil servants and money sent home by British residents in India at not less than £30,000,000 he asserted that the upper classes would suffer more from the loss of India than from the total loss of British foreign trade everywhere in the world. The profits on that trade amounted to only £ 18,000,000.

Though Brailsford believed it would not be worth the money and lives which the Germans would have to expend should they ever want to conquer India or any other British Colony, he disagreed with Angell's proposition that no German would gain from the conquest. Whatever governments might say about respect for private property and open doors for trade and investment, the facts were that contracts and jobs in any territory went mostly to citizens and firms of the controlling nation. In the event of a German conquest of India 'the actual investments of British capitalists would of course be respected. But the privately owned railways would tend to pass by purchase into German hands. German banks, assured of official patronage, would compete on favoured terms with the existing British banks, and would soon control the credit system of India. The profits of all the new loans required for public works and military works would fall to German financiers, and the immense gains from contracting would go exclusively to Germans. To Germans also would fall the large sum that now flows in pensions and salaries to England'. (pp. 165-66). Brailsford pointed to all these profits of empire as well known facts and did not understand how Angell could exclude them from his calculations. Brailsford's list does not, in fact, go beyond calculations of Britain's profits from Empire which the *U.S. Investor* had made in 1898.

The third of Angell's contentions — that maintaining huge armaments and diplomatic services did not help the big powers to win commercial advantages denied to the capitalists of weak states such as Belgium and Switzerland — Brailsford simply did not believe. It seemed inconceivable to him that German capitalists could have made such rapid progress in their penetration of Turkey without the prestige of Germany's military might behind them. And while British diplomatic representatives in China trying 'to obtain a concession for a British syndicate' would never be so ill-mannered as to 'threaten Chinese statesmen with the instant bombardment of a Chinese port', the Chinese would never forget that their ports had once been bombarded by British men of war. (pp. 167-68)

Finally, Brailsford berated Angell for utterly neglecting the separate interest of capitalist weapons manufacturers in exacerbating the arms race. He claimed that 'the British firms are so closely interlocked by the common ownership of minor firms, by common directorships' and by shares in other enterprises that they amounted to 'only four allied combinations'. (p. 89) Directors of these firms were not only well connected socially and politically to the governing class, but they were actually consulted as expert witnesses by the British Cabinet and the parliamentary committees which made decisions on the national armaments. The same thing was true elsewhere: 'In every country and across every border there is a powerful group of capitalists, closely allied to the fighting services, firmly entrenched in society, and well served by politicians and journalists, whose business it is to exploit the rivalries and jealousies of nations and to practise the alchemy which transmutes hatred into gold'. (pp. 92-93)

Brailsford intended that his point-by-point refutation of Angell's thesis should make a constructive contribution to ending the arms race. He believed Angell to be well-meaning but naive to think that the world's most powerful statesmen had been pursuing a dangerous and expensive policy merely because they all subscribed to an incorrect idea. To Brailsford, the events of the last fifteen years proved that the capitalists who had asked for vigorous policies of imperialism to create fields for surplus investment had found their governments ready to respond. Real profits were being made as a result of those policies. But Brailsford, like Hobson, also linked the new policy of imperialism for investment purposes to older efforts of the upper classes to make the state serve their private purposes. The explanation he offered of how the desires of the upper class were translated into action by the state was subtler and more convincing than Hobson's. In one or two sections of his book Hobson came near to saying that once the leading capitalists decided upon the policy they wished the government to pursue, they then issued appropriate orders to politicians and civil servants, and drummed up public enthusiasm for the policy in their newspapers. Hobson had also included rash statements about the supposed international conspiracy of Jewish financiers.[6]

6. Koebner and Schmidt, 263-64, grossly distort Brailsford's message, ascribing to him the thesis that 'Imperialism was state power in the service of Hebrew bankers and European industrialists, who desired to exploit cheap native labour. That was the reason why manufacturers and mineowners more and more looked to Africa'. Brailsford makes no mention of 'Hebrews' and concentrates attention on the Middle East and the armed peace, not on African labour.

In contrast Brailsford held that 'the explanation of the remarkable solidarity between the diplomatist and the financier in most modern Empires is not to be sought in any crude labels'. British foreign policy, for example had developed 'a purely bureaucratic character'; the various agencies of government had their traditional ways of conducting business and well-established axioms of policy. 'Certain assumptions became a tradition which was handed on from one generation of diplomatists to another. Such traditions are always plausible. They are constantly repeated, rarely questioned, and their subtle transformation under changing circumstances is apt to go unmarked'. (p. 52) The reason these agencies inevitably served the interests of the ruling class was not that they received daily packets of secret instructions from financiers in the City of London. It was that government agencies, the great banking and brokerage houses, the officer corps of the army and navy, were all staffed by members of the same privileged class. In Brailsford's opinion, it would not even be true to say that investment houses thought solely in terms of profit.

> It would be as false to say that the diplomatist is the sordid tool of finance, as it would be to say that the financier is the disinterested purse-bearer of patriotism. They belong to the same social world; they each submit to the vague influences which cause the world to turn its interest now to this corner of the world, and again to that. Each has his own formula to cover what he does. The financier knows that in pushing his business he is incidentally buying power for the empire. The diplomatist is convinced that he is serving his country by promoting 'trade'. However we explain it, the understanding between the City and Downing Street is admirably close. The City does not invest where investments would hamper our foreign policy; the Foreign Office will stand by the City where it has invested. (p. 220)

For everyone, it was 'part of the providential order of the universe that patriotism should profit the governing class'. The most significant fact of foreign policy in the twentieth century was that in all countries it was conducted by members 'of a ruling class which has become an investing class'. Though the foreign policy makers spoke and thought in the bureaucratic language of 'the official mind' which conceived the world in terms of 'a balance of power' and aimed to safeguard 'strategic interests', they never acted contrary to the perceived interests of the ruling investing class to which they belonged. Brailsford believed that in Britain the situation had recently worsened because Parliament had accepted the doctrine of 'continuity' in foreign policy which meant in practice that 'whichever party is in power, the Foreign Secretary will always be an Imperialist, a personality whom the *Times*, the City and the Conservative Party can unreservedly Trust'. (p. 132)

On the question of what should be done to curb imperialism, Brailsford agreed with Hobson that the ultimate solution was to strip the ruling class of the surplus capital that provided its strongest incentive for promoting an agressive foreign policy. But he also proposed some practical measures which could be taken in the meantime. The export of capital should be brought 'under public control through a classified register of foreign enterprises, loans and investments'. Opponents of imperialism could then identify dangerous enterprises and bring pressure on the government to refuse them any official support. The entire armaments industry should be taken over by the government and run as a public concern. Most important of all, Britain's foreign policy should be subject to 'the review of a number of unofficial minds'. Brailsford believed that Parliament reflected many interests besides those of the investing class and thought that the creation of a 'Commons Committee for Foreign Affairs' would be a step in the right direction. But the battle against 'the official mind' would not be finally won until it was forced to abandon the doctrine first enunciated by Lord Palmerston in his 'Don Pacifico' speech of 1850; i.e. the doctrine that a British 'subject residing or trading abroad is entitled to call upon the whole resources of diplomacy, backed if necessary by arms, to defend not only his personal safety but his material interest, if these are threatened by the people or government of the country in which he resides or trades'. (p. 53)

This doctrine, when extended to include government support of those who invested abroad, Brailsford regarded as the real essence of imperialism. He is very precise in his definition of imperialism: it is the 'constant acquisition of economic opportunity by political pressure'. The definition nicely encapsulates what all the recent theorists of imperialism had been talking about since the Spanish-American War. Imperialism was not the expansion of capitalism into new areas of the world nor was it the expansion of a nation's territory. Imperialism was the use of the state power beyond the state's own borders in order to acquire 'economic opportunity'. Like Hobson, Brailsford stressed that 'economic opportunity' covered not only the new policies consciously designed to create fields for investment but also the older policies which expanded opportunities for upper class employment in official and military capacities without consciously aiming at that result. Though Brailsford did not invent any new thesis concerning imperialism, his book should be remembered because it shows the direction that the theoretical discussion of imperialism took in Britain during the decade following the publication of Hobson's study. Discussion veered away from annexations to focus on the non-territorial forms of imperialism and on the arms race.

By the time Brailsford wrote, socialists in most countries agreed that appeals to reason along the lines of Angell's *Great Illusion* would not move the governments of Europe. Many hoped that the workers of all countries would call a general strike in the event that war should break out. Without the workers to fight and make weapons, war would be impossible. Brailsford opposed this programme on the ground that 'the armed peace', or 'the war of steel and gold' as he preferred to call it, was likely to continue for years and constituted a greater threat to the welfare of the masses than world war. He shared 'with Mr. Norman Angell the belief that war between European Powers for the possession of European soil or of old-established colonies has become an anachronism and is unlikely to occur'. (p. 163) Though the ruling classes of all nations would not give up their policies of imperialism, the evident attitude of all governments was timid rather than aggressive. 'Nowhere in Europe is this process of arming easy or uneventful. Everywhere it involves unpopular taxation, shaken credit, Cabinet crises, Parliamentary conflicts. A wanton enemy, a joyful aggressor, a primitive earth-shaking Imperialism there nowhere is in Europe today'. (p. 24.) More lamentable than the danger of war was the way that international tension and armaments were diverting attention and material resources from the task of social reform that needed to be undertaken everywhere. 'There is in all of us an uneasy sense that this international struggle is distracting the mind of society, which ought to be bent on the civilisation of our own barbarous way of life, while it dissipates on the engines of strife the resources that would suffice to raise the casual labourer and the sweated woman worker to a human level of comfort and freedom'.(p. 316) Having heard much the same thing from Hobson, the modern reader is likely to let his eye travel rapidly down the page to the bottom of Brailsford's concluding paragraph where he meets the words which chill the blood and tingle the spine: '*March, 1914*'.

CHAPTER 6
CENTRAL EUROPEAN SOCIALISTS AND IMPERIALISM BEFORE THE FIRST WORLD WAR

The war which had been so long in coming, the war Brailsford had thought might never come, all but destroyed the cherished hope of socialists that international 'working class solidarity' could triumph over the 'chauvinist militarism' of individual nation states. Many socialists had believed that, in the event of a general European war, class-conscious workers would desert the factories and the army, thus making it impossible for any country to carry on either business or warfare. They further hoped that in the ensuing chaos the working class would make a socialist revolution. Consequently, when war did actually begin socialist propagandists around the world looked expectantly to recognised leaders of the working class for a signal which would begin the general movement of resistance. In particular they looked to Germany, the homeland of Karl Marx and Frederick Engels, where there were millions of socialist voters and where the Social Democratic Party formed the largest single bloc of deputies in the national assembly. The news that on the fourth of August, 1914 the socialist deputies in the Reichstag had decided to vote *for* a bill to raise money for the German war effort created consternation and a split in international socialism which was never repaired. Because the acrimonious debates which surrounded that momentous decision were largely concerned with 'imperialism', they form an important chapter in the historical development of theories of imperialism.

For a long time the Germans had claimed a special eminence among Marxian socialists. The Germany party leader Karl Kautsky had known Marx and Engels well and was widely regarded as their true intellectual heir. H.M. Hyndman, the English Social Democrat who had his own ideas about who was in the vanguard of socialist thought, complained of this in a cantankerous letter to his friend

Gaylord Wilshire.

> I am rather sick of the Germans, Kautsky included .... what is the use of pretending that the Germans are completely the leaders in Socialism today when their doctrinaire utterances are falsified constantly? ... what is the use of talking of internationalism, when the party is becoming more and more national each year .... But among certain cliques it is as inadmissible to criticise Germans in Socialism, as it is to point out that Jews have their drawbacks.[1]

As far as the theoretical discussions of imperialism was concerned, Hyndman was quite right to challenge the German claim to pre-eminence. The first theoretical treatise in German which could rival the work of Wilshire or Hobson was not written until 1905 and not published until 1910. And just as American and British capitalists had preceded those two writers in proclaiming the economic necessity of imperialism, in Germany capitalist admirers of imperialism paved the way for socialist critics. The most important of the capitalist writers were Jacob Riesser and Otto Jeidels who in 1905 published highly influential books on the role of banking in the developing German economy.

Riesser lent his authority as a Professor in the University of Berlin and as a past president of the German Bankers Congress to his book, *Towards a Developmental History of the Great German Banks with Observations on the Concentration Movement.*[2] With massed charts and statistics, he aimed to show how the development of 'credit banks' with government assistance in the mid-nineteenth century had been of vital importance in the incredibly rapid industrialisation of the economy. Far from deploring the concentration of economic power in the hands of a few immensely powerful individuals, Riesser welcomed consolidation as an instrument for coordinating the activities of industry, finance and government in pursuit of Germany's

1. Hyndman to Wilshire, 25 April 1905, Wilshire Papers 1/13 U.C.L.A.

2. *Zur Entwicklungsgeschichte der deutschen Grossbanken* (Jena, 1905); 3rd. ed. *(The German Great Banks and their Concentrations in Connection with the Economic Development of Germany,* U.S. Senate, 2nd session, 61st Congress (Washington, D.C., 1911). Subsequent quotations are taken from this translation.

national goals of prosperity and greatness in world affairs. Much, he observed, had been asked of the great banks and they had responded magnificently.

> They had to assist by counsel and deed the business man crossing the seas as a pioneer of German trade. It became their function to support the industrial policy of the nation when it came to be considered in Germany as an economic necessity, and to promote the economic development of the colonies, as well as of German cable communications by a series of undertakings not promising immediate returns. They had to strengthen our financial, and with it our political influence abroad; nor was this accomplished without many a bitter experience. For in this field they met the competition of the majority of the great powers in the underwriting of foreign loans, the promoting of foreign undertakings, and the opening of international business relations, with the disadvantage that their rivals had entered the field long before them. By assisting German navigation, and establishing German banks abroad, they imparted to the German name a renown previously undreamed of thus extending by their activity the sphere of German business and political influence. Finally, by a cautious financial policy, they prepared our financial readiness for war, and for the carrying on of war. (pp. 11-12).

Riesser could not agree with the critics of consolidation finance and industry who lamented the passing of the era of laissez faire and free competition. (He believed the critics to be mostly composed of the owners of small and medium size enterprises who had been displaced by the growth of big business). (p. 548). Without government help the credit banks would not have been on hand to finance Germany's industrial revolution. Without the credit banks the periodical crises of the capitalist system — particularly the crises of 1873 and 1900 — would have been much more severe. He saw nothing sinister in the growing tendency for the representatives of the big banks to sit on the directorial boards of the great cartelised industries. It was only natural that the banks should wish to oversee the spending of the enormous amounts of capital they loaned to industry. And when the big banks invited captains of industry to sit on their own boards, it was 'not merely an act of courtesy... but also the manifestation of the mutual desire for an outward expression of the close business relationships that have been established'. (pp. 366-67).

Nor could Riesser agree with those who deplored overseas investments of German capital at a time when Germany herself needed capital for continued expansion. He pointed out that Germany was short of vital foodstuffs and raw materials and had to pay for these imports with either capital or the export of finished goods. Foreign investment in conjunction with an intelligent foreign policy could develop new sources of raw materials and profits which could be used to finance future imports. This could be particularly important if Germany's ability to export her products was further 'jeopardised by the growth of imperialistic and protectionist tendencies in countries which are at present our principal customers'. (pp. 536-37). If Germany was to continue her rise among the great powers in the age of 'world economy', *(Weltwirtschaft)* financial undertakings abroad were a necessity. Riesser deliberately uses the language of war. 'The skirmishes of the political advance posts', he announces grandly, 'are fought on financial ground'. (p. 543). Though he would not go so far as another writer who called the Franco-Russian alliance a 'bankers' creation', it was clear that Germany's rivals were using financial power to gain strategic advantages and that Germany must do the same. The British government, for example

> sought to prevent in every way the granting of a banking concession in Persia to the German *Orientbank* for fear that such a grant might lead to a diminution of its own political influence. The taking over of loans for China and Japan became an object of contention among all great nations, for the well known reason that financial influence merely paves the way for political influence. France and England are competing in Spain and Portugal — and nearly all the great powers in Turkey — to gain political influence by means of financial aid. Notwithstanding some painful experience in Argentina, the English banks and capitalists have been tenaciously lending financial support to the efforts of their Government to maintain the British political sphere of influence in that part of the world. (p. 544).

In his book on *The Relation of German Big Banks to Industry,* Otto Jeidels agreed with Riesser on the beneficial effects of German financial activity overseas.[3] In fact, he felt

3. O. Jeidels, *Der Verhaltnis der deutschen Grossbanken zur Industrie* (Leipzig, 1905).

that the banks should be doing more than they had been to promote the interests of Germany in every part of the world.[4] For Jeidels, expansion was more a matter of necessity than choice. Just as it had been natural at a certain stage of economic development for the big banks to assume a more direct role in the management of industrial enterprises, now it was necessary for the banks to develop overseas investments and to aid in the 'conquest' of 'economic regions'. 'The driving force of the banks' acitivity abroad is not national zeal but the necessity, which becomes even more imperative at a certain stage of capitalist development, of establishing abroad a favourable field for the investment of free German capital. (pp. 190-197).

References to defined periods in economic growth and 'stages of capitalist development' are commonplace in German economic literature at the turn of the century. They reflect the degree to which the basic concepts of Marx's *Capital* had penetrated German academic circles. For example, a thoroughly 'bourgeois' economist could write in 1904 that 'in relation to the German mining industry, the truth of the teachings of Karl Marx on concentration is definitely proved'.[5] The point on which the capitalist economic writers parted company with the socialists was on the question of whether concentration heralded the approaching end of the capitalist system. Riesser challenged the socialist prediction on the ground that so far no industry, no matter how centralised or cartelised, had yet been expropriated by the State. Germans, he said, still cherished 'individual independence' too much to allow the extinction of private ownership.[6] It would be unfortunate, he continued, if fears of eventual socialisation caused Germans to follow the Americans in passing laws against extreme concentration. If Germany was to secure the resources she needed overseas, concentration

4. See note on Jeidels in Riesser, 845.

5. H.G. Heymann, *Die gemischten Werke in deutschen Grosseisengewerbe* (Stuttgart, 1904) 278-79.

6. Edition of 1906, p. 302.

must proceed.

It is hardly surprising that socialists eventually noticed the capitalist literature linking aggressive foreign policy with economic necessity. On the contrary, it is surprising that German socialists took so long to develop their own theory of economic imperialism. At the time of the joint European and American expedition against the Boxers in China in 1900, some German Social Democrats had claimed to perceive in this new *Weltpolitik* the beginning of a new stage — the last stage — in capitalist development.[7] But it was not until 1905 that a young Austrian Marxist, Rudolf Hilferding turned the data provided by Riesser, Jeidels and other German capitalist writers into a comprehensive theory of imperialism.[8] In an article on tariff policy written for Kautsky's journal *Die Neue Zeit* in 1903 he suggested that the spread of high protective tariffs which was currently threatening the continuance of free trade in Britain had inaugurated the 'final phase' of capitalism.[9] Subsequently he expanded this idea into a five hundred page book on 'finance capital' which appeared in 1910 as volume three of a series of studies in Marxism published by the circle of Viennese socialists with whom he had been associated since his student days in the mid eighteen nineties.[10] Drawing not only on Jeidels and Riesser but also on recent British and American studies of trusts, Hilferding attempted to show, first, that the militarism currently threatening the peace of Europe could not be effectually combatted by a return to free trade, and second, that the consolidation movement in finance and industry was a major step forward toward socialism.

7. Lelio Basso, 'Analysis of Theories of Imperialism', in Bertrand Russell Peace Foundation, *Spheres of Influence in the Age of Imperialism* (Nottingham, 1972),p.

8. *Das Finanzkapital,* vol. III of *Marx-Studien, Blatter zur Theorie und Politik des Wissenschaftlichen Sozialismus* (Vienna, 1910).

9. 'Der Funktionswechsel des Schutzzolles, Tendenz der Modernen Handelspolitik', *Die Neue Zeit* (May, 1903) 274-81.

10. Tom Bottomore and Patrick Goode, *Austro-Marxism* (Oxford, 1978) 1-44.

What Hilferding had to say about the financial pressures on governments to pursue aggressive foreign policies did not go very far beyond what Wilshire had said several years earlier. The difference between Wilshire and Hilferding is more a matter of technique than substance. Wilshire painted with rough brushstrokes on a canvas the size of one of his Los Angeles billboards. The consolidation of capital in industry was personified by Rockefeller, the growing domination of financiers, by J.P. Morgan, and the forces of aggressive imperialism, by the war-hawks of the Republican Party. Wilshire described the antics of these cartoon characters for the purpose of wooing the average American voter to the cause of socialism. Hilferding on the other hand wrote in a dry academic manner for a small audience of socialist theoreticians familiar with the specialised language of Marxism. With masses of data and intricate argumentation he aimed to produce a treatise fit to stand beside the works of Marx and Kautsky.

The phenomenon documented by Riesser and Jeidels — the controlling position recently assumed by the big German banks in the direction of heavy industry — is the centrepiece of Hilferding's argument. He calls this situation the dominance of 'finance capital' and identifies it as a special stage in the historical career of capitalism. While he agrees with capitalist apologists of the consolidation movement that the emergence of cartels and big banks helped to cope with periodic crises of over-production, he believes that in the long run the trend towards monopoly creates grave problems for capitalism. In order to maintain control of prices and production in their home markets, the big capitalists favour high protective tariffs which will exclude products made in other countries. These tariffs in turn speed up the growth of cartels in all branches of business. (pp. 381-89). But the very maintenance of profits that the cartels and tariffs are designed to achieve is undercut by the increased costs generated by protectionism and the intensive development of the metropolitan economy. Faced with declining rates of profit and rising costs of raw materials at home, finance capital looks for opportunities abroad. Vast foreign sources of raw material are discovered but their exploitation is handicapped by shortages of willing workers and of political authorities amenable to capitalist methods of organising society. To solve these problems the exporters of capital seek forced labour and concessions; if they are unable to obtain them with their own resources they look to their own governments for help. (pp. 395-406). If they are successful in achieving their objectives, the capital exporters secure high profits based on cheap raw material and plentiful cheap labour. When the capital exporters of different developed nations come into conflict with each other in their attempts to carve out exclusive spheres of economic development beyond their own borders, imperialism is the result.

Because Hilferding is long on abstract concepts and short on concrete examples, it is easy to fall into confusion about what he means when he talks of imperialism. One matter, however, on which he is not vague is chronology. The era of imperialism under the aegis of finance capital commences *after 1895*. The capital exports and empires of earlier periods are not Hilferding's concern, and he provides no alternative to Hobson's account of how Britain acquired her colonies. In fact Hilferding portrays Britain as a late comer to imperialism. For the greater part of the nineteenth century Britain championed the cause of free trade and made no effort to organise her vast dominions into a coherent imperial system. It was only after the growth of monopoly and protectionism launched Germany and the United States into adventurous foreign policies that Rhodes and Chamberlain fought back with plans for imperial federation, new armaments and protective tariffs. (pp. 400, 475). This treatment of Britain as the imitator rather than the generator of the new Imperialist Politics emphasises the degree to which Hilferding identified trusts and cartels, militarism and protectionism as the hallmarks of imperialism.[11] This was only natural considering

11. See especially Hilferding's analysis of the way in which free trade hinders the growth of trusts and cartels, pp. 385-89.

his central European perspective. When allowance has been made for his very different circumstances it can be seen that his theory of the origins of imperialism closely resembles Wilshire's: imperialism arises from the attempts of financiers and monopolists in various countries to deal with problems of surplus capital and excessive productive capacity. Hilferding, however, says much more than Wilshire about *how* imperialism tries to prolong the life of the capitalist system. The power of the state, especially its military power, is used to assure access to foreign sources of raw materials and cheap labour.

He is also more precise than Wilshire in making predictions about the future. Wilshire merely pointed out that even with all the world as its stage, the growth of monopoly must eventually lead to a handful of capitalists with too much to sell confronting angry workers unable to buy their products. Hilferding pins his hopes for the future on a dramatic heightening of class consciousness among workers caused by the blatantly autocratic character of the imperialist state. Back in the days when the ideological champions of capitalism opposed the old ruling classes with the slogans laissez faire, free trade, peace and democracy, it had been difficult for socialists to expose the connection between capitalism and the state — to show how the state served the interests of the capitalists. However, as soon as economic expansion beyond political frontiers required assistance from the power of the state, the capitalists showed their true colours. Now they called for state interference in the economy for *their* benefit, for high tariffs instead of free trade, for heavy armaments instead of peace, for concentration of economic power in the hands of an oligarchy of finance capital instead of democracy. While the proletariat had received no positive benefits from free trade, the policy had at least not done them any positive harm. But under the regime of finance capital and imperialism, the workers suffer in a very direct way: they pay higher prices for food and manufactured goods protected by high tariff; their ability to bargain for higher wages is restricted by the close association of the bosses in trusts and cartels; they pay higher taxes to support bigger armies and navies; and, in the event of war, they risk life itself as conscripted soldiers. Hilferding also expected that as workers woke up to the necessity of seizing political power they would be joined by disgruntled defectors from other classes. Small businessmen destroyed or overshadowed by the growth of big business, office workers who realised that they had become insignificant cogs in a big machine, and middle class people who resented higher prices and higher taxes would also be attracted to socialism. (pp. 469-76).

Like Wilshire, Hilferding believed that the accelerating concentration of economic and political power would facilitate the transition from capitalism to socialism. It was, he wrote, 'an historical law' that precisely at the point at which the power of a ruling class reaches its apex, the revolutionary upheaval which overthrows that class begins. A successful revolutionary movement could seize effective control of economic power in Germany by simply seizing the six biggest banks which effectively controlled basic transport and industry. The power to control these branches of the economy carried with it the power to control all the rest. The 'dictatorship of the capitalist magnates' would give way to the 'dictatorship of the proletariat'. (pp. 476-78). Because he believed that imperialism was performing the dual function of heightening class conflict and concentrating economic power, Hilferding called it 'the final stage' of capitalism.

His book became an instant classic of central European Marxist thought. Without pretending to challenge Marx's basic teaching he updated it to take account of current great power politics. By introducing German and Austrian socialists to the bellicose conclusions of capitalist economists and financial journalists he did for his comrades what Wilshire had done for American and Hobson had done for British socialists. He transformed a capitalist theory of imperialism into a socialist theory of imperialism. Though the main lines of his analysis were unoriginal, his presentation of the problem of imperialism differed from that of his English-speaking predecessors by taking a central-European perspective. He was relatively unconcerned with overseas colonies and said little about how they had been acquired by the French and British. The growth of high tariffs, the Austrian drive for hegemony in the Balkans and Kaiser Wilhelm's challenge to British supremacy at sea were the matters uppermost in his mind. Nevertheless, his concept of imperialism is essentially the same as that set out by the English-speaking theorists. He too uses the word imperialism to describe the deliberate use of the state power, especially its military power, in order to advance alleged national economic interests in the world at large. His views received wide circulation because he constantly moved back and forth between Vienna and Berlin. In fact during the period when he was writing and revising *Das Finanzkapital* he was employed as a teacher at the Central Party School established by the German Social Democrats in Berlin for the purpose of educating young socialist activists. When the German authorities deported him in 1907, his position in the school was taken by the formidable Marxist theoretican Rosa Luxemburg, who in the course of the next six years developed an analysis of capitalist expansion which went far beyond Hilferding in placing the phenomenon of imperialism in a historical perspective.[12]

Rosa Luxemburg is one of the legendary figures of revolutionary socialism. The dramatic episodes of her life, beginning with her escape from Poland at the age of eighteen, only one step ahead of the police, and ending with her brutal murder by German troops in 1919, assured her a permanent place in the pantheon of socialist martyrs. This has tempted some writers to treat her as a romantic rebel who acted on the promptings of her heart rather than the calculations of her brain. Nothing could be more unfair. Rosa Luxemburg always insisted on the necessity of subordinating passion to reason in personal as well as political affairs. She did not marry her first

12. Peter Nettl, *Rosa Luxemburg* (Oxford, 1969) 262-65.

lover, the Polish socialist Leo Jogisches, because 'bourgeois marriage' had no place in correct theory. She did marry a man she did not love and hardly knew for the sole purpose of acquiring a German residence permit in 1897. After she broke her personal connection with Leo Jogisches because of his infidelity, she contined to work with him in political matters as though nothing had happened.[13] What mattered most to her in every situation was having a correct theoretical basis for practical action. With a natural flair for mathematics, a command of several languages and a doctor of laws degree from the University of Zurich, she felt herself to be as good as anyone in formulating correct theory — as good as Kautsky, as good as Lenin, even as good as Marx.

During her teaching years at the Central Party School she came to believe that Marx's analysis of the evolution of capitalism was incomplete because it failed to take into account capitalism's need for continuous expansion into new areas. In her book *The Accumulation of Capital* published in 1913 Luxemburg set out to remedy this deficiency and to show that the rise of imperialism .in the twentieth century was a natural consequence of a process of expansion which had been going on for centuries. Her attempt to demonstrate the failings of Marx's model of capitalist development as a closed system takes up more than three hundred pages in a four hundred and seventy page book and became the subject of heated debate among Marxist theoreticians. The point at issue in this debate is whether an economy based on capitalism *must* continually expand into non-capitalist areas in order to exist.[14] This highly abstract question could not be settled by an appeal to history because, whether or not capitalist economies *needed* to expand, the evident fact was that they *had* been expanding for centuries. The importance of Luxemburg's book to the development of theories of imperialism is not to be found in

13. Ibid 70, 257.

14. The consensus of opinion among Marxist and non-Marxists is that Luxemburg was wrong. See A. Brewer, *Marxist Theories of Imperialism* (London, 1980) 63-69.

its abstract discussion of necessity but in the final section on "The Historical Conditions of Accumulation" where the techniques of capitalist expansion are identified and illustrated by specific historical examples.

In this section Rosa Luxemburg demonstrates that, although she knew that passion must be subordinated to reason, she also knew how to use passion in the service of reason. Her writing is inflamed by indignation at the injustices perpetrated by expanding capitalism since the middle ages in almost every part of the globe. She denies absolutely the premise of Cobden and other mid-Victorian free traders that peaceful progress is possible in any society based on private ownership. Violence was, she asserted, a normal condition of life under capitalism. Violence had been necessary to drive Indians off agricultural land in the Americas, Africans off pastoral lands in South Africa, and self-sufficient farmers off grazing lands in Scotland so that a regime of capitalist agriculture could be introduced. Slaves had been captured in Africa to make plantations pay in the new world. Forts and gunboats had been used to pave the way for 'peaceful trade' in India, China and Japan. When capitalism needed 'free labour' for farms and factories it had forced peasants off the land. When capitalism needed self-sufficient peasant producers to grow crops and breed labourers, it kept them on the land. Sometimes the violence had been perpetrated by independent agents — frontiersmen, traders, slavers, landlords. Sometimes it had been perpetrated by agents of the State — *conquistadores,* colonial armies, gunboats, policemen. Sometimes it had been perpetuated by the impersonal fluctuations of the economic system itself — depressions, the ruination of small-scale craftsmen by imports of cheap factory-made goods, disastrous falls in world prices for agricultural commodities when new lands were brought into production in America, Russia and Australia. But whoever or whatever was directly responsible for individual instances of violence, the distinguishing feature of expanding capitalism since its inception had been 'catastrophe as a mode of existence'.

It is important to emphasise at this point that Rosa Luxemburg *does not use imperialism as a synonym for the expansion of capitalism.* Expansion had characterised the whole history of capitalism. Imperialism, 'The final phase of capitalism', arose only at the end of the nineteenth century when individual capitalist nations began arming themselves to the teeth and using protective tariffs, concessions, colonies, and other methods of 'economic monopolisation' to preserve for their exclusive exploitation 'what still remained open of the non-capitalist environment'.[15] It is equally important to emphasise that Luxemburg *does not equate the expansion of capitalism with the acquisition or founding of colonies.* The westward movement of American farmers, the northward movement of Boer farmers in South Africa, the building of railways in South America, the disastrous misuse of European loans by the rulers of Turkey and Egypt were all equally important aspects of the expansion of capitalism. The agents of this expansion had been countless and multifarious. Free trade had been one policy favorable to the expansion, imperialism was another.

Why, then, did imperialism — the 'policy of economic monopolisation and economic subjugation' with the aid of armaments and high tariffs — appear at the close of the nineteenth century? On this point Luxemburg is vague. She ignores the hypotheses of virtually all the theorists of imperialism from the *U.S. Investor* and Wilshire to Brailsford and Hilferding that surplus investment capital was responsible for the present wave of militarism. As far as she could see, the export of capital had been a characteristic of capitalism since the Renaissance. She also rejects the argument of many pro-imperialists in Europe that Britain's near monopoly of world trade in the nineteenth century could only be broken with the help of tariffs and aggressive foreign policies. German industry and foreign trade, for example, had flourished in the heyday of the alleged British monopoly. (p. 421). Insofar as her explanation for the rise of modern

15. *The Accumulation of Capital,* trans. A. Schwarzschild (London, 1951) 421.

imperialism can be separated from her overall analysis of capitalist expansion in *The Accumulation of Capital,* it appears to be that the current wave of militarism represented a quantitative rather than a qualitative change. Agents of capitalism had been using private and public force to extend their domination over non-capitalist areas for centuries. Even when the influence of pacifist free traders had been strongest, capitalist countries often resorted to force and war when they encountered obstacles to expansion. The teaching of Cobden and his allies, that a worldwide harmony of commercial interests could be achieved

never expressed the interests of capitalist accumulation as a whole. In England herself it was given the lie already in the forties, when the harmony of interests of the commercial interests of the commercial nations in the East were proclaimed to the sound of gunfire in the Opium War which ultimately, by the annexation of Hongkong, brought about the very opposite of such harmony, a system of 'spheres of interest'. On the European Continent, Free Trade in the sixties did not represent the interests of industrial capital, because the foremost Free Trade countries of the Continent were still predominantly agrarian with a comparatively feeble development of industry. Rather, the policy of Free Trade was implemented as a means for the political reconstruction of the Central European states. (pp. 447-48).

However, once a number of states had acquired strength enough to challenge Britain's industrial supremacy there arose in each of them a party which wanted high tariffs to protect them from competition at home, and aggressive foreign policies aimed at carving out exclusive areas for future exploitation beyond their own frontiers. Because this policy necessarily required the equipping of formidable armies and navies, it was doubly attractive to capitalists. Armaments themselves constituted new sources of profits, gained at the expense of workers and other taxpayers who had to pay for them. All of this ominous activity was speeded up by the realisation among the advanced capitalist powers that there were only a few non-capitalist areas still available for exploitation by an exclusive systems. In the long run, however, the policy is self-defeating. 'The more ruthlessly capital sets about the destruction of non-capitalist strata at home and in the outside world, the more it lowers the standard of living for the workers as a whole, the greater also is the change in the day-to-day history of capital. It becomes a string of political and social disasters and convulsions, and under these conditions, punctuated by periodical economic catastrophe of crises, accumulation can go on no longer'. Thus in the end Rosa Luxemburg reached the same conclusion as Wilshire and Hilferding — that capitalism could not go on much longer. But she reached this conclusion without propounding a theory of imperialism grounded on specific features of contemporary capitalism such as the growth of monopolies, the rise of big banks or the export of capital. Her historical research convinced her that there was nothing particularly new about the use of the state power to further capitalist expansion. Modern protectionism and militarism represented simply the culmination of a long historical process. The so-called peace of the free trade era had been an aberration in capitalist development and even that era had been a great deal less peaceful and free than most people realised.

For socialists seeking a simple mechanistic explanation of why Europe teetered on the edge of war, Rosa Luxemburg's book was not very satisfying. It presented a brash challenge to Marx's mathematical equations. It implied that protective tariffs and the arms race were as much a product of specific decisions made by the rulers of central European powers as of 'historical necessity'. It offered no firm predictions about the short-term prospects for peace or war. Furthermore, she had specifically denied that the survival of German or Austrian capitalism depended upon successful aggression against any other capitalist country. This left it open for someone to argue, as Hobson had suggested a decade before, that the leading capitalist nations might somehow overcome their current mutual antagonism and combine to place an iron yoke around the necks of the rest of humanity. This possibility was discussed by Karl Kautsky in a short but very important article written a few weeks before war broke out in 1914.[16]

Luxemburg once complained that instead of the concrete facts which could stir victims of capitalism to action, Kautsky offered only boring, featureless constructions of history in the abstract.[17] This is a fair description of his article 'Der Imperialismus'. He is maddeningly vague about dates and names and countries as he sets out a highly schematic account of capitalist expansion. Kautsky begins by agreeing with Luxemburg that there has been a 'constant drive of the industrialised capitalist countries to extend the agricultural zones involved in trade relations with them', and agreeing with Hilferding that 'imperialism was particularly encouraged by the system of capital export' which grew up towards the end of the nineteenth century. However, Kautsky departs from both Luxemburg and Hilferding by pointedly refusing to describe imperialism as the 'final stage' of capitalist development. While asserting that the drive to expand was 'one of the very conditions of the existence of capitalism', Kautsky maintained that the drive could assume 'the most varied forms'. Imperialism was one form of the drive, 'another form preceded it: *free trade*'. Why, he asked, could not capitalist expansion take another form in the future?

After all, the present effort of advanced capitalist countries to create exclusive zones of exploitation and defend them with modern armaments was costing them a great deal of money — so much money, in fact, that capital exports were actually declining. Even before the War, it was clear that since the Balkan War [of 1912] the arms race and the costs of colonial expansion had reached a level that threatened the rapid increases of capital accumulation and thereby capital export, i.e., the basis of imperialism itself. 'Industrial accumulation at home still advances continously, thanks to

16. 'Der Imperialismus', *Die Neue Zeit* (11 Sept. 1914), translated with a very misleading introduction in *New Left Review* LIX (1970) 39-46. Subsequent quotations refer to this translation.

17. Nettl, *Rosa Luxemburg*, 276.

technical progress. But capital no longer rushes into export'. (p. 45). World war could obviously cripple the ability of both winners and losers to exert their influence beyond their own borders. Furthermore, the internecine strife of the great powers could make it easier for backward countries to repeat the success of America, Germany and Japan in developing their own industrial economies and threatening the old capitalist countries with their exports. Kautsky thought it quite possible that sooner or later the big capitalist powers would see the senselessness of their competition in trade and armaments. If they buried the animosities of the past, they could combine their strength and maintain a stranglehold on the backward agrarian regions of the world until at some distant time they reached the theoretical limits of expansion. Kautsky called this possible unification of capitalist states 'ultra-imperialism' and attempted to put it into the context of general Marxist theory. 'What Marx said of capitalism can also be applied to imperialism; monopoly creates competition and competition monopoly. The frantic competition of giant firms, giant banks and multi-millionaires obliged the great financial groups, who were absorbing the small ones, to think up the notion of the cartel. In the same way, the result of the World War between the great imperialist powers may be a federation of the strongest, who renounce their arms race'. (p. 46). Though Kautsky went on to say that socialists 'must struggle against' ultra-imperialism 'as energetically as we do against imperialism', his article struck a good many socialists as a very odd thing to write just as the world was exploding. Only two years earlier Kautsky had made a vigorous attack on Norman Angell's thesis that the export of investment capital could be managed without armaments or war. Now, when he might have joined others in denouncing capitalism for plunging the world into a nightmarish era of perpetual war, when he might have called for a general strike to stop the big war machines before they began to roll, he speculated irrelevantly that an era of peace might be just around the corner. Kautsky's failure to give a decisive lead to anti-war forces at a critical moment in history paralleled the failure of the whole Social Democratic Party in the Reichstag. Their decision to support the German war effort in opposing the 'barbarous aggression' of 'reactionary Russian Tsarism' in turn reflected the general disintegration of the supposed 'international solidarity' of socialism. In England, H.M. Hyndman's campaign against 'The German Menace' had split the Social-Democrats even before the outbreak of war. Across the Atlantic, Wilshire wrote in support of American involvement in the war 'against German imperialism'.[18] Nowhere was there a large-scale socialist resistance to the war; in every country a majority of socialists found a convenient foreign scapegoat to justify their temporary cooperation with their erstwhile enemies of the ruling class. The impotence of the socialist movement to hinder what was everywhere described as an imperialist war provoked a round of bitter mutual recriminations and a further development of socialist theories of imperialism.

18. H.H. Quint, 'Wilshire's Magazine', *American Radical Press 1880-1960,* ed. J.R. Conlin, I (Westport, 1974) 72-81. N. Etherington, 'Hyndman, the Social Democratic Federation and Imperialism, *Historical Studies* XVI (1974) 89-103.

CHAPTER 7
EXPLAINING THE GERMAN 'BETRAYAL'; LUXEMBURG, BUKHARIN AND LENIN

Emigres from countries where socialism was weak and where it was suppressed by autocratic governments were especially bitter towards the leadership of the German Social Democrats. They had counted on Germany as the most advanced capitalist state with the biggest socialist party to begin a world-wide revolution. Kautsky's journal *Die Neue Zeit* (Modern Times) had been *the* international forum of theoretical socialism. One reaction to the coming of war was to pick over the theoretical writings on imperialism which had emanated from Germany. Where had these works gone wrong?

The Russian Bolshevik Nickolai Bukharin blamed Kautsky and Luxemburg for putting too much emphasis on the overseas manifestations of imperialism and consequently neglecting the struggle among the great powers for the redivision of Europe. Luxemburg, he asserted, had identified imperialism with colonialism and had implied 'that a fight for territories that have already become capitalist' or 'a fight for already "occupied" territories is not imperialism'.[1] This criticism was grossly unfair. In the first place, Luxemburg's book of 1913 had been, as the title implied, a treatise on the place of expansion in the accumulation of capital over the course of several centuries; it was not a book specifically on imperialism. Its purpose was to provide the historical background to imperialism. In the second place, there was no socialist in Germany who had more bravely denounced the war effort than Rosa Luxemburg. She and Karl Liebknecht, the son of a famous pioneer socialist, broke entirely with the official party and formed the "Spartacus" group which called upon the workers to refuse all cooperation with the German war effort. Before, during and after her imprisonment (1915-1916) she wrote inspiring, highly effective anti-war pamphlets.

1. R. Luxemburg and N. Bukharin, *Imperialism and the Accumulation of Capital*, ed., K.J. Tarbuck (London, 1972) 253.

However unjust, the criticism directed against her did perform the useful function of forcing her to clarify her analysis of imperialism, a word which she had only occasionally used in her 1913 book. Her two pamphlets, 'The Accumulation of Capital — An Anti-Critique' and 'The Crisis in The German Social Democracy' make her views plain. On the subject of chronology she is precise. The imperialist period of capitalist expansion is defined as the period 'that Marx did not live to see', the 'imperialist development of the last twenty-five years' (i.e. since 1893). This period had been prefigured by 'a strong tendency toward colonial expansion beginning 'as early as the eighties' but only developed fully in a series of wars 'beginning with the Chinese-Japanese War in 1895'.[2] Far from identifying imperialism exclusively with the acquisition of colonies, she lists several 'typical external phenomena of 'imperialism': 'competition among capitalist countries to win colonies and spheres of interest, opportunities for investment, the international loan system, militarism, tariff barriers, the dominant role of finance capital and trusts in world politics'.[3] Like Brailsford, Luxemburg calls attention to Turkey as an example of the way in which imperialism can actually work *against* the acquisition of colonies. 'It is obvious from the foregoing that the interests of German imperialism demand the protection of the Turkish State, to the extent at least of preventing its complete disintegration. The liquidation of Turkey would mean its division between England, Russia, Italy and Greece among others and the basis for a large scale operation by German capital would vanish'.[4]

She scoffed at the idea that the need to possess particular pieces of overseas territory had been the real reason for tensions between European powers. England's free trade

2. Luxemburg, *The Crisis in the German Social-Democracy* (New-York, 1919), 34-35. This was the work commonly known as the 'Junius Pamphlet'.

3. *Imperialism and the Accumulation of Capital*, 60.

4. Junius Pamphlet', 43-44.

policy and her colonial empire had been 'cornerstones for German industrial growth' because they provided huge markets for German goods.

> Far from standing in each other's way, British and German capitalist development were mutually highly interdependent, and united by a far-reaching system of division of labour, strongly augmented by England's free trade policy. German trade and its interests in the world market, therefore had nothing whatever to do with a change of front in German politics and with the building of its fleet.
>
> Nor did German colonial possessions at that time come into conflict with the English control of the seas. German colonies were not in need of protection by a first-class sea power. No one, certainly not England, envied Germany her possessions. That they were taken during the war by England and Japan, that the booty had changed owners, is but a generally accepted war measure, just as German imperialist appetites clamor for Belgium, a desire that no man outside of an insane asylum would have dared to express in time of peace. Southeast and Southwest Africa, Wilhelmsland or Tsingtau would never caused any war, by land or by sea between Germany and England. In fact, just before the war broke out, a treaty regulating a peaceable division of the Portuguese colonies in Africa between these two nations had been practically completed.[5]

Luxemburg believed that 'Germany's interest in other people's colonies was based not on the economic value of those colonies in themselves but on the desire to present a general challenge to the power of other capitalist states. For example, when international pressure forced Germany to retract its demands for special privileges in Morocco she accepted as compensation a tract of African territory adjacent to her Kamerun colony. 'In the end Germany was satisfied with the French Congo region, and in accepting this admitted that it had no special interests to protect in Morocco itself. This very fact gave to the German attack in Morocco a far reaching political significance. The very indefiniteness of its tangible aims and demands betrayed its insatiable appetite, the seeking and feeling for prey — it was a general imperialistic declaration of war against France'.[6] From this point of view the distinguishing feature of imperialism, the

5. Ibid 38-39.

6. Ibid 49-50.

characteristic that marks it out as a phase of capitalist development separate from earlier expansion, is the conflict between capitalist powers at home in Europe. 'What distinguishes imperialism as the last struggle for capitalist world domination is not simply the remarkable energy and universality of expansion but — and this is the specific sign that the circle of development is beginning to close — the return of the decisive struggle for expansion from those areas which are being fought over back to its home countries. In this way imperialism brings catastrophe as a mode of existence back from the periphery of capitalist development to its point of departure'.[7]

When Rosa Luxemburg looked for the cause which had transformed the expansion of capitalism from a harmonious joint undertaking to a bitter contest culminating in war, she placed the blame squarely on Germany. For a very long time international rivalry had been a 'secret underhand war of each capitalist nation against each other'. At the same time a perceptive observer might have perceived 'that the wind that was sown in Africa and Asia would return to Europe as a terrific storm, the more certainly since increased armament of the European states was the constant associate of these Asiatic and African occurrences'. What had been required to whistle up the tempest had been a 'centralised axis, a conflict of sufficient magnitude' to weld competing powers into conflicting alliances. That sinister lightning rod was 'the appearance of German imperialism'. In Germany since the foundation of the empire' in 1871 one could study the development of imperialism' condensed 'into the shortest possible space of time'. In Germany, banking was more concentrated, monopolies grew bigger and faster. And no monopoly grew stronger than steel, 'the branch of capitalist endeavour most interested in government orders, in militaristic equipment and in imperialistic undertakings'. Atop the whole awesome machine sat autocracy. 'Germany is under a personal regime, with strong initiative and spasmodic

7. *Imperialism and Accumulation*, 147.

activity, with the weakest kind of parliament, incapable of opposition, uniting all capitalist strata in the sharpest opposition to the working class. It is obvious that this live, unhampered imperialism, coming upon the world stage at a time when the world was practically divided up, with gigantic appetites, soon became an irresponsible factor of general unrest'.[8]

With this analysis Rosa Luxemburg finally achieved a formulation which deserves to be called a theory of imperialism. It differs significantly from earlier theories. Her theory is that imperialism resulted from the endeavours of rising capitalist powers, particularly Germany, to secure foreign fields for expansion in a world already virtually partitioned among rival powers in earlier decades. It differed from previous chapters in the expansion of capitalism inasmuch as it was a movement for the *re*partition rather than the partition of the globe. The new era began about 1895, when Germany set out to challenge British supremacy at sea, and culminated in the World War.

By the time Luxemburg made her final statement on imperialism she was far more concerned with the present and the future of international socialism than with achieving a nice theoretical exactitude in judgments on the past. When the Social-Democrats in the Reichstag announced on the fourth of August 1914 that 'in this hour of danger, we will not desert our fatherland', they had, in her view, betrayed the German people.

It was their duty to speak loudly and clearly, to proclaim to the people of Germany that in this war victory and defeat would be equally fatal, to oppose the gagging of the fatherland by a state of siege, to demand that the people alone decide on war and peace, to demand a permanent session of Parliament for the period of the war, to assume a watchful control over the government by parliament, and over parliament by the people, to demand the immediate removal of all political inequalities, since only a free people can adequately govern its country, and finally, to oppose to the imperialist war, based as it was upon the most reactionary forces in Europe, the programme of Marx, of Engels, and Lassalle.[9]

8. 'Junius', 35-36.

9. Ibid 108.

Unless socialists of every country took up that programme Luxemburg prophesied a very dark future for humanity. The world stood at a crossroads: 'either the triumph of imperialism and the destruction of all culture, and, as in ancient Rome, depopulation, desolation, degeneration, a vast cemetery; or, the victory of socialism'. Without the revolution one hardly dared hope even for the defeat of the reactionary Hapsburgs and Ottomans. That would entail 'the bartering of their peoples to the highest bidder — Russia, England, France or Italy'. A shift of power of that magnitude would probably also mean 'the liquidation of Persia and a redivision of China' which 'would bring the Anglo-Russian as well as the Anglo-Japanese conflict into the foreground of international politics'. Even worse, a victory of the allies 'would lead to new feverish armaments in all nations — defeated Germany, of course, at the head — and would introduce an era of undivided rule for militarism and reaction all over Europe, with a new war as its final goal'.[10]

How quickly war had blighted long-standing socialist hopes for the future of humanity. The Russian emigre Vladimir Illych Lenin chimed in with the prevailing mood in a review of Luxemburg's pamphlet on 'The Crisis in the German Social Democracy' which he called 'a splendid Marxist work'.[11] The decades ahead might be even grimmer than Luxemburg had feared:

> ...*if* the *European* proletariat remains impotent, say, for twenty years; *if* the present war [W.W.I] *ends* in victories like Napoleon's and in the subjugation of a number of viable national states; *if* the transition to socialism of non-European imperialism (primarily Japanese and American) is also held up for twenty years by a war between these two countries, for example, then a great national war in Europe would be possible. It would hurl Europe *back* several decades. That is improbable, but *not* impossible, for it is undialectical, unscientific and theoretically wrong to regard the course of world history as smooth and always in a forward direction, without occasional gigantic leaps back.

10. Ibid 18.

11. Lenin, 'On The Junius Pamphlet' July 1916 *Collected Works* XXII (Moscow, 1964) 310

Lenin can be excused for being somewhat pessimistic at this point in his career. Though in a matter of months he was to emerge as the architect of one of the world's most astonishing revolutions, at the moment he was sheltering from the storms of war in neutral Switzerland. One of the tasks he set himself during this frustrating exile was to sort out the underlying causes of the present war and Kautsky's betrayal of international socialist solidarity. His working hypothesis was that imperialism provided a common explanation for both disasters.

Lenin was not the first Russian to write on imperialism; he was not even the first Russian Marxist. His Bolshevik comrade Bukharin had attempted to refute Kautsky in 1915 in an article which had a good deal of trouble getting into print. Lenin wrote a short introduction in December of the same year, but both article and introduction were subsequently lost. The article turned up in 1917, but Lenin's introduction was not found until 1927.[12] Bukharin's execution as an enemy of the State in one of Stalin's great purges ensured that the work would remain little known outside scholarly circles. It probably deserved a better fate. It is more readable than Lenin's subsequent publication and takes a broader view. It directly addresses theorists outside the Marxist camp, including Norman Angell and H. N. Brailsford.

Lenin's introduction states concisely the general problem. Why had 'an epoch of comparatively "peaceful capitalism"' during which that system 'was in a position to develop comparatively tranquilly and harmoniously . . . spreading over tremendous areas of still unoccupied land' suddenly ended? Bukharin's broad answer was that in the course of many decades individual, self-contained economic systems had gradually become part of a single world economy. Integration in the market place had not, however, been accompanied by integration in the political arena. Sovereignty resided in a multiplicity of 'national states' each of which was

12. *Imperialism and World Economy*, written in 1915, published after the Russian Revolution with a forward by Lenin. English edition, n.d.

directed by a small clique of capitalists. There was, in Bukharin's words, a structural 'conflict between World Economy and the limitations of the "National State"'. Each national clique sought profit by protecting its own home base with high tariff walls while insisting on its right to sell freely in territory under the domination of competing cliques. When unimpeded access was denied each clique came to see 'war as the only solution of the problem'.

Bukharin specifically endorsed Brailsford's refutation of Norman Angell's attempt 'to influence the ruling classes by logical reasons'. (pp. 100-101). 'The Englishman Brailsford' was 'correct' in contending that a policy which did nothing for the well-being of the majority of citizens in every nation was nevertheless of direct benefit to 'individual groups (large financiers, cartels, bureaucracy, etc.)'. (pp. 61-62, 100-101) The arms race would go on until the contradiction between a world economy and national states was eliminated through an international revolution '*abolishing* state boundaries and merging all the peoples into one Socialist family'. (p. 167) Bukharin had more trouble confuting Kautsky's suggestion that a mutual agreement among 'the state capitalist trusts' could restore capitalism to its former peaceful ways. Imperialism, the constant struggle to obtain economic advantage through the use of armed force, was a necessity not because of logic, but because the relative positions of the players in the murderous game would never stabilise enough for such a mutual agreement to be arranged. Therefore, 'a series of wars is unavoidable'.

Bukharin's pamphlet has little to say about colonial policy, except to note that because of 'a special combination of historic conditions, imperialism in Great Britain expressed itself in a movement 'towards combining the disunited parts of the state organism, towards fusing the colonies with the metropolis, towards forming a vast single empire with a general tariff wall'. (pp. 79-80) At the very end of his pamphlet, however, Bukharin made a peculiar and unsubstantiated assertion. He charged that the colonies of the great powers yielded 'a colossal income' which made it possible to raise the wages 'of the European and American workers'. Thus 'moderate internationalists' like Hobson were wrong to contend that the interests of both the industrial bourgeoisie and the workers were harmed by colonial adventures. (pp. 164-67) Lenin put this argument to polemical use against Kautsky.

Lenin's book *Imperialism: The Highest Stage of Capitalism* has been enshrined as a classic of socialist thought by the Revolution that made him famous. It has been lovingly edited by Soviet scholars, translated into every major language, read and studied by millions of people who know no other book on imperialism.

Scholars owe a debt of gratitude to those who have religiously preserved Lenin's relics because among them are the notebooks he compiled during his study of imperialism. These notebooks reveal that Lenin set out to read virtually everything that had yet been written on his subject. In his neat methodical handwriting he filled notebook after notebook with excerpts from books and articles written in French, German, English and Russian. When he found references to other publications he copied those into his notebooks as well, so that eventually his bibliographical lists ran to hundreds of items. (Lenin's compilation of source materials is still probably the best starting point for anyone interested in studying the global relationship between finance and foreign policy in the period 1898-1915.)[13] If only he had not been confined in his reading by the limitations of Swiss libraries, his lists would have eventually lead him to the writings of the American economists who gave Gaylord Wilshire his theory of imperialism. Scattered among the lists, for example, are C.A. Conant's article of 1898 on 'The Economic Basis of Imperialism', J.W. Jenks's book on trusts, Brooks Adams' analysis of 'American Imperialism' and Paul Reinsch's book *World Politics.* Read together they would have given Lenin everything which Wilshire got from *United States Investor.*

13. 'Notebooks on Imperialism, *Collected Works XXXIV* (Moscow, 1968).

Even without them, however, Lenin was able to follow Hilferding's lead to a wealth of material written in German by unashamedly capitalist authors testifying to the causal connections between modern capitalism and the international rivalry of nations.

Unlike Wilshire, who was accustomed to finding ammunition for the socialist cause in capitalist journals, Lenin was evidently surprised at the openness with which his class enemies expressed their imperialist objectives. He gleefully transcribed *their* statistics, *their* arguments, *their* conclusions along with his own reactions, expressed in exclamation marks and snide marginal comments: 'ha-ha!!'; 'reads like a schoolboy's exercise book'; 'N.B.N.B.'; 'Scoundrel of the first order and vulgar to boot'; 'dull-witted, smug, complacent bourgeois apologist'; '!!ha-ha!!'; 'a triumphant swine'. Nevertheless, he read on, uncovering in the process a good deal of new material unknown to Wilshire, Hobson, and Hilferding. The importance to Lenin of these non-socialist writers can be shown quantitatively by picking out from the authors listed in the index to his *Notebooks*, those sources from which he copied more than five pages and which he used for two or more footnotes in the final draft of his book on imperialism. In this way Lenin's sources can be reduced to just fifteen vital items. Some of the fifteen are well-known contributions from the political left: Marx, Engels, Hobson, Hilferding, and Kautsky's journal *Die Neue Zeit.* But the majority are capitalists — bankers, economists and statisticians. From Theodore Vogelstein, who wrote dull, wise books on new methods of industrial organisation in steel and textiles, Lenin took a three-stage periodisation of the growth of monopoly; the third and highest stage began in 1900. Riesser provided Lenin with a wealth of material on the critical role of big banks in the twentieth century. Jeidels confirmed that 'the driving force of the banks' activity abroad was not national zeal, but the necessity, which becomes more imperative at a certain stage of capitalist development, of establishing abroad a favourable field for the investment of free German capital'.[14] Lenin found plentiful examples of the nefarious operations of the international loans system in the German bankers' journal *Die Bank.* Dr. Sigmund Schilder, 'secretary of a trade museum', provided him with proof that these unsavoury practices were particularly rife in the colonial dominions and 'spheres of influence' lately taken over by the great capitalist powers.[15] Dr. Gerhard von Schulze-Gaevernitz, 'enthusiastic admirer of German imperialism' and noted 'exponent of present-day bourgeois political economy' confirmed that 'the British creditor keeps Japan in political vassalage, Argentina in colonial dependence and Portugal in unconcealed debt bondage'.[16] Lenin found the imperialist character of the first World War openly proclaimed by the Swedish Germanophile, Gustaf Steffan, who asserted that 'world history teaches us that empires tend to divide up each other after they have more or less divided among themselves the "no master" areas in all parts of the globe'. The 1914 war he continued 'is therefore really a world war — a war to give the new German empire a share in ruling the world, a war in which the leading role is played by the mistress of the world, Great Britain, while the next most powerful world powers — Russia and France — are interested participants'.[17]

With these old and new sources at his disposal, Lenin set out to expose the villainy of 'social-chauvinists' in all countries who had failed to perceive the true character of the war. By the time he had finished his book, he felt he had beyond any possibility of doubt 'proved ... that the war of 1914-1918 was imperialist (that is, an annexationist, predatory, war of plunder) on the part of both sides'.[18] This was a very

14. 'Notebooks', 171.

15. 'Notebooks' 96, 106-108.

16. Ibid 58, 60, 68; 'Imperialism, the Highest Stage of Capitalism', *Collected Works* XXII 211, 278, 303

17. 'Notebooks', 259-60.

18. 'Imperialism', 189.

broad view to take of imperialism, as Lenin himself fully realised. There had, he recognised, been many eras of imperialism in world history. 'Colonial policy and imperialism existed before the latest stage of capitalism, and even before capitalism. Rome, founded on slavery, pursued a colonial policy and practised imperialism. But "general" disquisitions on imperialism, which ignore, or put into the background, the fundamental difference between social economic formations, inevitably turn into the most vapid banality or bragging, like the comparison: "Greater Rome and Greater Britain". Even the capitalist colonial policy of *previous* stages of capitalism is essentially different from the colonial policy of finance capital'.[19] The Seven Years' War of the eighteenth century had also been 'an imperialist war (which is possible on the basis of slavery and primitive capitalism as well as on the basis of modern highly developed capitalism)'.[20] He was not, however, concerned to discuss either the history of the expansion of capitalism or previous forms of imperialism. He therefore barely mentioned the problems studied by Rosa Luxemburg and offered no alternative to Hobson's explanation of Victorian colonial expansion in terms of vested interests. Indeed, he was so little concerned with the growth of nineteenth-century colonial empires that he made an extraordinary error when discussing British expansion. Using a chart from an American book on *The History of Colonization* he concluded that 'for Great Britain, the period of the enormous expansion of colonial conquests was that between 1860 and 1880'. In so doing he overlooked the author's explanation that in 1880 the British government for the first time included the hinterlands of the Australian and Canadian colonies in its published statistics.[21]

This did not matter in the least to the argument which Lenin intended to make. His aim was not to show how or why

19. Ibid 260.

20. 'On the Junius Pamphlet', 310.

21. 'Imperialism', 255; **Henry C. Morris** *History of Colonization* (New York, 1900) 85-88.

the world had come to be divided up among capitalist powers but to show the disastrous effects of competition between various blocs of capital upon a world *already divided up.* From his reading he had concluded that the vital watershed of recent world history had been the period '1898-1900'. Since that time, 'the economic and also the political literature of the two hemispheres has more and more often adopted the term "imperialism" in order to describe the present era'. As a Marxist Lenin took it for granted that the determining factor in human history was the configuration of economic forces and therefore began his explanation with an analysis of those forces in the era which 'neither Marx nor Engels lived to see', the 'imperialist epoch of world capitalism which began not earlier than 1898-1900'.[22] Using mostly his German capitalist sources and Hilferding, Lenin described in his first three chapters the process by which the growth of monopolies and finance capital had ended the era of free competition. This analysis brought together for the first time the argument developed by American capitalists in the wake of the Spanish-American War and the argument made by Hilderding in *Finance Capital.* Lenin then proceeded to describe the growth of capital exports from the developed countries, agreeing with his predecessors that the exports were necessary for the continued growth of capitalism. In his fourth chapter he compiled from many sources a table showing that 'the export of capital reached enormous dimensions only at the beginning of the twentieth century'.[23] Everywhere in the world competing blocs of capitalists were seeking secure and exclusive areas for investment, trade and the extraction of essential raw materials while at the same time they were attempting through protective tariffs to keep foreign interests from poaching on their established preserves.

The best possible guarantee of exclusive control for any 'capitalist association' was the establishment of colonial

22. 'Imperialism and the Split in Socialism', Oct. 1916 *Collected Works* XXIII (Moscow, 1964) 111.

23. 'Imperialism', 242.

overlordship by the association's own government. But this was not easy to achieve in the period of enormous capital exports following 1900 because the world had already been virtually partitioned. There were no more 'free lands', no more 'stateless' territories to be acquired with a minimal show of force. Moreover, the political division of the world was out of tune with distribution of economic power. The tiny states Holland, Belgium and Portugal held vast colonial possessions entirely disproprotionate to their economic or military strength. The stagnating powers Britain and France had inherited huge empires from their forefathers, while the rising economic giants where the growth of monopoly was most striking — the United States, Germany and Japan — had virtually no colonies. This situation led to a predatory scramble for control of the decaying states of the Middle East and Far East as well as an escalating arms race. Considering that further expansion by the up and coming powers could only be achieved at the expense of the old powers, war in 1914 had been more or less inevitable. 'The question is', Lenin concluded, 'what means other than war could there be *under capitalism* to overcome the disparity between the development of productive forces and the accumulation of capital on the one side, and the division of colonies and spheres of influence for finance capital on the other?'[24]

Having reached that grim conclusion about the past, Lenin turned his attention to the problems of the present and future which were his main concerns. First, there was the question of Kautsky. No words were harsh enough to describe the crimes of this 'renegade', this 'opportunist', 'archtrickster' and 'swindler'. And no article in the history of socialism had been so damaging to the cause as Kautsky's brief speculations on the possible rise of 'ultra-imperialism'. Modern readers may find the passion of Lenin's attack puzzling. After all, Kautsky had not endorsed either imperialism or 'ultra-imperialism'. On the contrary, he had said that socialists must vigorously oppose them. What was

24. Ibid 275-76.

the harm in Kautsky's little article? For Lenin, the harm consisted in Kautsky's suggestion that war was a temporary aberration rather than a permanent feature of modern capitalism. Peace had reigned among the major capitalist powers in the free trade era; it might reign again under 'ultra-imperialism'; therefore Socialists could wait out the current war and make their revolution some other time. Lenin diagnosed a permanent anaemic disorder in Kautsky's brand of socialism. In 1909, Kautsky had said a war was coming and that then the workers would make the revolution. In 1914, he said that peace was coming and *then* the workers would make the revolution. For Kautsky the time was never quite ripe.

In order to combat Kautsky's suggestion that imperialism might be just a passing phase in the history of capitalism, Lenin insisted that in the twentieth century *imperialism was capitalism.* Armaments, tariffs, wars and rumours of war would continue until capitalism had been finally conquered by socialism. This was the meaning of the title he gave his book, a title which has given rise to much confusion since Lenin's death. When he wrote that 'in its economic essence imperialism is monopoly capitalism' he was not intending to state a meaningless tautology or to give a new definition to the word imperialism. Like most other writers of this era, he understood imperialism to be the deliberate use of the state power to seek economic advantages in the world at large. More than most socialists he believed that the state was in a very direct sense 'the executive committee of the ruling class' and so did not bother to make fine distinctions between the aggressive actions of governments and the 'plundering', 'predatory' behaviour of monopolies. But his main concern throughout the book was to prove that after the critical period 1898-1900, armed aggression and international tension were the inescapable companions of further capitalist development. That is the meaning of his phrase, imperialism is capitalism.

Burning with hatred for Kautsky and all self-deluding armchair revolutionaries, enraged at the failure of international socialism to take advantage of the present opportunity, Lenin now used the proposition first advanced by Bukharin to suggest a deeper reason for 'opportunism' and 'social — chauvinism'. He charged that working class leaders had been bribed by the capitalists.

> As this pamphlet shows, capitalism has now singled out a *handful* ... of exceptionally rich and powerful states which plunder the whole world simply by 'clipping coupons'. Capital exports yield an income of eight to ten thousand million francs per annum . . .
>
> Obviously, out of such enormous *superprofits* (since they are obtained over and above the profits which capitalists squeeze out of the workers of their 'own' country) it is *possible to bribe* the labour leaders and the upper stratum of the labour aristocracy. And that is just what the capitalists of the 'advanced' countries are doing; they are bribing them in a thousand different ways, direct and indirect, overt and covert.[25]

This was not only an extremely serious charge to make against his former comrades, it opened a new chapter in theorising about imperialism. At the turn of the century some capitalists had recommended imperialism as a method of opening fields for the investment of surplus capital some had even speculated that without those new fields capitalism might find itself in desperate straits. Wilshire and other socialists took the capitalists at their word, observing that Marx had predicted that this sort of situation would arise sooner or later. No one before Bukharin and Lenin, however, had asserted that imperialism had *already* temporarily solved the problems of capitalism by generating 'superprofits' over and above profits acquired in the course of ordinary business in ordinary capitalist economies.

Lenin did not show in detail how the alleged 'superprofits' were generated. He simply pointed to statistics showing the burgeoning growth in certain countries of income from foreign investments. The trouble with this line of argument is that Lenin himself supplied ample evidence that the bulk of the income derived from foreign investments in

25. From the preface to the French and German editions, 6 July 1920, 'Imperialism', 193-94.

each of the major capitalist countries came from other capitalist countries. These could not be fairly counted as 'superprofits'; they were simply profits. Lenin may have realised that he was on shaky ground in his charges of bribery for he went on to invoke the authority of Engels and Hobson to support his case. As early as 1858 Engels had complained to Marx that 'the English proletariat is actually becoming more and more bourgeois', and had attributed this to the peculiar circumstance that Britain 'exploits the whole world'. Later in the century he again blamed the distinctly unrevolutionary character of the British working class on the higher wages earned by the tiny 'upper stratum' of workers, the so-called 'labour aristocracy'.[26] What had happened earlier in England was, Lenin asserted, now happening everywhere. He did not explain, however, where the states of Central Europe, who derived very little income from foreign investments and as yet only aspired to exploit vast new territories, managed to turn up the funds to bribe Social Democrats into supporting their imperialist adventures. It was, after all, the cowardice of the Central European Marxists (and non-Bolshevik Russian Socialists) that he was attempting to explain in terms of bribery.[27]

Hobson was of even less real use as a buttress for Lenin's argument on bribery. Lenin claimed that 'one of the shortcomings of the Marxist Hilferding is that on this point he has taken a step backward compared with the non-Marxist Hobson'.[28] It is true that Hobson placed special stress on the 'parasitism' of the investing classes, but it was a gross distortion of Hobson's entire book to claim that he had demonstrated the existence of a source of capital available for

26. Quoted in 'Imperialism', 283-84. See also F. Engels' preface to the revised edition of *The Condition of the Working Class in England in 1844* (London, 1892) 8.

27. Neither could his argument explain British working-class attitudes to war and imperialism since 1899. See R. Price, *An Imperial War and the British Working Class* (London, 1972).

28. 'Imperialism', 276.

bribing the working class. On the contrary, one of Hobson's principal objectives had been to expose the falsity of the imperialists' boast that everyone would benefit economically from an aggressive foreign policy. Hobson tried to show that imperialism had not paid, that it could not benefit anyone except the miniscule investing class and that it positively obstructed the material advancement of everyone else. To be sure, Hobson had also sketched a nightmare vision of the future akin to Kautsky's prophecy of 'ultra-imperialism' which envisaged a peaceful parasitic Europe feasting on the prostrate economies of the developing world. But this vision had been grounded on little more than Hobson's reading of Roman history. The Romans had grown parasitic while entertaining the metropolitan masses with bread and circuses; a united Europe might do likewise. By quoting part of Hobson's Roman analogy out of context, Lenin made it look as though Hobson had been writing about the present economic situation.[29]

One important consequence of Lenin's decision to use the 'super-profits' of imperialism as an explanation of Kautsky's 'opportunism' was a view of future developments that contrasted sharply with the predictions of previous Marxist theorists. Hilferding, for example, had predicted that the advent of imperialism powered by finance capital would heighten class conflict by revealing close connections between the state and the ruling class which had been concealed during the heyday of free trade; consumers, office workers, store keepers and small-scale manufacturers would join forces with manual workers in opposing high prices, high taxes, autocratic government and war. Rosa Luxemburg had likewise anticipated that the horrors of European war would create a revolutionary spirit in the working classes of the most developed coutries before the capitalist combines had reached the theoretical limits of their exploitation of other continents. Her charge against the majority of the Reichstag Social

29. Compare, for example, 'Imperialism', 279 with Hobson, *Imperialism, A Study* (London, 1902) 205.

Democrats was that they had missed a heaven-sent opportunity to speed on the revolution. Her hope was that the Spartacus group might yet save the day by raising the revolution in the country where most Marxists had always supposed it would begin. Because Lenin believed that the working class leaders of the advanced capitalist countries had all been more or less 'bribed' into impotence he could not be so hopeful about the prospects for revolution in those countries. He accordingly looked elsewhere.

Contemplating the future from his Swiss vantage ground, Lenin considered four possibilites. The first was the pessimistic vision quoted above of a Europe hurled 'back several decades' by another great war. The second was the achievement against all odds of a form of ultra-imperialism. 'Can it be denied...that a new phase of capitalism is "imaginable" in the abstract *after* imperialism? No it cannot. Such a phase can be imagined... There is no doubt that the trend of development is *towards* a single world trust absorbing all enterprises without exception and all states without exception'. But, Lenin was quick to add, 'this development proceeds in such circumstances, at such a pace, through such contradictions, conflicts and upheavals' that 'inevitably imperialism will burst and capitalism will be transformed into its opposite *long before* one world trust materialises, before the "ultra-imperialist", world-wide amalgamation of national finance capitals takes place'.[30] A third possibility, which seemed to Lenin to be just as unlikely, was that the imperialist powers might take Hobson's advice and eliminate their surplus of capital by developing agriculture and raising 'the living standards of the masses, who in spite of the amazing technical progress are everywhere still half-starved and poverty-stricken'. If 'capitalism did these things', he sneered, 'it would not be capitalism'.[31] There was, however, a forth possibility that gave a glimmer of hope in a darkening world. About one billion people, Lenin observed, 'live in the

30. Preface to Bukharin's Pamphlet, Dec. 1915, *Collected Works* XXII, 107.

31. 'Imperialism', 241.

colonies and semi-colonies' presently dominated by finance capital. Everywhere 'national liberation movements' were 'growing or maturing'. It was 'not only probable but *inevitable*' that 'national wars of liberation' would be waged in the future against the imperialist powers. There could be, for example, 'an alliance of Persia, India and China against one or more of the imperialist powers'.[32] Or if a revolution occurred in Russia, there could be first 'a civil war against the bourgeoisie' bringing an end to Russian participation in the World War, followed by a later 'national war' against imperialism.

If Lenin had expressed these sentiments in Russia instead of Switzerland in 1916, he would certainly been clapped into gaol by the Czarist authorities for traitorously attempting to undermine the war effort. When a revolution overthrew the Czar less than a year later, it occurred to the German High Command that if Lenin were returned to Russia, he might just succeed in his aim of getting Russia out of the war. In April 1917, they arranged for Lenin to be sped safely through German territory to St. Petersburg where he began his agitation for 'bread and peace'. By March, 1918, Lenin's Bolsheviks were the masters of Russia and Russia was out of the war.

32. 'On the Junius Pamphlet', 310-17.

CHAPTER 8
ASSESSING THE PROSPECTS FOR PEACEFUL CAPITALISM, THORSTEIN VEBLEN AND JOSEPH SCHUMPETER

Ironically, as the Russians were withdrawing from the war in the name of anti-imperialism, American troops were arriving in Europe ready to fight and die in the same cause. President Wilson called his people to war with ringing promises to rid the world of the menace of aggression once and for all. The world must be made 'safe for democracy'; the rights of all nations to 'self-determination' must be guaranteed; there should be a 'dismemberment' of empires, a 'peace without annexations', and a League of Nations to see to it that the carnage of the last three years would never be repeated. Some of the President's critics pointed out that nowhere in this list of high sounding objectives was there a mention of capital exports or profits. A Senator from Nebraska voiced his sorrowful conviction that 'we are going into war upon the command of gold . . . we are about to put the dollar sign upon the American flag'. Was the United States an avenging angel sent to destroy imperialism or one more cut-throat villain on the world stage? If, as the Spartacists and Bolsheviks contended, capitalism based on national states could not avoid war, then Wilson's moralism was a sham. If, on the other hand, capitalist states could throw off their current infatuation with arms, then Wilson offered hope. Two of the great synthesising economic philosophers of the twentieth century attacked the problem with similar techniques and came up with ambiguous predictions. One was an American, Thorstein Veblen. The other was an Austrian, Joseph Schumpeter. Both believed in the economic interpretation of history but insisted that the current behaviour of nations was determined not only by present economic conditions but also by the economic conditions of previous historical epochs. Both were drawn to comparisons between peaceful Britain and Imperial Germany.

Veblen was an academic hobo who eked out a nomadic

and precarious existence on the outskirts of respectable university life in America. Even after his book *The Theory of the Leisure Class* made him famous he found it difficult to hold a job. His notorious womanising scandalised college administrations and his lectures repelled students (one colleague observed that he spoke slower than any man alive).[1] Yet he commanded great respect among the prosaic profession of economists through books which were original to the point of peculiarity. *The Theory of the Leisure Class* (1899) explained the behaviour of American businessmen on the principle of 'conspicuous waste'. Their extravagant lives were in his view determined not by real wants or needs, but by ancient patterns of behaviour persisting from earlier stages of human evolution. He was enough of an economic determinist to believe that changes in the system of production eventually destroyed social usages appropriate to earlier eras. However, he maintained that force of habit ('habituation' as he called it) was difficult to overcome, even in the dog-eat-dog business of buying and selling for profit. Thus modern business practice displayed many archaic features.

This economic theory of history was Darwinian rather than Marxian. Veblen employed it to examine bosses, workers, and politicians in contemporary society as if they were biological specimens. He kept a studied detachment from his subjects, appearing to regard indignation as irrelevant to the enquiry. Would a zoolologist be indignant at the rapacity of wolves or the pecking order of chickens? On three occasions Veblen employed his method to study the causes of modern imperialism and to forecast the prospects for peace in the decades to come. Each time he arrived at a different result.

1. The most charming account of Veblen's life and work is still Robert Heilbroner's essay in *The Worldly Philosophers* (New York, 1961) 181-213. A more extensive recent study is J. P. Diggins' *The Bard of Savagery: Thorstein Veblen and Modern Social Theory* (New York, 1978). J. A. Hobson wrote a short book, *Veblen* for a series on social thinkers. It does not give special notice to Veblen's views on imperialism, perhaps because Hobson does not appear to have read his *Theory of Business Enterprise.*

In *The Theory of Business Enterprise* (1904) he considered the arms race, starting from the premise that 'constitutional government has, in the main, become a department of the business organisation and is guided by the advice of the business men'.[2] Business men gained popular approval for foreign policies which lined their own pockets by harnessing two 'sentiments' which had grown up in medieval Europe under very different economic conditions:
1) patriotism which habituated 'the common man' to believe 'that he has some sort of metaphysical share in the gains which accrue to the businessmen who are citizens of the same "commonwealth"';
2) property whose acquisition had come to be regarded not only as expedient for the owner, but meritorious as an action serving the common good'.
To Veblen, 'the current policy of war and armaments' was 'an extreme expression of business politics'. (pp. 291-92) Having discovered that the power of the armed state could be used to make better business deals, they proceeded to demand that aggressive policies be adopted. Because government was a 'department of the business organisation', it did what was asked of it.

This was a much cruder analysis of capitalist imperialism than that advanced by Hobson in 1902 or by Brailsford in 1914. However, Veblen felt no need to buttress it with quotations or other evidence. It was, he said, 'little else than a recital of commonplaces: the facts and their connection are matters of common notoriety'.[3] His reason for reviewing 'the motives and aims of a war policy' on behalf of business interests was to project 'the immediate future of business enterprise'. (p. 297) He saw no reason to suppose that the arms race would cease. Once several states had decided to arm

2. *The Theory of Business Enterprise* (New York, 1904 and 1934), 287. Business enterprise was Veblen's term for capitalism.

3. Veblen cited Hobson in his footnotes and once reviewed *Imperialism, A Study* for *The Journal of Political Economy* (March, 1903). See J. Dorfman, ed., Thorstein Veblen, Esssays Reviews and Reports (Clifton, New Jersey, 1973), 508-11.

themselves for the purpose of seeking or defending business advantages, they were committed to acquire weapons of destruction at least equal to the weapons of their rivals. The progression was practically unstoppable.

In this cumulative diversion of effort to warlike ends a point is presently reached beyond which the question of armament is no longer, What amount of warlike expenditure is needed to extend or maintain business traffic? but rather, What amount will the nation's resources bear? But the progression does not stop at that point; witness the case of Italy, France, and Germany, where the war drain has visibly impaired the industrial efficiency of the several nations concerned, but where the burden still goes on growing, with no stopping place in sight. (pp. 298-99)

That the arms race eventually became irrational for business as a whole was as obvious to Veblen as to Norman Angell, but he could see several reasons why the business community did not call a halt when the critical point was reached. In the first place, businessmen generally acted as individual profit seekers, not as guardians of the collective welfare of the business community. As long as there were profits to be made by dealing in armaments, military contracts or loans raised by the state to pay for its expanded role, there would be businessmen ready to make deals, even with the avowed enemies of their own nations. In the second place, the growth of militarism bred servile habits of subordination and discipline which were useful to the large scale industrial establishments of modern capitalism.[4] Discipline and servility were useful counterweights to 'social unrest' among the workers. (p. 393) In the third place, when business gave its support to 'war and armaments and imperialist politics' it uncorked genies who could not easily be forced back into their bottles. The 'sentiment of patriotism', which 'habituation' had preserved even after it had ceased to be economically useful, and which businessmen revivified to serve the cause of their 'imperialist politics' could not be readily dampened. In order to make a modern state ready for war, warriors must be recruited. In Europe war leaders were

4. Compare the similar point made by the editor of the *U. S. Investor,* above, p.10.

drawn overwhelmingly from old aristocracies and landed gentry left over from the feudal system.

> The barbarian virtues of fealty and patriotism run on national or dynastic exploit and aggrandisement, and these archaic virtues are not dead. In those modern communities whose hearts beat with the pulsations of the world-market they find expression in an enthusiasm for the commercial aggrandisement of the nation's businessmen. But when once the policy of warlike enterprise has been entered upon for business ends, these loyal affections gradually shift from the business interests to the warlike and dynastic interests, as witness the history of imperialism in Germany and England. The eventual outcome should be a rehabilitation of the ancient patriotic animosity and dynastic loyalty, to the relative neglect of business interests. This may easily be carried so far as to sacrifice the profits of the businessmen to the exigencies of the higher politics. (pp. 394-95)

The capitalists who called imperialism into existence might at length become its victims.

The future would depend on the operation of forces in contradiction with each other. Neither modern industrial technology nor the organisation of business were in tune with the archaic 'regime of status, fealty, prerogative, and arbitrary command'. If the nations remained on a war footing without actually fighting, businessmen would at first welcome the protection of large fortunes and the suppression of working class movements which such a regime would favor. In the longer run, however, the revival of a hierarchical society would slowly destroy 'those cultural features that distinguish modern times from what went before, including a decline of business enterprise itself'. If, on the other hand, the world slipped over the edge into war, the people who died would include a disproportionate number of the warlike elements of society. Thus there would be 'a gradual selective elimination of that old-fashioned element of the population that is by temperament best suited for the old-fashioned institutitonal system of status and servile organisation'. (p. 396) However, if that happened there would be nothing to check the growth of discontent among the have-nots who would eventually overthrow the whole system. Though he had taken a very different path, Veblen managed to arrive at a conclusion very similar to Lenin's. Twentieth-century imperialism was the beginning of the end for the capitalist system.

Nevertheless, when the first World War erupted, Veblen did not say I told you so. *Imperial Germany and the Industrial Revolution* (1915) identified special warlike propensities in the German state which differentiated it from its principal enemy, England. The industrial revolution had developed relatively slowly in England. In the course of three centuries the English people and the English constitution had adapted to the neeeds of the new technological conditions. Pomp and circumstance had given way to business as usual as the dominant objective of the state. Merchants and workers alike had become 'habituated' to take 'a matter of fact' view of the world. They had lost most of the servile, obsequious attitudes which the medieval state had demanded of its subjects. Things were very different in Germany where the industrial revolution came late and suddenly. The 'dynastic state' was still intact, supported by an arrogant landed aristocracy, an autocratic constitution and long-established habits of groveling humility in the lower classes. It put the immense potential of the new forces of production to work on behalf of its own ancient goals of limitless power and conquest.

Veblen regarded every 'dynastic state' as 'necessarily of a competitive or rapacious character'. Once Prussia had obliterated the dynastic ambitions of competing principalities in a political union that was also an economic union, she swaggered abroad with insatiable appetites. 'With the new departure of 1870' Germany commanded universal attention as a 'singularly striking, not to say unique, instance of exuberant growth'.[5] The aggressive policies of Imperial Germany were demonstrably harmful to the interests of individual Germans. The high tariff policy in particular limited the profitability of business and industry.

> the country would have been better off, simply in point of material prosperity and in the rate of its economic progress, if no such barrier as the Imperial frontier had been kept up; but the immediate result would have

5. *Imperial Germany and the Industrial Revolution* (London, 1915), 58, 71, 76.

been such a specialisation of industry and such trade relations as would have left the community dependent for a large and indispensable part of its current consumption on foreign countries; from which it would follow that the Empire would be relatively vulnerable in case of war, at the same time that the community, the people, would be much more reluctant to go to war. Such a policy would, in other words, nowise comport with the strategy of dynastic politics. (p. 172)

A 'side issue' of the high tariff policy 'fortified also by visions of imperialistic magnitude' was 'the colonial policy of the Empire since Bismarck's retirement'. In pursuit of self-sufficiency in raw materials the German states developed colonies which were costly to acquire, irksome to administer and profitless to all but a handful of insignificant traders. (pp. 178, 198-99) All of this could be done because the dynastic state overawed subjects who had not yet acquired the 'matter of fact' mentality that longer acquaintance with the new machine technology would breed. At last 'the pursuit of the Imperial policy . . . led Christendom into an unexampled war'. (p. 257)

What of the future? In the short run success for the German 'adventure in imperialism' would mean a substantial 'impairment and arrest of Western civilisation at large'. In a wider view, however, Veblen predicted that 'the current war will necessarily be accounted an untoward episode'. The guiding philosophy of the dynastic state was 'an atavistic revulsion' against the modern world. If it continued to guide German development the Empire would soon destroy its ability to wage successful war against constitutional states of the English type. If, on the other hand, German business and workers wriggled out from under the dead-weight of hereditary autocracy, they would gradually force the state to assume a more modern form. (pp. 221, 231, 257) Either way German imperialism was doomed.

But what of the capitalist-backed imperialisms of Western Europe and America whose fatal diseases Veblen had confidently diagnosed in *The Theory of Business Enterprise?* Had he revised his opinions because Britain had rejected Chamberlain's concept of imperialism and the United

States had stayed out of war in 1914? Whatever the reason, the prospects for peaceful capitalism in those countries are not canvassed in *Imperial Germany.* In February 1917, two months before his own nation entered the war, Veblen finished a book which contrasted the fortunes which mankind might anticipate in the event of 1) a victory for the dynastic states and 2) a victory by a league of consitutional democratic states. With characteristic perversity he entitled his second wartime tract *An Inquiry into the Nature of Peace and the Terms of its Perpetuation.*

Following the line of argument sketched out in *Imperial Germany,* Veblen ruled out the possibility of a lasting peace being concluded between the principal disturbers of the world's peace — Germany and Japan — and their enemies. It was in the nature of the dynastic states to seek dominion and now that they were equipped with industrial power they would employ that power for aggressive purposes unless and until they were stopped by a superior power. If they triumphed they would impose their archaic systems of government on mankind. Those systems would, if continued for very long, stifle the modern industrial system.

Veblen believed that a victory by the constitutional democracies could conceivably result in a new era of peace and progress. A 'league of peace' constucted on the lines suggested by President Wilson and others would neeed to be formed to 1)force the dismantling of the dynastic states; 2) eliminate exclusive citizenship which was the prinicipal focus of the outmoded 'sentiment of patriotism'; and 3) demolish tariffs and other restrictions on trade which gave privileged business cliques an incentive to support aggressive policies. There was, however, a sting in the tail of Veblen's assessment of the prospects for peaceful capitalism. Without militarism and war to discipline the masses, there would be an unprecedented antagonism between social classes. Because the have-nots possessed an overwhelming superiority in numbers, they would abolish the capitalist system — unless they were opposed by arms. Thus, unless 'rights of ownership and the price system' were abolished along with dynastic states and patriotism, the future would still be characterised by war: the class war.[6]

By 1919 the Great War had eliminated some of the possibilities which concerned Veblen. Dynastic states fell like ninepins till only Japan remained to test whether the marriage of industrial capitalism and ancient privilege could survive in twentieth-century conditions. Sitting in Vienna among the ruins of the house of Hapsburg, Joseph Schumpeter ventured to suggest that imperialism was a spent force. The approach he used to arrive at this conclusion was strikingly similar to Veblen's but the terminology he used was borrowed from the language of central-European Marxism. In an extended essay on *The Sociology of Imperialism* he proposed to prove his theory on the basis of 'the economic interpretation of history' whose methodology he had learned during the days when he and Hilferding had moved in similar circles in Vienna.[7]

There are, Schumpeter explains at the beginning of his essay, two ways to practise the economic interpretation of history — a good way and a bad way. The good way takes a long view of the subtle process by which 'the relations of production' operate to 'shape life in general'. 'I do not doubt in the least, he wrote, 'that this powerful instrument of analysis will stand up here in the same sense that it has with other, similar phenomena' provided only that 'it is kept in mind that customary modes of political thought and feeling in a given age can never be mere "reflexes" of, or counterparts to, the production situation of that age. Because of the persistance of such habits, they will always, to a considerable degree be dominated by the production context of past ages'. (pp. 7-8) In other words, the behaviour of peoples and nations will be conditioned as much by the economic needs of

6. *The Nature of Peace* (New York, 1917 and 1945), 363-67.

7. Joseph Schumpeter, *Imperialism and Social Classes,* trans. H. Norden, ed. Paul M. Sweezy (Oxford, 1951). The introduction by Schumpeter's student, Sweezy, is especially good in a placing the economist in the context of Marxist thought. See also T. Bottomore and P. Goode, *Austro-Marxism* (Oxford, 1978) 24-25. Subsequent quotations are taken from the Norden translation.

bygone years as by the needs of the present. The bad way of practising the economic interpretation of history, on the other hand, tries to explain human behaviour solely in terms of 'the economic class interests of the age in question'. This, according to Schumpeter is where Hilferding and other exponents of 'neo-Marxist theory' went wrong in their explanation of imperialism. That explanation 'views imperialism simply as the reflex of the interests of the capitalist upper stratum, at a given stage of capitalist development. Beyond doubt that is by far the most serious contribution toward a solution of our problem. Certainly there is much truth in it ... But let us emphasise ... that it does not, of logical necessity, follow from the economic interpretation of history'. (p. 8) Schumpeter, then, sets out to give an explanation of modern imperialism which considers the economic forces generated in previous ages as well as the dominant forces of the present.

First he struggles with the problem of defining imperialism at a time when the word 'has been abused as a slogan to the point where it threatens to lose all meaning'. Despite this abuse he finds in 'common usage, even in the press' that 'whenever the word imperialism is used, there is always the implication — whether sincere or not — of an aggressiveness, the true reasons for which do not lie in the aims which are temporarily being pursued; of an aggressiveness that is only kindled anew by each success; or an aggressiveness for its own sake, as reflected in terms such as "hegemony", "world domination", and so forth'. (p. 6) This leads him to offer this formulation: 'imperialism is the objectless disposition on the part of a state to unlimited forcible expansion'. At first glance this definition may appear to be quite out of line with that explicitly or implicitly embodied in other writings: the use of the state power, including its military power in order to pursue economic advantages in the world at large'. The discrepancy is more apparent than real, however. In his 'definition' Schumpeter simply leaps ahead to the conclusion reached by most previous theorists, i.e., that in the modern world no nation gains real advantages from the practice of imperialism; that only small cliques of interested parties within a nation can hope to gain. 'No one', Schumpeter claims, 'calls it imperialism when a state, no matter how brutally and vigorously, pursues concrete interests of its own; and when it can be expected to abandon its aggressive attitude as soon as it has attained what it was after'. His view of the 'objectless' character of imperialism therefore resembles Rosa Luxemburg's analysis of Germany's truculent behaviour toward Morocco where 'the very indefiniteness of its tangible aims and demands betrayed its insatiable appetite'.[8]

Thus, Schumpeter's problem is essentially the same as the problem confronted by his predecessors. How has it come about that a number of nations actively pursue policies that are harmful, even disastrous to the great majority of their citizens? Hobson's solution to the problem was to locate aristocratic and financial interests who bamboozled the rest of the people through the control of the principal instruments of propaganda. Norman Angell's solution had been to argue that most people great and small in most countries had been deluded into believing that war paid. Schumpeter agrees with Angell that 'current fallacies, especially of an economic character, may serve to create the semblance of an adequate, concrete interest in the mind of the people'. (p. 5) But his own solution to the problem of imperialism is more along Hobson's lines. He sets out to discover the minority interests who do have something to gain from imperialism and to explain how they manage to press their hapless fellow countrymen into supporting their policies.[9]

The first step in his investigation is to test the 'neo-Marxist' hypothesis of capitalist imperialism by looking at the recent history of the world's two most indubitably

8. Above, p. 125

9. Bernard Semmel, *The Rise of Free Trade Imperialism* (Cambridge, 1970) 217, 222-25, has also called attention to similarities between Hobson and Schumpeter.

capitalist countries, Britain and the United States. The surprising conclusion that he reaches is that in both countries imperialism never really got beyond the stage of slogans. British imperialism was launched as a 'catch phrase of domestic policy' in the speech by the Conservative leader Disraeli at the Crystal Palace in 1872. For Schumpeter the imperialist features of Disraeli's 'Imperial Federation' plan are 'its protective tariff, its militarist sentiments, its ideology of a unified 'Greater Britain', all of which 'foreshadowed vague aggressive trends that would have emerged soon enough if the plan had ever passed from the sphere of the slogan into the realm of actual policy'. (p. 13) Disraeli, however, *spoke,* did not *act* after he became Prime Minister in 1874; 'his foreign policy moved wholly within the framework of Conservative tradition'. Though imperial federation never wholly vanished as a slogan — 'as early as the [eighteen] nineties it meant a great deal to the youth of Oxford and Cambridge' — it did not become a force to be reckoned with until Joseph Chamberlain took up the cause of an Empire-wide protective tariff. Schumpeter recognises as well as Hobson that Chamberlain's scheme

had much to offer to a whole series of special interests — primarily a protective tariff and the prospect of lucrative opportunities for exploitation, inaccessible to industry under a system of free trade. Here was the opportunity to smother consumer resistance [to higher prices caused by tariffs] in a flood of patriotic enthusiasm. Later on, this advantage weighed all the more heavily in the balance, for certain English industries were beginning to grow quite sensitive to the dumping tactics employed by German and American exporters. Equally important was the fact that such a plan was calculated to divert the attention of the people from social problems at home. But the main thing, before which all arguments stemming from calculating self-interest must recede into the background, was the unfailing power of the appeal to national sentiment. No other appeal is as effective, except at a time when the people happen to be caught in the midst of flaming social struggle. All other appeals are rooted in interests that must be grasped by reason. This one alone arouses the dark powers of the subconscious, calls into play instincts that carry over from the life habits of the dim past. (p.14)

In 1902 Hobson had feared that precisely these forces were

dragging the nation into an unprecedented orgy of imperialism. In 1919 Schumpeter, with the benefit of hindsight, is able to point out that Chamberlain and his allies had suffered a total defeat. 'England rejected him, turning over the reins to the (Liberal) opposition by an overwhelming majority. It condemned the Boer War, did everything in its power to "undo" it, proving that it was merely a chance aberration fron the general trend ... The rejection of imperialism meant the rejection of all the interests and arguments on which the movement was based'. (pp. 17-18)

The outcome of the campaign for imperialism in America had, according to Schumpeter, resulted in an even more resounding defeat. At the time of the Spanish-American War, the United States saw 'a particularly strong emergence of capitalist interests in an imperialist direction'. Later, 'Theodore Roosevelt and certain magnates of the press actually resorted to imperialism — and the result, in that world of high capitalism, was utter defeat, a defeat that would have been even more abject, if other slogans, notably those appealing to anti-trust sentiment, had not met with better success'. Readers who have grown used to identifying imperialism with the acquisition of colonies may be surprised by Schumpeter's exclusion of Britain from the tally of imperialist states. For Schumpeter, however, imperialism is not simply a matter of annexing territory. That Britain, a trading nation dependent upon far flung lines of ocean communication, should have acquired colonies in the past was perfectly natural. However, as long as these colonies were not cordoned off by tariff barriers as 'objects of exploitation in a sense different from that in which independent countries can be exploited', Britain could not be numbered among the aggressive imperialists. This kindly appraisal of Britain's imperial domain reflects not only the further shift away from the study of colonies in discussions of imperialism during the war, but also the pro-British cast of mind common to a great many Viennese intellectuals in the last days of the Austro-Hungarian Empire. Schumpeter has no doubt about who was responsible for the outbreak of world war. Like Veblen, he blames the Hapsburgs and their ally, the Hohenzollern rulers of Germany. Exposing their imperialism, their insatiable appetites, their glorification of war is as much the object of his essay as the refutation of 'Neo-Marxist' theory.

Having established by an appeal to British and American history that highly developed capitalism cannot goad nations into imperialism without the aid of other forces, Schumpeter considers ancient forms of aggression. He proposes to show that 'a common basic trait emerges in every case, making a single sociological problem of imperialism in all ages'. (p. 8) The common trait which he discovers in all the ancient imperialisms — Egyptian, Assyrian, Persian, Arab — is the rise of a dominant social class whose perpetuation and prestige depended upon war and conquest. Once such a class, great or small, existed it would promote objectless, unlimited forcible expansion regardless of the cost. It would not, of course, always own up to or even recognise the objectless character of its aggression. It would cloak its class interest in appeals to honour and glory and the national destiny. As long as the warrior class could maintain the active or passive support of the rest of the nation, it would push forward in its career of aggression. Its imperialism was grounded beyond question upon an economic interest, but that interest was the maintenance of class domination rather than the attainment of any of the announced objectives which served as pretexts for war.

Schumpeter points to the use of a similar class-based imperialism in the absolute monarchies which appeared in Europe at the end of the Middle Ages. Taking France as an example, he describes the militarising effects of the monarchy's pursuit of total state power which culminated in the absolutism of Louis XIV.

> In France, as elsewhere, the absolutist national state meant the military organisation of the martial elements of the nation, in effect a war machine .... Now that national unity was achieved, now that ... no external enemy

offered a serious threat any longer, there might have been disarmament — the military element might have been permitted to recede .... But the foundations of royal power rested on this military character of the state and on the social factors and psychological tendencies it expressed. Hence it *was* maintained, even though the causes that had brought it to the fore had disappeared. Hence the war machine continued to impress its mark on the state. Hence the King felt himself to be primarily a war-lord, adorned himself preeminently with military emblems. Hence his chief concern was to maintain a large, well-equipped army, one that remained active and was directly tied to his person. (p. 72)

The war machine was also Louis' means of coping with the landed aristocracy at whose expense the centralisation of power had been achieved. At home on their estates they still had the power to stir up trouble, even civil war. At the court of Versailles, however, or in the army the energies of the nobility were directed towards ends which did not threaten the monarch. Schumpeter finds in this state of affairs the real reason for Louis' court extravagance and his exhausting, pointless wars which historians have so often censured. 'Unless the nobles were allowed to revolt, they had to be kept busy. Now all the noble families who were amusing themselves at Versailles could look back on a warlike past, martial ideas and phrases, bellicose instincts. To ninety-nine out of a hundred of them, "action" meant military action. If civil war was to be avoided, then external wars were required'. (p. 76) The pattern established in France was repeated everywhere in Europe where the monarchy triumphed in its quest for centralised power. Everywhere aggression became part of the 'settled order of life'; everywhere the aristocracy revelled in the pomp and circumstance of glorious war.

With the gaudy tapestry of continental absolutism as his backdrop Schumpeter is now able to unveil his own solution to the problem of imperialism in the early twentieth century. It is an extremely elegant solution which manages to incorporate most of the strong points of the alternative theories of imperialism which it is intended to refute. Its fundamental premise is similar to Veblen's notion of the advance of 'matter of fact' ways of thought under the regimen of machine technology. Capitalism — the pre-eminent force which 'began to shape the society and impress its stamp on every page of social history only with the second half of the eighteenth century' — exercised a rationalising influence on every society it touched. Capitalism stimulated the development of new 'class types' which multiplied with astonishing speed: the industrial and financial bourgeoisie; the worker; the 'professional' and intellectual class; the 'rentier, the beneficiary of industrial loan capital'. Each of these class types was 'inevitably democratised, individualised, and rationalised' by the 'capitalist mode of production'. 'Trained to rationalism, these peoples left no sphere of life unrationalised, questioning everything about themselves, the social structure the state, the ruling class'. (pp. 88-89) As Schumpeter sees it, the questioning spirit ignited by capitalism sweeps through societies like a laser beam illuminating ungainly customs and traditions with an un-flattering bright light, cutting away the props of every institution that will not stand up to the test of present utility. He expects it eventually to penetrate even the dark corners of the subconscious and enfeeble the aggressive instincts lurking there 'that carry over from the life habits of the dim past'. His reasoning here is similar to that used by Angell and Veblen to make the same point. 'Everything that is purely instinctual, everything insofar as it is purely instinctual, is driven into the background by this development ... instinctual tendencies can survive only when the conditions that gave rise to them continue to apply, or when the "instinct" in question derives a new purpose from new conditions. The "instinct" that is *only* "instinct", that has lost its purpose, languishes . . .' (p. 89) Capitalism, Schumpeter continues, is under most circumstances as hostile to the war-mongering behaviour of states as it is to the irrational aggressive instincts of the individual. This can be demonstrated not only in British and American history but also in abstract economic reasoning. The arms manufacturers and allied interests who *do* profit from warlike activities constitute only a fraction of the whole capitalist class. The temporary gains made by some workers in some industries are likewise far outweighed by the losses in both life and livelihood which war imposes on the vast majority of workers. *However,* Schumpeter admits, as he approaches the crux of the matter, there are circumstances in which capitalism abandons its ordinary peaceful character and turns nasty. Those are the circumstances Hilferding described in which nations impose protective tariffs, cartels arise and an international competition ensues aimed at securing exclusive territories for exploitation.

Schumpeter agrees with a great deal of Hilferding's analysis. He agrees that trusts and cartels shielded from competition over-produce and seek to dispose of their excessive production by 'dumping' it on foreign markets at below-cost prices. He agrees that *'organised* capital may very well make the discovery that the interest rate can be maintained above the level of free competition' through a concerted policy of capital exporting. He agrees that this organisation of capital was facilitated by 'a close alliance between high finance and the cartel magnates, often going so far as personal identity'. He agrees that 'the ordinary "small" capitalist foots the bill for a policy of forced exports, rather than enjoying its profits'. He agrees that 'the customs area of a trustified country generally pours a huge wave of capital into new countries' where 'it meets other, similar waves of capital, and a bitter costly struggle begins but never ends'. (pp. 105-07) In short, Schumpeter fully acknowledges the existence of 'capitalist imperialism'. He paints as black a picture of its character as any previous theorist. At the climax of imperialism capitalist powers in Europe see concrete advantages in conquering adjacent territories.

> it is sufficient for the industry of the conquering state to be superior to that of the one to be subjugated... to make it possible to treat the subjugated state, perhaps not quite, but very much like a colony . . . the conqueror can face the subjugated nation with the bearing of the victor. He has countless means at his disposal for expropriating raw material resources and the like

and placing them in the service of his cartels. He can seize them outright, nationalise them, impose a forced sale, or draft the proprietors into industrial groups of the victor nation under conditions that ensure control by the domestic captains of industry. He can exploit them by a system of quotas or allotments. He can administer the conquered means of communication in the interests of his own cartels. Under the pretext of military and political security, he can deprive the foreign workers of the right to organise, thus not only making cheap labour in the annexed territory available to his cartels, but also holding a threat over the head of domestic labour.

Thus we have here, within a social group that carries great political weight a strong, undeniable, economic interest in such things as protective tariffs, cartels, monopoly prices, forced exports (dumping), an aggressive economic policy, an aggressive foreign policy generally, and war, including wars of expansion with a typically imperialist character. Once this alignment of interests exists, an even stronger interest in a somewhat differently motivated expansion must be added, namely an interest in the conquest of lands producing raw materials and foodstuffs, with a view to facilitating self-sufficient warfare. Still another interest is that in rising wartime consumption. A mass of unorganised capitalists competing with one another may at best reap a trifling profit from such an eventuality, but organised capital is sure to profit hugely. Finally, there is the political interest in war and international hatred (as a diversionary tactic) which flows from the insecure position of the leading circles. They are small in numbers and highly unpopular. (pp. 109-11)

Wilshire, Hilferding, Luxemburg, Lenin, Veblen and even the editor of *U.S. Investor* believed that this catastrophic state of affairs could not continue indefinitely; the victims so outnumbered the beneficiaries of capitalist imperialism that the whole system must be overthrown. Schumpeter admits their first premise but denies their conclusion. Yes, the imperialist policy of ‘export monopolism’ is ‘essentially untenable’. A general rush to exclude foreign products from domestic markets injures more traders than it helps. The businessmen who suffer as the result of tariffs, artificially high prices and war outnumber those who gain. Whatever gains may accrue temporarily to some workers in the form of higher wages and social reform are far outweighed by the losses they suffer in their roles of consumers and soldiers. Growing indignation will produce enormous political unrest. *But,*

Schumpeter asserts, it is not true that imperialism constitutes the unavoidable final sickness of capitalism. 'It cannot be emphasised sharply enough', he writes, that 'export monopolism does *not* grow from the inherent laws of capitalist development'. (p. 117) If it did, Britain would have adopted Joe Chamberlain's tariff programme. And if imperialism were an inescapable companion of 'export monopolism', then high tariff, trust-ridden America would have elected Teddy Roosevelt President in 1912. Schumpeter simply did not believe that there was any evidence to indicate that monopolies were an efficient form of organisation in most industries. In order to thrive they needed careful nurturing by the State. He also denied that tariffs were an inevitable product of the evolving capitalist system. Again the survival of free trade Britain makes the point. It therefore follows that one must seek for the origins of recent imperialism in the origins of the high tariff policy which made 'export monopolism' possible. Where were there forces strong enough to impose the policy against the real interests of capitalists and workers?

With the assurance of an accomplished showman Schumpeter steps back, turns and points dramatically to the historical background of continental European absolutism. In America which had never known a ruling nobility, and Britain where the absolutist aims of the sovereign had been frustrated by Parliamentary supremacy, capitalism had mostly had its own way. Not so in central and eastern Europe. There the advance of capitalism had been conditioned by the demands of the autocratic state and the land-holding aristocracy. Capitalists could not strut and brag in that courtly atmosphere as they did in Manchester or Chicago. They bowed and scraped and pleaded for favours. Developing a point made by Jacob Riesser in his book on the rise of the big German banks, Schumpeter stresses that without the state central European capitalism could not have developed as it did.

The industrial organism, such as it was, would not have been able to withstand free competition. Even where the old barriers crumbled in the autocratic state, the people did not all at once flock to the clear track. They were creatures of mercantilism and even earlier periods, and many of them huddled together and protested against the affront of being forced to depend on their own ability. They cried out for paternalism, for protection, for forcible restraint of strangers, and above all for tariffs. (p. 121)

The monarch gave them what they wanted but exacted a pound of flesh in return. He insisted that they stay in their lowly social place and conform to the ethos of the ruling class — the ethos, that is, of 'the war-oriented nobility'. The bourgeoisie therefore conformed as best they could to the world view of their masters, rejected the pacifist internationalism of Cobden and shouted the slogans of nationalism, militarism, and forcible expansion.

...the submission of the bourgeoisie to the powers of autocracy, its alliance with them, its economic and psychological patterning by them — all these tend to push the bourgeois in a nationalist direction; and this too we find prevalent, especially among the chief exponents of export monopolism. The relationship between the bourgeoisie and militarism is quite similar . . . The continental bourgeois . . . was used to the sight of troops... He had no power at all to abolish the army... In his 'artificial' economic situation and because of his submission to the sovereign, he thus grew disposed toward militarism, especially where export monopolism flourished. (pp. 126-27)

Here then is Schumpeter's final solution to the problem of modern imperialism. Capitalist imperialism is made possible by the continued domination of some States by a ruling class imbued with warlike habits which served the economic and political interests of the monarchy in another age. By using what he regards as a more sophisticated economic interpretation of history — one that takes account of past as well as present economic interests — Schumpeter arrives finally at an optimistic assessment of the future prospects for capitalism and for peace. He predicts that the 'untenability' of imperialism will lead not to the overthrow of capitalism as Hilferding expected, but to the overthrow of the autocratic ruling classes of central and eastern Europe. Freed from that burden imposed by the past, international capitalism could resume its fundamentally peaceful ways. 'This diagnosis also bears the prognosis of imperialism. The precapitalist elements in our social life may still have great vitality; special circumstances in national life may revive them from time to time; but in the end the climate of the modern world must destroy them' (p. 129)

* * *

When Schumpeter published his essay in 1919, the world appeared poised to put his predictions to the test along with the predictions of everyone else who had ventured to theorise about imperialism in the course of the last two decades. The old autocratic dynasties were everywhere overthrown. Gone were the Hapsburgs, the Hohenzollerns, the Romanovs and the Ottomans. Would militarism disappear with them as Schumpeter predicted? Or would Lenin's successful revolution in Russia be quickly followed by the downfall of capitalism and wars of national liberation throughout the world? (Rosa Luxemburg and the Spartacists took to the streets in Germany in the hope that it would). Or would the leading capitalist powers, chastened by the horrors of world war, combine under Woodrow Wilson's banner of a League of Nations and create an economic order resembling what Hobson had called inter-imperialism and Kautsky had called ultra-imperialism? As it turned out, none of these prophets got it quite right. In fact the world seemed such a different place after the war that theorising about imperialism declined and the word was used less and less in popular literature on international relations. It would be several decades before anyone undertook to invent a new theory of imperialism and when theorising did begin again the word had undergone a further metamorphosis. It is therefore just as well at this point to summarise the theories propounded between 1898 and 1919. The chart below cannot, of course, do justice to the complexity of all the theories, but it will provide useful points of reference and comparison for the discussion of subsequent developments in later chapters. Implicit in every theory is the same definition of imperialism: the use of the state power, especially military power, to pursue alleged economic advantages in the world at large. This definition does not by any means cover all the meanings assigned to the word in the pre-war period; as Schumpeter saw, by 1919 the word was in danger of losing all meaning in the popular press. But something like this definition will fit all the writers discussed here. Though Hobson stressed the strength of imperialist tendencies in Britain and Schumpeter stressed their weakness, though Kautsky saw war between European powers as a passing phase of capitalist development and Lenin saw it as a more or less permanent condition, all four of them were writing about the same thing. It is important not to be misled into thinking otherwise by statements about the causes or consequences of imperialism which resemble but are not in fact definitions : 'imperialism is the highest stage of capitalism'; 'imperialism is the objectless disposition on the part of a state to unlimited forcible expansion'; imperialism is 'the return of the decisive struggle for expansion from those areas which are being fought over back to its home countries'; imperialism 'is a debasement of... genuine nationalism by attempts to overflow its natural banks and absorb the near or distant territory of reluctant and unassimilable peoples'. From the *U.S. Investor* in 1898 to Schumpeter in 1919, all the theorists are grappling with the same phenomenon, the adoption of aggressive foreign policies by a number of nations accompanied by the spread of high tariffs, an arms race and an unfriendly competition for the acquisition of positions of dominant influence in less developed countries.

CHAPTER 9
CONCISE EXPOSITION OF CLASSIC THEORIES OF IMPERIALISM

1898-99 U.S. Investor, C.A. Conant (American business and economic writers)

STATEMENTS ABOUT THE PAST	None
STATEMENTS ABOUT THE PRESENT	'A congestion of capital' exists. 'The problem of finding employment for capital... is now the greatest of all the economic problems that confronts us'. The Spanish American War gives America the opportunity to solve this problem.
STATEMENTS ABOUT THE FUTURE	In the new economic era marked by 'a congestion of capital' and trusts, continued economic progress will require the use of the armed might of the State to open and maintain foreign fields of investment. A social and political revolution may occur if monopolies continue to grow.

1900-1901 H. Gaylord Wilshire (American businessman and Socialist editor)

STATEMENTS ABOUT THE PAST	None
STATEMENTS ABOUT THE PRESENT	Over-production led capitalists to form trusts which in turn restricted opportunities for investment. The 'Republican Party, which is the political expression of the organized wealth of the country' favors a policy of imperialism in order to secure outlets for this surplus capital in foreign countries.

Statements about the past, present and future

STATEMENTS ABOUT THE FUTURE	Imperialism and warfare between the great powers can only provide temporary relief for the problems of the capitalist system. As more and more of the world is subjected to domination by monopolies, pressure for a socialist revolution will grow until it is irresistible. Monopolies can be easily transferred to national ownership.

1898-1903 Ethel R. Faraday and other British economic and Financial writers; Joseph Chamberlain

STATEMENTS ABOUT THE PAST	None
STATEMENTS ABOUT THE PRESENT	Challenges to Britain's pre eminent economic position from other countries organized according to the German 'imperial ideal' since 1870 can only be met by the abandonment of Free trade and the the consolidation of Britain's Empire into a self-sufficient unit protected by tariffs.
STATEMENTS ABOUT THE FUTURE	Without adoption of the 'German conception of empire', Britain will decline into a second rate State and face possible social upheaval at home. Imperialism is an economic necessity.

1902 J.A. Hobson (British economist and social thinker)

STATEMENTS ABOUT THE PAST	The growth of the British Empire in the tropics during the second half of the 19th century carried on the process which

Richard Cobden and other Radicals had attacked in the early Victorian era. The growth of the tropical empire throughout the 19th century was the work of self-interested minority interests: bureaucratic, military, philanthropic, business and financial. It benefited those interests and harmed the rest of the nation. These minority interests attracted support from other groups by successfully appealing to irrational 'atavistic' 'aggressive instincts' surviving from an earlier era in human evolution.

STATEMENTS ABOUT THE PRESENT

Wilshire correctly identified the 'taproot' of contemporary imperialism as the need of investors to secure outlets for accumulated capital. In most countries the investment interest is the most powerful advocate of an aggressive foreign policy.

STATEMENTS ABOUT THE FUTURE

Imperialism is not an economic necessity. Much of the impetus toward imperialism can be eliminated 'by removing the unearned increments of income from the possessing classes and adding them to the wage-income of the working classes or to the public income'. If this is not done the struggle among European nations for dominant positions in Asia will increase along with a perilous arms race. If by some chance the imperialist powers can settle their differences, they may combine to exploit the rest of the world ('inter-imperialism'). Europe will then decline as Rome declined when she parasitically lived on the resources of her empire. If, on the other hand, anti-imperialist forces succeed in overcoming imperialism, the work of developing parts of the world where the people are not ready for self-government can be done using the methods of indirect rule pioneered by able British colonial administrators.

Statements about the past, present and future

1904-05 J. Riesser, O. Jeidels (German writers on economic affairs)

STATEMENTS ABOUT THE PAST	Government fostering of big banks was an essential prerequisite of Germany's rapid industrialisation. The big banks, strengthened by consolidation during economic crises, had a vital role to play in promoting German interests abroad.
STATEMENTS ABOUT THE PRESENT	'The driving force of the banks' activity abroad is the necessity at a certain stage of capitalist development, of establishing abroad a favorable field for the investment of free German capital'.
STATEMENTS ABOUT THE FUTURE	The process of consolidation in finance and industry must proceed if Germany is to development, of establishing secure the resources she needs in other lands.

1905-10 R. Hilferding (Austrian socialist, later German politician)

STATEMENTS ABOUT THE PAST	None
STATEMENTS ABOUT THE PRESENT	Monopoly organisations in industry and finance — products of capitalism's struggle to deal with periodic crises of overproduction — favor high tariff barriers in order to maintain steady profits and rates of production. The imposition of these tariff barriers speeds up the growth of monopoly but at the same time limits the profitability of domestic enterprises. Big capital, organized and led by the big banks (finance

capital) therefore turns to capital exporting. The advantages sought by capital exporters are new markets, cheap raw materials and cheap labor. Imperialism is the product of the competition between capital exporters of different nations for exclusive control of developing regions beyond their own borders.

STATEMENTS ABOUT THE FUTURE

Imperialism backed by 'Finance capital' represents the final stage in the development of capitalism. It paves the way for the advent of socialism by : (1) increasing class conflict between the few who benefit from protective tariffs and aggression on the one hand and the many who suffer from those policies; and (2) concentrating the control of basic industries in a few organisations which can be easily seized by the nation in the course of a social revolution.

1909-10 Norman Angell (British journalist and crusader for peace).

STATEMENTS ABOUT THE PAST

None

STATEMENTS ABOUT THE PRESENT

Imperialism and the arms race which is its inevitable companion are caused by the mistaken belief that nations can become richer by conquering territory. Under modern conditions nations cannot enrich themselves by conquest. Outlets for surplus investment capital are needed but can be got without aggression. 'Aggressive instincts' which also motivate warlike activities are being gradually eliminated by economic progress.

Statements about the past, present and future

STATEMENTS ABOUT THE FUTURE	Peace and disarmament can be obtained without overthrowing capitalism if international arrangements for 'collective security' are made.

1914 H.N. Brailsford (British journalist & Socialist)

STATEMENTS ABOUT THE PAST	Reiterates the Cobden-Hobson argument that the British 'ruling class' built the British Empire and was its chief beneficiary.
STATEMENTS ABOUT THE PRESENT	Foreign policy in all countries in the 20th century is conducted by members 'of a ruling class which has become an investing class'.
STATEMENTS ABOUT THE FUTURE	The only effective way to overcome aggressive tendencies in international relations is to strip the investing class of surplus revenue and to democratise the conduct of foreign policy by subjecting it 'to review by unofficial minds'.

1913-16 R. Luxemburg (Polish Socialist active in Germany 1897-1919

STATEMENTS ABOUT THE PAST	Since its inception capitalism has needed to expand in order to live. Sometimes the expansion has been peaceful, sometimes not. Sometimes it has been managed with the use of the armed might of the State, sometimes not. But with or without armed force, the process has always been traumatic

for those newly subjected to the capitalist system. Sometimes capitalism has actually worked against colonial expansion by European States.

STATEMENTS ABOUT THE PRESENT

The age of imperialism began about 1895, when the capitalist system had penetrated nearly every corner of the globe. The struggle to gain exclusive control of 'what still remained open of the non-capitalist environment' increased international tensions. The rise of imperial Germany after most of the world had been subjected to control by other states introduced 'an irresponsible factor of general unrest'. Imperialism is distinguished by "the return of the decisive struggle for expansion from those areas which are being fought over back to its home countries'.

STATEMENTS ABOUT THE FUTURE

International tension will continue until a social revolution occurs in the leading capitalist states. If there is no revolution, the end of World War I will 'introduce an era of undivided rule for militarism and reaction all over Europe, with a new war as its final goal'.

1914 K. Kautsky (German Socialist leader)

STATEMENTS ABOUT THE PAST

The drive to expand was 'one of the very conditions of the existence of capitalism'. Free trade was the characteristic expression of this drive in the 19th century.

STATEMENTS ABOUT THE PRESENT

Imperialism, which is the current expression of capitalism's drive to expand, is actually damaging to many capitalist interests.

Statements about the past, present and future

STATEMENTS ABOUT THE FUTURE	After World War I, capitalist countries might combine to end their competition in armaments and commerce. Through an 'ultra-imperialism' they could peacefully exploit the rest of the world.

1915 N. Bukharin (Russian Bolshevik ideologist)

STATEMENTS ABOUT THE PAST	None
STATEMENTS ABOUT THE PRESENT	There is a structural conflict between the integrated 'World Economy' and the limitations of sovereign 'national states' Income from colonies enables capitalists in Europe to raise the wages of the workers. The characteristic British form of imperialism is the drive for an Imperial customs union.
STATEMENTS ABOUT THE FUTURE	A series of wars between capitalist national states is 'unavoidable because the relative strength of rival powers will never remain stable long enough for a lasting peace to be concluded.

1916-17 V.I. Lenin (Leader of the Bolshevik faction of Russian socialists)

STATEMENTS ABOUT THE PAST	'Colonial policy and imperialism existed before the latest stage of capitalism, and even before capitalism'. But the economic factors behind colonial policy and imperialism differ markedly in different

eras. 'Even the previous stage of capitalism is essentially different from the colonial policy of finance capital'. Lenin does not go into details on previous forms of imperialism.

STATEMENTS ABOUT THE PRESENT

The rise of monopolies (trusts and cartels) and finance capital (big banks and other organised blocs of capital able to shift investments from industry to industry) inaugurate the 'imperialist epoch of world not earlier than 1898-1900'. The basic cause of World War I is that new capitalist powers, Germany in particular, appeared after the world had been practically divided up into states and spheres of influence. There is therefore a disparity between economic strength and territorial control. Earnings from the exploitation of foreign lands are used to bribe 'the labour aristocracy' (especially 'opportunists' and leaders like Kautsky) into supporting aggressive policies.

STATEMENTS ABOUT THE FUTURE

Imperialism and the wars it provokes are inescapable features of life in the era of monopolies and finance capital. Only warfare against the capitalist system in the form of a) socialist revolutions in advanced capitalist countries and b) 'wars of national liberation' elsewhere can bring this disastrous epoch to a close. Until these forces defeat capitalism there will be continual warfare.

1904-17 T. Veblen (American Economist)

STATEMENTS ABOUT THE PAST

The process by which organised states arose in medieval Europe required the constant employment of armed force for aggressive purposes. Warlike classes dominated most states during the transition to industrialism and portions of those classes survived in positions of power. Sentiments of patriotism and militarism were fostered in the masses in the course of centuries which could at any time be invoked to support wars from which most people derived no visible benefit.

STATEMENTS ABOUT THE PRESENT

The arms race and World War I are the result of two quite different forces. In the industrialised constitutional democracies of Western Europe and North America, dominant business interests discovered that high tariffs backed by the force of the armed state created unique opportunities for profit and could help to discipline the working classes who had become disenchanted with the current division of the fruits of industrialisation. They harnessed powerful 'sentiments' from earlier eras of European history to serve their special interests. Once aroused, these sentiments could not be controlled. In 'dynastic states' such as Imperial Germany the late arrival of the industrial revolution enabled the old ruling class to turn the immense potential of machine technology to serve its own ancient objectives of conquest.

STATEMENTS ABOUT THE FUTURE

Unless tariffs are abolished and the sentiment of patriotism curbed through the elimination of exclusive citizenship, destructive arms races and wars will continue. If peace were achieved through those means, the egalitarian thrust of the masses would no longer be curbed by military discipline and warfare between classes would replace warfare between nations.

1919 J. Schumpeter (Austrian economist, later Professor of Economics in the United States).

STATEMENTS ABOUT THE PAST	There have been many instances of imperialism since the beginning of recorded history. The common factor in every instance has been the growth of a social class with a vested interest in aggressive, warlike enterprises. The social groups generated by capitalism — bourgoisie and workers — have more to gain from peace than from war. This is shown by the fact that imperialist movements failed in both Britain and America, the countries where capitalism has been most influential.
STATEMENTS ABOUT THE PRESENT	Modern Imperialism, which has culminated in World War I, has its origins in the survival of court and aristocratic circles accustomed to aggressive European absolutism in the 17th and 18th centuries. On the continent of Europe, especially in central and eastern Europe, this class continued to hold supreme power in the state even after the advent of capitalism and industrialisation. The ruling class imposed protective tariffs which gave *some* capitalists an interest in forming cartels and supporting imperialist policies. Support for these policies also came from some other groups with no rational interest in imperialism but who possessed 'atavistic' aggressive instincts acquired in earlier eras of human evolution. Capitalist imperialism is therefore a transient phenomenon.
STATEMENTS ABOUT THE FUTURE	With downfall of the old aristocratic ruling classes, the progressive rationalization of all areas of human life and the "decay" of aggressive instincts, imperialism can be expected to disappear. Capitalism can survive for some time to come without high tariffs, "export monopolism" and the further growth of trusts and cartels.

CHAPTER 10
THEORIES OF IMPERIALISM BECOME 'THEORIES OF EMPIRE'

From C.A. Conant and the *U.S. Investor* to H.N. Brailsford and V.I. Lenin, those who speculated about the meaning of imperialism between 1898 and 1918 had been activists whose efforts to understand the world were motivated by the desire to change it. Most were propagandists trying to predict the future rather than academic historians trying to explain the past. Inevitably their propagandistic purposes had affected their definitions as well as their explanations of imperialism. So it would be with the most influential writers on imperialism after World War I. Because the whole configuration of international relations had altered dramatically, discussions of imperialism took a new course. During the next twenty-five years imperialism — once regarded as the mighty fulcrum of world affairs — came to mean little more than colonialism. The notion that capitalists who required outlets for 'surplus' funds had called upon the armed state for help was accordingly transmuted into the notion that the great colonial empires had been created as fields for investment. Stated in this way, the theory of investment-powered imperialism is not so much an over-simplification of history as an anachronism. The largest of Europe's colonial empires had been mostly built before anyone, capitalist or socialist, had begun to talk of surplus funds seeking outlets. It was therefore bound, eventually, to be attacked by professional historians who specialised in imperial and colonial history. Their attacks, which began in earnest in the late nineteen thirties, would, paradoxically, help to perpetuate the very theory whose credibility they set out to destroy.

The development of this monumental misunderstanding began in 1919 with the publication of Leonard Woolf's influential book. *Empire and Commerce in Africa, A Study in Economic Imperialism.* Woolf, though he was thirty-nine when the book appeared, had little knowledge of the pre-war debates on imperialism. While others had been writing about empires, he had been helping to run one as an officer in Britain's Colonial Service in Sri Lanka from 1904 to 1911. By his own account he was a briskly efficient, tough administrator who was more than once the subject of official complaints to the Governor by a local native welfare organisation. When he left the service, it was to marry one of the most brilliant novelists of his generation and to plunge directly into the heady, hectic literary world of Virginia's 'Bloomsbury Set'.[1] Over the next few years he discovered that his own talents lay in political journalism. Gradually he gravitated to the left, getting to 'know well Norman Angell and the group of young men ... who were tremendously influenced by his remarkable personality and his remarkable book *The Great Illusion'*[2]. In the nineteen twenties he replaced H.N. Brailsford as a leader writer for the *Nation,* a weekly paper whose staff included J.A. Hobson and other distinguished Liberal intellectuals. In their company Woolf confessed that he 'felt very much the new boy' and 'a bit of fraud' because 'they were so high-minded'. He also became a member of the executive committee of the socialist Fabian Society where, because of his background in the Colonial Service and his study of Africa, he was treated 'more or less as the Fabian and Labour Party "expert" in international and imperial questions'.[3]

These personal links connected Leonard Woolf to the most influential pre-war English critics of imperialism and put him at the very centre of intellectual life in the inter-war decades. His writings on Africa and imperialism, however, represent a sharp break with the past. This went unnoticed at the time because he so faithfully reflected the new and urgent

1. Leonard Woolf, *Growing, An Autobiography of the Years 1904-1911* (London, 1961) 12-111. For a different perspective on Woolf's experience with colonial government see T. J. Barron, 'Before the Deluge: Leonard Woolf in Ceylon', *Journal of Imperial and Commonwealth History* VI (1977) 47-63.

2. Woolf, *Beginning Again, An Autobiography of the Years 1911 to 1918* (London, 1964) 233.

3. Woolf, *Downhill All the Way, An Autobiography of the Years 1919-1939* (London, 1967) 218-19.

concerns of his liberal and radical contemporaries. As he recalled later it seemed to him that

> There were in fact two vast, ecumenicál problems which threatened ... mankind and are interrelated: first the prevention of war and the development of international government; secondly the dissolution of the Empires of European states in Asia and Africa which would cause as much misery to the world as war unless the Goverments of the great imperial powers recognised the inevitability, and deliberately worked for an orderly transference of power to the native populations, educated for self-government by their rulers.[4]

Though this formulation pronounces the problems of war and colonialism to be 'interrelated', it does not actually relate them in any structural way; it merely relates them as co-generators of human misery. Woolf makes no profound connections based on 'surplus' investment capital or any other underlying common factor. He excludes the non-colonising nations from the imperialist camp and writes for the most part as though imperialism and empire building are synonymous. His critique of imperialism is, therefore, far removed from Lenin's and those of the Central European Socialists, a group for which Woolf had little sympathy. The first genuine communist he met was Theodore Rothstein who had once been a member of H.M. Hyndman's Social-Democratic Federation but by 1919 was serving as virtual 'Bolshevik ambassador to Britain'. 'Rothstein', Woolf wrote later, 'was the first of these modern civilized savages, these communist fanatics, that I came across. Outside the circle of his Marxist religion he seemed to me a nice man and highly intelligent; inside the magic circle he was a cross between a schoolman and a dancing dervish. He would expound the gospel of Marxism-Leninism to me at great length in that dreadful jargon of meaningless abstractions which has become the language of communism'.[5]

The opening pages of Woolf's *Empire and Commerce in Africa* reveal the vast gulf which separates his ideas from the

4. Ibid 195-96.

5. Ibid 18-19.

ideas of the Central and Eastern-European socialists. He begins by tracing the roots of modern imperialism to seventeenth century mercantilists who first enunciated the principle 'that the power and organisation of an individual State should be directed against the world outside the State for the economic purposes of the world within the State'.[6] This formula, which Brailsford and most of his Edwardian contemporaries would have simply called imperialism, is subdivided by Woolf into three forms of state action. One of these is protectionism, another is 'economic imperialism' and the third is 'other forms', including 'peaceful penetration' of territories 'under State influence or control'. War and threats of war between developed countries do not appear anywhere among his three categories. His definition of 'economic imperialism' is restricted to colonial questions:

'Economic Imperialism'. Under this term I include the international economic policy of the European States, of the U.S.A., and latterly of Japan, in the unexploited and non-Europeanised Territories of the world. The policy of Economic Imperialism includes colonial policy and the acquisition by the Europeanised State of exploitable territory, the policy of spheres of influence, and the policy of obtaining economic control through other political means. These various kinds of policy are all distinguished by one important characteristic; they all aim at using the power and influence of the European form of the State in the economic interests of its inhabitants in lands where the European form of State has not developed. I call it imperialism because the policy always implies either the extension of the State's territory by conquest or occupation, or the application of its dominion or some form of political control to peoples who are not its citizens. I qualify it with the word economic because the motives of this imperialism are not defense nor prestige nor conquest not the 'spread of civilisation', but the profit of the citizens, or some of the citizens, of the European State.[7]

Early theorists of imperialism would have regarded this as a very odd definition. Lenin and Bukharin would have attacked it vigorously as they attacked anyone who identified imperialism with 'mere colonialism'. Schumpeter's entire analysis of imperialism — which was grounded on the

6. *Empire and Commerce,* 14-15.

7. Ibid 19.

assumption that Britain, the United States and the Low Countries had never practised imperialism — is rendered irrelevant by Woolf's definition. But what earlier theorists might have thought of his definition was not uppermost in Woolf's mind in 1919. He was agitating for reform and devolution in Britain's empire; his definition served his immediate propagandist purpose.

Woolf also marshalled the whole history of nineteenth-century colonial expansion in support of his case — something no previous theorist had done. In the process he played fast and loose with chronology. At one point he writes that 'the beliefs and desires which produced the economic imperialism of *the last half of the nineteenth century* are no new phenomenon in the world'. Later he observes that 'the history of *the last ninety years* ' [i.e., since 1839] 'offers in simplest and clearest form the facts and effects of a policy of economic imperialism'. Elsewhere he argues that '*in 1880* a conscious policy of economic imperialism hardly existed'. Another paragraph opens with the claim that 'it was in *the ninth decade of the nineteenth century* that economic imperialism fully and finally established itself', and finishes with the conclusion that 'after 1880 European policy is dominated by rival imperialisms, colonial policies, spheres of influence, commercial treaties, markets and tariffs'.[8] A careful reader will eventually discover that Woolf offers very little evidence to support his wild generalisations about the motives for colonial annexations before 1880, and that his most telling quotations are drawn from empire builders of the eighteen nineties.[9] But the average reader will go away with the impression that, in Woolf's opinion, all of Europe's dealings with the non-European world in the nineteenth century were undertaken for economic reasons.

8. Ibid 21, 24, 37, 55, my italics.

9. For example, Frederick Lugard's claim in 1893 that 'the Scramble for Africa was due to the growing commercial rivalry, which brought home to civilised nations the vital necessity of securing the only remaining fields for industrial enterprise and expansion'. Quoted in ibid 26.

Another novelty of Woolf's book is its use of Africa as a test case. The first capitalist writers who held imperialism to be a necessity as an outlet for surplus capital wrote at a time when most of Africa had already been appropriated by European claimants. Hobson had said next to nothing about Africa, believing as he did that 'the great test of Western Imperialism is Asia'. Later writers, particularly the central Europeans had concentrated their attention on the events leading to the World War. Woolf, in sharp contrast, chooses Africa as his subject because it

> is one of the finest fields for the study of economic imperialism, of the interaction between European policy and commerce in non-European countries ... It is a peculiarly fine field for study, not only because the actions and reaction are crowded into the space of a few years ... The African policy of European States was more conscious, more open and unabashed and less complicated and obscured by ancient traditions, vested interests, properties, and political expediencies than has been the case in other continents.[10]

His conclusion after a lengthy region by region survey of modern Africa was that Europe's 'policy of grab' had paid very few dividends. The nations who had scrambled for Africa had gained no real power or prestige from their activities, their competition had embittered international relations, and the fabled riches of the dark continent had turned out to be fool's gold. Only a small number of white settlers and officials had benefited from an ill-conceived adventure which had imposed forced labour and political servitude on countless unoffending peoples. This conclusion, strikingly similar to Hobson's verdict on the profits of empire building, is reached with even less resort to arguments based on economic 'necessity'. Woolf does not point to a glut of surplus capital or a crisis in the evolution of capitalism as the reasons for Europe's involvement in Africa. He singles out instead 'the beliefs and desires' of the human beings who were in a position to make and execute national policies. 'The policy of interference is finally determined by an agent or two of the Government's in Africa ... a few high officials in the Foreign and Colonial Offices, and a politician, a Secretary or a

10. Ibid 53.

Minister of State. These men are only the last levers which put in motion the power of the State: they are themselves set in motion by another small group of persons, the financiers, traders and capitalists, who are seeking particular economic ends in Africa'. There was no suggestion, however, that the officials and statesmen who were responsible for interference in the final analysis had been 'bought' by capitalists.

> There is indeed little, if any evidence of actual corruption of statesmen or government officials in the colonial adventures of European States. What happened is that the governing group is subjected to a persistent and powerful pressure from the small and influential profit-seeking group, and even when, as not infrequently happens, it is actually opposed to the immediate aims of the financial and capitalist interests, it yields to the pressure ... There is clear evidence that our Foreign Office was not eager to support all Sir William Mackinnon's schemes and interests ... Yet our policy, whether under Lord Salisbury or Lord Rosebery or Lord Kimberley, was indisputably shaped by Sir William Mackinnon and his co-directors. This was possible because at need the Company could exert pressure from so many different classes. Public opinion, as expressed in *The Times'* leading articles, was consistently behind Sir William Mackinnon. Wires, only waiting to be pulled, ran between the board room of the Company and the Archbishop of Canterbury and the Church of Scotland, wires which were as invisible to Lord Salisbury as they were to the Archibishop and 'The Moderators and other dignitaries'. The invisibility of the wires, when pulled at crucial moments, adds to their effectiveness.[11]

Empire and Commerce in Africa changed the way English-speaking peoples thought and wrote about imperialism. It joined Hobson's study as a standard work on the subject. Because it supplied far more historical detail than Hobson's book, it was much more useful as a reference. In subsequent years most scholars would take for granted the innovations Woolf had made in the definition and explanation of imperialism, namely,

1) The separation of imperialism from broader questions of militarism, protectionism and war.
2) The restriction of imperialism to denote only situations in which 'the power and influence of the European form of the state' was brought to bear on 'lands where the

11. Ibid 319-21.

European form of State has not developed'.

3) The extension of imperialism back into the past to include most if not all European colonising activities in the nineteenth century.
4) The use of the Scramble for Africa as *the* test case for assessing the motivation of imperialist powers.
5) A greatly increased emphasis on the role of trade and trading companies in promoting colonialism. In this he departed dramatically from all previous theorists, including Hobson, who had regarded trade as a negligible factor in promoting colonial annexations.

A consequence of these changes was a shift of attention away from Central Europe, America and Japan towards the old empires of Britain and France. This suited Woolf's overriding propagandist purpose which was the transfer of ownership of Europe's overseas colonies either to the indigenous peoples or to a truly international body which could look after their interests until they were 'ready for independence'.

Woolf continued to promote this aim through his own books *(Economic Imperialism* (1920), *Mandates and Empire* (1920), and *Imperialism and Civilization* (1928) as well as through books on the same theme published by his Hogarth Press. These books maintained the new emphasis on the nineteenth century as the great age of imperialism. In *Economic Imperialism* Woolf clarified his own chronology by insisting that it was 'about 1870' that 'Europe had just become ripe for economic imperialism'. *Imperialism and Civilization* identified imperialism as 'an aspect of the conflict or clash of different civilizations in the nineteenth century'.[12] Norman Leys's book on Kenya, published by the Hogarth Press in 1924, ascribed later nineteenth-century colonialism partly to a need for tropical raw materials, partly to the completion of the industrial revolution in Europe and North America which made it 'increasingly difficult to find in these parts of the world, ways of profitably re-investing the profits of capitalised

12. *Economic Imperialism* (London, 1928) 29-30; *Imperialism and Civilization* (London, 1928) 29-30.

industry', and partly to the rise of socialism as a political movement 'that threatened the profits derived from industries in Europe'.[13] Leys was a doctor whose statements about colonial and African history were based on information he acquired second-hand. Much more convincing testimony about the reasons for the building of Europe's empires in Africa came from Lord Olivier whose book *The Anatomy of African Misery* was published at Woolf's Hogarth Press in 1927.

Like Woolf, Olivier had actually participated in the making and ruling of the British Empire. His career in public service began in the Colonial Officc in 1882, prospered with his subsequent appointment as Governor of Jamaica, and culminated in service as Secretary of State for India in Britain's first Labour government. His observations on colonialism and 'capitalist imperialism' are especially interesting because he was a life-long socialist and member of the Fabian Society. But, like Leonard Woolf, he had taken no part in pre-war debates about imperialism and so fell easily in with the new trend of identifying imperialism with colonialism.[14] As he saw it, British policy in Africa underwent a profound change during the eighteen nineties. Before that date 'British interests in India demanded that British control should be maintained' in South Africa, but there was no important push for territorial expansion. The government of African colonies had been conducted for the most part according to liberal maxims which counteracted the illiberal political and economic schemes of self-interested white settlers and businessmen. During the nineties, Olivier continued, there was increasing pressure from private interests for government patronage of vast companies formed for the purpose of 'opening up' the allegedly bountiful resources of the African interior. 'Qualified advisors of the British Government at the time' had pointed out the dangers

13. *Kenya* (London, 1924) 71.

14. In 1918 he linked W.W.I and colonialism by arguing in *The League of Nations and Primitive Peoples,* p. 4, that 'The World War came about ... because the general politics of Europe had taken on the character and colour of the "scramble for Africa"'.

to the welfare of African peoples posed by the new policy but 'that Government was satisfied to believe that the appointment on the directorate and as administrators of men of distinguished names and high character' would ensure that justice was done. Drawing on his own insider's knowledge of policy making in the nineties, he claimed that 'during the period of its elaboration in South East Africa, an obscure conflict was waged between those older [liberal] traditions of the Colonial office ... on the one side, and the British Imperialist politicians and financiers and expansionist Afrikanders, abetted by the British Government of the period and by the Foreign Office on the other. The capitalist-commercialists and the Afrikander policy won'.[15]

Lord Olivier amplified this analysis in *White Capital and Coloured Labour* (1929), yet another product of the Hogarth Press. He repeated his charge that 'Those ... who with colonial knowledge, were in touch with the facts at the time, realised quite clearly and with concern that about 1890 British colonial policy was breaking away from its traditional principles'. The reason for the break was the rise of what Olivier now called 'capitalist imperialism'.

> whereas a great part of the British Empire was colonised not capitalistically but by the emigration of men and women who went to work for themselves, other parts of our colonies were colonised capitalistically; actually, in fact, by joint stock companies or grantees of large blocks of land, assigned to them by the Crown for estates with the intention of exploiting them through the use of slave labour, whilst practically the whole of our recent colonisation in Africa, to speak only of that continent, has been essentially capitalist colonisation in precisely the same sense, financed by European syndicates and investors, and the active directing work of it done by men who go out as landowners or farmers and employers and organisers of labour, the labour which they expect to employ being not specifically chattel slave labour but the labour of native black men.[16]

This sketch of the rise of a new era in the development of the

15. *The Anatomy of African Misery* (London, 1927).

16. *White Capital and Coloured Labour* (London, 1929) 14-15. This book was presented as a revised edition of one published in 1906 but is in fact an almost wholly different work. The earlier book does not analyse 'capitalist imperialism'.

British Empire, while more cautious and convincing than the vast generalisations of Leys and Woolf, nevertheless reinforced many of the essential features of Woolf's critique of imperialism. It was solely concerned with colonies, assigned a central role to trading and mining ventures, and cited Africa as the prime example of imperialism in action. Though it specifically excluded most nineteenth-century empire building from the category of capitalist imperialism, it confused an important question of chronology by identifying that type of imperialism as a phenomenon of 'the last forty or fifty years'.[17] The variation of ten years would be crucial for later historians. Ascribing the advent of new axioms of imperial policy to the eighteen nineties appeared on the surface to be reasonable interpretation of well-known facts. Pushing the triumph of those axioms ten years farther back in time was a dubious operation which was bound to raise the eyebrows of later historians. Olivier had offered his own personal experience as evidence that colonial policy in this earlier period continued to reflect the liberal dogma of the mid-nineteenth century. (Ironically the reiteration of precisely this view in the nineteen sixties would be hailed by many historians as a triumphant refutation of 'the socialist theory of capitalist imperialism'.)

While British writers were redefining the concept of imperialism to suit the needs of a new generation of reformers, American professors were busily dissecting and embalming it. Once imperialism had been reduced to the question of colonies, it seemed reasonable to treat American imperialism as largely a thing of the past. Almost all the overseas territories of the United States had been acquired as a result of the Spanish-American War. A sizeable proportion of public opinion held that they should be relinquished as soon as possible. And although American military and naval power had grown enormously since 1898, that power had rarely been used as the *United States Investor* and other early enthusiasts for imperialism had hoped it would be used, i.e.,

17. Ibid.

for the frank pursuit of economic advantages beyond the Atlantic and Pacific oceans. When the United States had intervened in the affairs of the old world, it had done so in the name of anti-imperialism. It promoted the 'Open-Door' in East Asia. It entered the first World War with the professed aims of 'making the world safe for democracy', safeguarding the rights of small nations, and securing a 'peace without annexations'. To be sure, American activity in Latin America had grown increasingly high-handed but this could be explained as zealous devotion to President Monroe's ancient doctrine that the United States should be Latin America's guardian against European interference. For all these reasons imperialism had come to be regarded by Americans as a bygone mistake rather then as a burning contemporary issue. Most books on the subject were written by academics who concentrated their attention on the rise of European colonial empires. What critics referred to as U.S. 'dollar diplomacy' in Latin America was treated as a special case of 'economic imperialism', a term to which the Americans ascribed an entirely new meaning.

The main lines of post-war American thinking were brought together in a popular college textbook by Parker Thomas Moon, a professor of international relations at Columbia University. Moon's *Imperialism and World Politics* went through an amazing twenty-one printings between 1926 and 1966; it therefore probably ranks second only to Lenin's tract as a maker of public opinion. No doubt the ripples of its impact are still felt in American schools. In a breezy, often racy style, Moon offered categorical statements about the causes of imperialism, a region-by-region survey of world politics, and a set of conclusions about the morality of imperialism that sat squarely on the ideological fence. He would, he said, view imperialism 'both as an achievement and as a world problem'. Imperialism was an achievement because it had brought development to 'barbarous negro tribes' and 'the attractive "South Sea Islanders", whose surf boards, and dances, and, idleness, and picturesque customs have kindled the imagination of urbanized Americans'. Without the 'dollar diplomacy' practised by the United States in Latin America there would have been more dictators, 'more subsidized revolutions and counter-revolutions in backward countries — in a word, more anarchy'.[18] On the other hand, imperialism was a problem because the competing economic systems of the great modern empires posed a threat to world peace — a threat which would only finally disappear when the concept of 'international trusteeship' over 'backward' peoples had been established in place of the concept of colonial empires 'owned' by individual nations. This was a process which thc United States was particularly qualified to assist because she had never been 'converted, certainly not wholly converted, to European imperialism'.[19]

Moon listed just five causes which had impelled European nations to acquire colonies: 1) 'surplus' manufactured goods; 2) the nineteenth-century revolution in transportation and communication; 3) the demand of industrial nations for tropical products; 4) the appearance of surplus capital seeking overseas outlets; and 5) the popularity of economic nationalism after 1870.[20] Imperialism, he concluded, 'naturally ensued, once it was assumed that government should promote business. For then it follows that nations many legitimately reach out for colonial empire, in order to preempt markets for their surplus manufactures, protect investments of their surplus capital, obtain business and coaling stations for their shipping, and secure raw materials. Such is the logic which combined with economic facts makes imperialism a necessity'.

Moon presented this list as a set of propositions to be copied down by students rather than a series of statements to be debated by historians. Though he follows Woolf in reducing imperialism to empire building in the nineteenth and

18. *Imperialism and World Politics* (New York, 1926) 76, 374, 536.

19. Ibid 56, 565-66.

20. Ibid 28-34.

early twentieth centuries, he significantly broadens the case by including surplus capital in his list of causes. On this point Hobson seems to have been his authority rather than any of the pre-war socialist theorists. Moon made full and free use of Hobson's *Imperialism,* frequently copying whole phrases word for word without any acknowledgement to the author.[21] His knowledge of socialist theorists, on the other hand, was limited. What he did know he did not like. It was 'not the whole so-called "capitalist class", as many an earnest Socialist would have us believe, but only a minority of business interests' who 'are directly interested in imperialism'. He challenged socialist predictions that imperialism would inevitably raise up rival economic blocs, generate new wars or end in the formation of a single consortium exploiting the world's resources for the benefit of a small oligarchy.[22] He regarded his own explanation of empire building as a value-free assessment rather than any sort of left-wing doctrine.

Moon also introduced his readers to an entirely new concept of 'economic imperialism'. Leonard Woolf, like all the European writers who preceded him, had regarded state action as an essential attribute of imperialism. Economic imperialism aimed 'at using the power and influence of the European form of the State' to win economic advantages in other lands. Moon, though he does not give a precise definition, tends throughout his book to use economic imperialism to describe forms of domination achieved through the instrumentality of business activity without the aid of any state. For example, 'the Amazon, protected by the Monroe Doctrine against European annexation, was subjected to economic imperialism, almost as if it were a colony' when rubber plantations were established. The activities of the Firestone company in Liberia and the United Fruit Company in Central America are cited as similar cases.[23]

21. Compare, for example, Moon, 61 with Hobson (1902) 53, 66.

22. Ibid 58, 536-39.

23. Ibid 29, 110, 431.

Somewhere between the 'naked' or 'pure imperialism' marked by annexations and the purely corporate domination which Moon calls economic imperialism fall cases such as the American relationship with Cuba. 'Toward Cuba the United States practised not naked imperialism but a more subtle imperialism, which left to the Cuban people a very considerable amount of self-government, and which sought its profits in the economic prosperity and political stability of Cuba'.[24]

One of Moon's early reviewers complained that it was 'certainly misleading to describe by the same word, imperialist, both the European statesman who plans cold-bloodedly to seize 1000 square miles of territory in Africa and the university instructor who invests $1000 in a French government bond'.[25] Indeed it was. Wilshire and Hobson had argued that overseas investment on a grand scale *promoted* imperialism but neither they nor anyone else before World War I had contended that investment or private business activities on foreign soil were in themselves the active process of imperialism. To this day, the meaning of economic imperialism remains ambiguous. It may mean any of three things: 1) the use of the power of a state beyond its own borders to serve the interests of private profit seekers; or 2) the use of state power to secure real or supposed economic advantages for the state; or 3) financial, commercial or industrial operations by foreign- based companies in any part of the world, which tend to limit the ability of the indigenous people to conduct their affairs as they wish.

Part of the reason that the new, enlarged meaning of economic imperialism won wide acceptance was that it was incorporated into a general definition of imperialism by one of America's greatest historians, William L. Langer. At the outset of his two volume study, *The Diplomacy of Imperialism 1890-1902,* he included in his definition 'the rule or control, political or economic, direct or indirect, of one state, nation or

24. Ibid 422.

25. Review by Blakeslee, *American Historical Review* XXXII (1927) 597-99.

people over other similar groups'. Most subsequent writers brave enough to attempt a general definition have employed some variation on Langer's phrasing. Few of them, however, have possessed Langer's profound appreciation of the complexities of the historical process. His own academic American contemporaries persisted in following Moon in the quest for neat formulae. Henry Elmer Barnes, a professor of sociology wrote in 1930 that it was

conventionally assumed that the imperialistic process is essentially the following:

1). Merchants and bankers recognize the opportunities for pecuniary gain in certain relatively backward political and economic areas.

2). Their penetration is followed by appeals to the foreign offices of their respective states.

3). These requests lead immediately to military intervention and the political administration of such areas.[26]

This grossly oversimplified monocausal explanation of the growth of modern colonial empires was paralleled by the development of similar pat explanations for American foreign policy provided by a vigorous body of researchers during the inter-war years.[27] The results of both types of research were taken up by anti-imperialists on the other side of the Atlantic and incorporated in the British critique of historical imperialism developed by Woolf and his followers. Leonard Barnes demonstrated in *The Duty of Empire* that the English could be just as simplistic in their treatment of the past.[28] Barnes continued the trend of pushing the 'age of imperialism' back into the nineteenth century and identifying it with the control of undeveloped tropical regions. 'The

26. *World Politics in Modern Civilization* (New York, 1930) 188.

27. M. M. Knight, *The Americans in Santo Domingo* (New York, 1928), and *Morocco as a French Economic Venture* (New York, 1937); L. H. Jenks, *Our Cuban Colony* (New York, 1928); C. D. Kepner and J. H. Soothill, *The Banana Empire* (New York, 1935); M. C. Marsh, *The Bankers in Bolivia* (New York, 1928); S. Nearing and J. Freeman, *Dollar Diplomacy* (New York, 1925).

28. London, 1935.

lengths to which economic imperialism was prepared to go almost defy belief. In the twenty years [1880-1900] ... the partition of Africa was completed. Great progress was made with the partition of Turkey, Persia, and China ... After 1900 the great imperialist racket passed its peak, though the decline was gradual and enlivened by frequent spasms of renewed activity'. (p. 188)

Thus increasing numbers of educated people were taking for granted that capitalism's need for expansion and investment opportunities had created a drive for overseas colonies in the final decades of the nineteenth century, a drive that was largely over by the turn of the century. That is to say, they used a theory originally devised to explain global politics *after 1900* to explain colonial annexations *before 1900.* This was a gross distortion of the ideas of both the capitalists and the socialists who formulated Edwardian theories of imperialism. But by the late nineteen thirties capitalists had mostly given up publicly promoting aggression; many socialists found the new distorted versions of the theory of economic imperialism more practically useful than the originals.

Even the beneficiaries of Lenin's Bolshevik revolution in Russia failed to prevent the spread of misshapen versions of their founder's theory of imperialism as 'the highest stage of capitalism'. The reasons for this surprising turn of events can all be ultimately traced to the internal and external difficulties faced by the Soviet Union after the Revolution. Before the World War Lenin had argued strenuously that nationalists could be useful, though temporary, allies of socialist revolutionaries.[29] They were useful allies because of their power to weaken the principal capitalist powers by creating disturbances on the exposed flanks of their over-extended spheres of influence. They were temporary allies, however, because they were not generally class-conscious representatives of the proletariat. Once the revolution was

29. See his highly ambiguous 'Critical Remarks on the Natonal Question', *Collected Works* XX (Moscow, 1964) 19-51. Reinforcement for the view presented here is provided by the anti-Stalinist Marxist, Bill Warren, *Imperialism: Pioneer of Capitalism* (London, 1984), especially 85, 108-09.

over the vanguard of the proletariat would take charge.

The question of the role to be played by nationalist revolutionaries pressed itself upon the fledgling Soviet government with special urgency. Contrary to Bolshevik expectations, the revolution in Russia did not precipitate a world-wide convulsion of capitalist systems. In the aftermath of the great war capitalism shuddered in Western Europe but it did not fall. Had a socialist revolution swept the world there would have been — from Lenin's point of view — no further need for an alliance between the vanguard of the proletariat and nationalists struggling to establish independent states. The dictatorship of the proletariat would commence. As it was, however, Lenin faced the difficult task of establishing the dictatorship of the proletariat within the Soviet Union while encouraging nationalist revolutions in the capitalist world beyond its borders. In practical terms this meant suppressing local nationalist movements while encouraging foreign ones. Thus the nationalist leaders of ethnic minorities in the southern and eastern regions of the U.S.S.R., who had hoped that the Bolsheviks would end the Russian hegemony imposed by the Tsars, were bluntly told that they were to take their orders from the revolutionary workers of Moscow and Petrograd. There were to be no pan-Muslim or pan-Turkish breakaways. As Lenin's agent in Central Asia candidly appraised the situation in 1921, 'It was inevitable that the Russian revolution in Turkestan should have a colonialist character. The Turkestani working class, numerically small, had neither leader, programme, party nor revolutionary tradition. It could therefore not protest against colonialist exploitation. Under Tsarist colonialism, it was the privilege of the Russians to belong to the industrial proletariat. For this reason, the dictatorship of the proletariat took on a typically colonialist aspect'.[30] This frank admission that colonialism could be carried on by socialists did not conflict with anything which Lenin had written in *Imperialism, the Highest Stage of*

30. Helene C. d'Encause and Stuart R. Schram, *Marxism and Asia* (London, 1969), 32.

Capitalism. Imperialism and Colonialism were two different things. There was no contradiction between the fierce denunciation of the aggressive foreign policies pursued by 'moribund' capitalist powers and the establishment of the dictatorship of the proletariat over 'backward peoples'.

Confusion could, and did arise, however, with respect to the conduct of the 'struggle against imperialism' being carried on by peoples far away from the U.S.S.R. Did that struggle have a central or a subordinate place in the continuing socialist revolution? Should communists work with or against bourgeois nationalist revolutionaries in the remaining European colonial empires? These momentous questions were debated by Lenin himself and the Indian communist leader M. N. Roy at the Second Congress of the Comintern in 1920.[31] Roy gave a specifically colonial meaning to Lenin's thesis that the profits from overseas investments provided capitalist countries with the means to bribe the labour aristocracy. European capitalism, according to Roy, 'draws its chief strength less from the industrial countries of Europe than from its colonial possessions'. By 'exploiting the masses in the colonies, European imperialism will be in a position to give concession after concession to the labour aristocracy at home'. It followed that only 'the breaking up of the colonial empire, together with a proletarian revolution in the home country' could succeed in overthrowing the capitalist system in Europe, Therefore communists should put themselves at the head of all those forces who were struggling to free themselves from colonial subjugation. It seemed self-evident to Roy that the leadership of these movements should be in the hands of class-conscious leaders of the proletariat like himself.

To a European Marxist of the old school Roy's remarks appeared distinctly heretical. They not only implicitly challenged the leading role of the industrial workers of developed economies, they advocated cooperation with non-socialist reformers — a tactic that had always been

31. Ibid 150-67.

suspect among revolutionary socialists. The Italian delegate Serrati accused Roy's argument of presenting 'a grave danger for the position of the communist proletariat in the advanced countries, which should remain hostile to all forms of class collaboration, especially in a pre-revolutionary period'. Serrati contended that 'no act of national liberation carried out by bourgeois-democratic groups — even if methods of insurrection are employed — is a revolutionary act'. It is 'carried out either on behalf of a national imperialism in the process of formation, or in the context of the struggle of the capitalist imperialism of one state against the state which dominated the country in the first place'. In this analysis Serrati faithfully preserved the pre-war meaning of imperialism, the meaning Rosa Luxemburg had in mind when she described Balkan politics as a clash of Austrian, Italian and Serbian imperialisms.[32] If India or Turkey or China were to escape domination by imperialist powers without going through a socialist revolution, their independence would signify only that they had themselves become imperialist, using the power of the state to enrich their own capitalist class. Their relations with other imperialist states would necessarily be antagonistic, tending towards war.

In an earlier time or another place, Lenin might have applauded the rigour of Serrati's case. But at the moment the overwhelming fact of international relations was 'the struggle waged by a small group of imperialist nations against the Soviet movement and the Soviet states, at the head of which stands Soviet Russia'. In this struggle the Soviet Union needed all the help it could get, including everyone opposed to that 'small group of imperialist nations'. The Bolsheviks had supported Russian liberals when they 'acted against tsarism'. They could support bourgeois liberation movements now. To that extent Lenin agreed with Roy. Indeed, he went beyond Roy in arguing that communists should support 'bourgeois-democratic' movements in 'backward

32. Rose Luxemburg, *The Crisis in the German Social Democracy* (New York, 1919) 101.

countries'.[33] He was therefore unwilling to endorse Roy's view that the international communist movement should invariably support national liberation movements with proletarian leaders at their head. That might not always be the best method of defending the Soviet movement against 'the small group of imperialist nations'. Lenin was not about to let future Soviet foreign policy be dictated by the theories of either Serrati or Roy.

Nor was Lenin impressed by Roy's ingenious twist of his own argument that the 'superprofits' earned abroad by imperialist powers were used to bribe domestic working class leaders into quiescence. 'Comrade Roy', Lenin asserted, 'goes too far when he asserts that the fate of the West depends exclusively on the degree of development and the strength of the revolutionary movement in the Eastern countries'. Roy was not only mistakenly attributing the source of the alleged superprofits solely to colonial or semi-colonial countries, he was challenging the leadership role of the European communist parties in the world revolution. Lenin made it clear that the 'oppressed nationalities' outside Europe were wanted as soldiers, not generals. It was not the U.S.S.R. who must look to them for salvation; it was they who were 'learning from bitter experience that their only salvation lies in the triumph of Soviet power over "world imperialism"'. Of course, in a conflict of opinion between the founder of the Soviet State and an obscure expatriate Indian agitator, the views of the former must prevail. The report of the Comintern commission on the national and colonial question acknowledged the strength of Roy's argument by making minor modifications in terminology but endorsed Lenin's position. It is important to notice, however, that the report avoided questions of definition. Serrati could leave the

33. Lenin eventually agreed to a compromise wording of the resolution on the national and colonial question. The resolution spoke of 'national-revolutionary' rather than 'bourgeois-democratic' movements. Nevertheless, Lenin insisted that 'there is not the slightest doubt that every nationalist movement can only be a bourgeois-democratic movement, for the bulk of the population in backward countries are peasants who represent bourgeois-capitalist relations'. (Ibid, 157).

Congress unshaken in his conviction that for the workers of Italy the central problem of imperialism was the threat to the peace of Europe posed by the unresolved antagonisms among the capitalist powers. Roy could depart equally unshaken in his conviction that the central problem was the British Empire. Soviet policy and propaganda, could, as circumstances changed, make use of both points of view.

The shifty use of words to serve shifting needs flourished under Lenin's successor, Josef Stalin, who elevated pragmatic foreign policy to a lofty point of principle under the slogan 'Socialism in One Country'. In part, Stalin devised his slogan as a weapon against his internal rivals in a struggle too convoluted to be summarised here. But, aside from that internal wrangle, the slogan expressed a realistic attitude towards the Soviet Union's position in an uncertain, mainly hostile world. Struggling to maintain a firm grip on the multi-national empire built by the Tsars, Stalin needed a slogan which justified tough measures against domestic ethnic nationalist movements while appearing to respect the principle of national self-determination. Committed by rhetoric and tradition to world revolution, he needed a slogan which made the strength of the U.S.S.R. the fundamental condition for that revolution. Too weak to withstand a serious onslaught by the western capitalist powers, he needed a slogan which advertised his wish to live in peace with them without abandoning his commitment to the overthrow of their economic system. Believing that any anti-colonial and anti-western movements weakened the ability of the great powers to attack the Soviet Union, he needed a slogan which justified support for those movements even when they were avowedly anti-communist. 'Socialism in one country' served all those needs.

With respect to the ethnic minorities of the U.S.S.R., Stalin tried to consolidate socialism in one country with a policy that would have been readily understood by any enlightened British colonial ruler of the period. Peoples 'backward economically and culturally' were at the present time 'incapable of making full use of the rights and opportunites afforded them by national equality of rights; ... incapable [also] of rising to a higher level of development and thus catching up with the nationalities which have forged ahead unless they receive real and prolonged assistance from outside'.[34] In other words, they were not ready for independence. The worthy efforts of the Russian proletariat to render 'prolonged assistance' had run into trouble from people who had 'not yet managed to rid their minds of old national grievances'. Among them there was 'a certain national aloofness and the absence of full confidence' in 'measures proceeding from the Russians'. Indeed 'in some of the republics ... this defensive nationalism becomes converted into agressive nationalism'. In other words, there was resistance to rule from Moscow. Wise administrators must take care not to antagonise local nationalists by haughty displays of 'Great-Russian chauvinism'. Wherever possible, 'the organs of the national republics and regions should be staffed mainly with people who know the language, manner of life, habits and customs of the peoples concerned'. In other words, Indirect Rule was to be the preferred method of administration. Meanwhile, missionary work should go vigorously ahead. Party workers were to 'develop a literature based on Marxist principles in the native languages', to 'form advanced Marxist study circles', to 'intensify work among youth', and to 'strengthen the University of the Peoples of the East and its local branches'.[35]

With respect to the potential threat from capitalist Europe, Stalin based the defense of socialism in one country upon an analysis of imperialism which closely conformed to Lenin's original theory. That is, it took for granted that, 'since the beginning of the twentieth century', the need of the developed capitalist powers for external markets and investment opportunities had generated 'inevitable conflicts

34. Josef Stalin, 'National Factors in Party and State Affairs, *Collected Works* V (Moscow, 1953) 190-96.

35. Ibid.

within such states and inevitable wars between them'. 'The law of uneven development in the period of imperialism' would continue to produce 'periodic redivisions of the *already divided world* through military conflicts and catastrophic wars'.[36] The only difference between the pre-war and post-war world was that socialism had been established in the U.S.S.R. It was only to be expected that the capitalists would struggle to regain this territory; they needed it as a field for investment and to extinguish a revolution which inspired the discontented workers in their own nations. Stalin therefore expected that the internecine struggles of the capitalist powers would be punctuated from time to time by attempts to present a united front against the Soviets. He blamed friction between the U.S.S.R. and its immediate neighbours on the clandestine efforts of western capital to provoke the bourgeois nationalist governments of Poland, China, Rumania, Hungary, etc. into attacks which would weaken the ability of socialism to survive in one country.[37] These expectations of the future, based on Lenin's theory of imperialism, were used by Stalin to justify a three-pronged strategy of defense: building up a strong military force at the expense of Soviet citizens' standards of living; maintaining pressure on neighbouring states notwithstanding the Leninist commitment to the rights of small nations; pursuing, in the name of peace, a pragmatic, even Machiavellian foreign policy which looked for advantages wherever they were to be found.

On the role of colonial revolutionaries in the world revolution — the question which divided Lenin and Roy at the Second Congress — Stalin took an ambiguous stance. In 1918 he called the undeveloped countries of the East 'imperialism's reserves'. Without attempting to appraise their precise economic value in prolonging the life of the capitalist system, he claimed that

The imperialists have always looked upon the East as the basis of their prosperity ... That, in fact, explains why, while fighting in Europe and *prating*

36. *Collected Works:* V, 185-86; IX, 105, 111-13; X, 281-82.

37. *Works:* IX, 328-34; X, 293-95; IV, 181-85.

> about the West, the imperialists have never ceased to *think* of China, India, Persia, Egypt and Morocco, because the East was always the real point at issue. It is this that chiefly explains why they so zealously maintain 'law and order' in the countries of the East — without this, imperialism's far rear would not be secure.[38]

Whatever 'far rear' might mean, Stalin deduced from his analysis that 'it is the duty of the Communists to intervene in the growing spontaneous movement in the East and to develop it further, into a conscious struggle against imperialism'. His later pronouncements deliberately blurred the existing class divisions among the peoples of 'the East' in order to justify support for any sort of anti-colonial or anti-Western movement. By 1924, Stalin had attached this policy to the concepts of 'the dictatorship of the proletariat' and 'socialism in one country' through a dubious analogy. Just as the dictatorship of the proletariat in Russia, according to Stalin, amounted to a revolutionary alliance between the proletariat and 'the labouring masses of the non-proletarian classes which are led by the proletariat', so the world revolution required 'a revolutionary alliance, a revolutionary bloc, between the proletariat of the advanced countries and the oppressed peoples of the enslaved colonies'.[39] The Soviet Union would of course, be at the head of the proletarian forces; the 'oppressed peoples' would be whomever Stalin chose to support in the undeveloped world. And he would give most help to those whose activities strengthened the power of 'socialism in one country'.

It is far beyond the scope of this book to describe the astonishing twists and turns of foreign policy which world communism justified on the basis of Stalin's catch-all slogan: how the Comintern forced the Chinese communists into a disastrous alliance with Chiang Kai-shek's Kuomintang, how the South African Party (with Soviet blessing) asked 'Workers of the World to Unite for a White South Africa', how the French communists threw their weight *against*

38. *Works* IV 174-75.

39. *Works* VI 379-82.

independence for the colonies in the hope that the non-European masses would help to bring about the Revolution in France, how Stalin concluded a non-aggression pact with Hitler when Europe was in flames, how the internal colonial policy developed in the U.S.S.R. during the twenties was extended to most of Eastern Europe at the end of World War II. It would be absurd to explain these events as the rational consequences of abstract theories. But the constant appeal to Lenin's theory of imperialism by communist leaders between the World Wars did have an important impact on discussions of theories of imperialism in general. The original meaning of Lenin's theory was preserved in communist analyses of European politics. Outside Europe, however, the Comintern practice of supporting all kinds of anti-colonial movements gave Lenin's pamphlet a huge circulation among people who had no knowledge of the Edwardian context in which complex theories of imperialism were first developed and who had little interest in the politics of Europe or North America. For this big new audience imperialism simply meant empires and spheres of influence. If they were party leaders like Roy in India or Mao in China they ascribed to Lenin the double edged doctrine that the advanced capitalist nations depended for their very survival on keeping their colonies (or 'semi-colonies'), and that therefore liberation movements were indispensable agents in the struggle to establish socialism. If they were non-communist nationalists, they used Lenin's pamphlet to expose the philanthropic pretensions of European empire builders. It showed that colonies had been acquired to serve the needs of European capitalism and were maintained as a source of 'superprofits'. One did not have to be a communist or even a socialist to regard this as a valuable ammunition in a struggle for self-determination.

By the mid-nineteen thirties, anti-colonial nationalists in Asia, Africa and Latin America had taken parts of Lenin's theory as expounded by Comintern agents and attached them to the historical critiques of colonialism elaborated by Leonard Woolf in Britain and by political scientists in the

United States. Combining these disparate elements into a single theory created the hybrid creature which is known to present day historians as 'the economic theory of imperialism'. Hundreds of examples could be cited to show the uses which colonial agitators, nationalists and revolutionaries made of the hybrid theory. But the gist of all of them is embodied in George Padmore's account of how Europe came to rule Africa:

> The conquest of Africa reflects the whole trend of the development of economic imperialism. We saw that in the early centuries when the European powers only wanted to trade with the Africans, they did not attempt to annex their lands. Colonial annexation only arose at a particular historic period in the development of capitalism, namely the nineteenth century, when the Industrial Revolution had sufficiently developed in Western Europe to create a demand for independent sources of raw materials that could not be obtained in the home country, overseas markets for surplus commodities, and, later on, outlets of the investment of surplus capital, where the natural resources and cheap labour guaranteed greater profits than in more developed capitalist countries.
>
> Hand in hand with economic imperialism go military and naval intervention. For in order to acquire colonies and spheres of influence, and afterwards safeguard those interests, the imperialists of the oppressing nations send their armies, navies and air forces into the territories of the oppressed nations to prevent the Natives from driving away the foreign robbers.[40]

The educated eye will recognise at once the elements from which Padmore has constructed his story. From Luxemburg and other Marxist studies he has borrowed the notion that capitalism had to expand to acquire markets, resources and labour. From Hobson and his contemporaries he draws the argument that Europe needed investment outlets for surplus capital. From Leonard Woolf he takes the assumption that imperialism and colonial annexations are synonymous. From Woolf too he takes the assertion that Europe's nineteenth-century scramble for Africa is the classic example of economic imperialism. On the other hand, it is from Angell, Lenin, Luxemburg and other agonised observers of the first global war that Padmore takes the idea

40. *How Britain Rules Africa* (London, 1936) 32-33.

that rivalries for economic advantage lead to militarism and war.

The various elements,however, do not fit together very well. Rosa Luxemburg and Lenin would have vigorously denied that capitalism's need for expansion required colonial annexations, particularly in the nineteenth century. No one spoke of outlets being required for surplus investment capital until most of Africa and the rest of the undeveloped world had been appropriated by western empire builders. That a competition for colonies anywhere outside Europe least of all in Africa, was the principal cause of European militarism and war would have struck all of the pre-war theorists of imperialism as a ludicrous exaggeration. Padmore's sketch of the causes and consequences of Europe's appropriation of Africa is a scarecrow figure, stitched together from ragged bits of theoretical cloth cut from the castoff arguments of earlier eras. Without logical coherence or any solid grounding in historical fact, it is a lifeless thing stuffed with straw. But because it served the present purposes of left and right wing ideologues it would stand for decades to come as a sacred object to be defended by the left, and as a devilish idol to be assaulted by the right. Social scientists of the nineteen forties, fifties and sixties who spoke loosely of 'the theory of capitalist imperialism' or the 'theory of economic imperialism' would have such scarecrow figures in mind rather than the classic theories of Hobson, Conant, Lenin, Hilferding, Luxemburg or Schumpeter.

CHAPTER 11
THE PATRIOTS FIGHT BACK; THE ROUND TABLE TRADITION IN IMPERIAL HISTORIOGRAPHY

To those who administered and believed in Europe's colonial responsibilities the 'theory of economic imperialism' appeared to be more than a straw man. It was a hulking Frankenstein's monster which moved and breathed and could break up empires. Such men generally knew little of the great quarrels which divided communist, socialist and liberal critics of empire. They lumped the critics together as a common enemy. Sir David Petrie, Director of the Intelligence Bureau in British India from 1924 to 1931 took a policeman's view of Soviet theoreticians in his book, *Communism in India 1924-1927*.[1] When Petrie read reports of the second Comintern Congress he perceived no differences of opinion among the delegates. M. N. Roy seemed to him to be the puppet rather than the challenger of Lenin. He believed that the Soviets had inherited from the tsars the ambition of displacing Britain as the ruler of India. Afghanistan had 'received the early attention of M. N. Roy and his Bolshevik masters, probably as marking an important stage on the way to India'. The 'Reality of the Bolshevik Menace' was proved by Zinoviev's statement that '"The Indian Proletarian Mass" must be utilised by us as a reserve and bulwark for the Comintern in Asia'.

Bolshevik operatives were everywhere. They were in Saudi Arabia where 'it would be strangely unlike the Soviet agents' if they failed to utilise the 'unique opportunities' offered by millions of pilgrims streaming to Mecca from India, Malaya, Java and Russia. They were in India itself where an American Professor of Christian Ethics at Union Theological Seminary gave speeches which 'asserted that Communism was not a menace to humanity', 'severely condemned the profit system', and 'betrayed admiration of the Soviet regime in Russia'.

1. (Calcutta, 1972) ed. M. Saha. Originally published in an official edition of 165 copies in 1927. The quotations used in this chapter come from pp. 2-3, 169, 180-181, 186, 203, 232, 234-35, 245-47, 281, 292.

Petrie had learned from 'an authoritative American source' that the Christian professor 'regarded Bolshevik principles as correct and likely to prevail throughout the world', that 'he and The Fabian Club' supported 'a revolutionary and anarchical association', and that he had 'made characteristic extremist statements in support of the anti-foreign student movement in China'. Another agitator whom Petrie believed to be doing the work of the Comintern was the veteran British socialist Tom Mann, who had 'made a very objectionable speech' at a conference in China. Mann had gone so far as to claim 'that there are three hundred and twenty million Indians who are dominated by Great Britain, who are robbed of freedom' and 'whose efforts at 'Liberty are stamped out'. Petrie perceived that the spread of communist propaganda about 'imperialism' had fostered anti-European sentiment even among 'bourgeois elements' who were steadfastly opposed to communist aims. For all these reasons, Petrie feared that the 'germ' of communism was 'bound to multiply, even as that of an infectious disease' unless the government resolved that wherever it appeared 'it should be met and stamped out like the plague'. 'In pursuance of their despicable schemes', 'Moscow's allies in England' had spread their propaganda among Indian students at Oxford. Even the case-hardened veteran of the Punjab Police blanched at this 'particularly odious' attempt 'to debauch these young Indians before they had reached years of discretion'.

Petrie, as it happened, need not have worried about Oxford. The ancient university was quite capable of defending itself against subversive theories of imperialism. This was due in no small part to an extraordinary academic and intellectual legacy left by the empire builders of South Africa. From Cecil Rhodes himself came the Rhodes Trust which looked after Rhodes scholars drawn to Oxford from all over the English-speaking world and which financed other, less well known schemes for strengthening 'Empire sentiment'. From Alfred Beit, Rhodes' old partner in diamond and gold mining, came endowments for South African universities and professorships of history in British universities. Among the trustees of Rhodes' will was Lord Milner, prime mover of British policy in South Africa before and after the Boer War. Milner's South African staff, his so-called 'kindergarten', contributed bright young imperial patriots who formed the nucleus of the Round Table Movement, an organisation dedicated to promoting closer ties between the various parts of the Empire.[2] In the course of time, the Round Table came to include among its affiliates most of the leading historians of the Empire and Commonwealth. Academic members in Britain included: Reginald Coupland (Beit Lecturer and later Beit Professor of History at Oxford); Alfred Zimmern, (Professor of International Relations at Oxford); and Lionel Curtis, (Beit Lecturer at Oxford and a founder of the Institute of International Affairs, London). Among the Canadian Members were: A. L. Burt, (Rhodes Scholar and later Professor of History at the University of Alberta and Minnesota); Vincent Massey, (Lecturer in Modern History at the University of Toronto); G. M. Wrong and George Glazebrook; (both Professors of History at the University of Toronto). George Louis Beer was a correspondent in the United States. W. K. Hancock, another Rhodes Scholar, was a member while serving as Professor of History at Adelaide and later at Birmingham University. South African historians of the Round Table included Eric Walker and W. M. Macmillan.

These men were more than great historians. Like ideal Rhodes Scholars, many of them were also practical men of affairs with first-hand knowledge of government. Curtis moved from Oxford to the Colonial Office as Permanent Under Secretary for Irish Affairs in 1921, George Louis Beer attended the Versailles Peace Conference as the American expert on colonial affairs and later became a member of the Mandates Commission. Massey rose to become Governor General of Canada; Hancock would one day write

2. The movement is described with a rare mixture of sympathy and detachment by John E. Kendle's *The Round Table Movement and Imperial Union* (Toronto, 1975).

constitutions for East Africa. And behind the practically-minded historians stood real statesmen and financiers. Lord Milner and L. S. Amery remained in close contact with the movement they had helped to launch. The Rhodes Trust gave financial support; so did a bevy of peers of the realm and Sir Ernest Oppenheimer, head of the South African conglomerate which succeeded to Rhodes' mining interests. There is no better way to enter into the mental world of the first generation of professional historians of the British Empire than to thumb through the pages of *The Round Table,* monthly journal of the movement to which so many of them belonged.[3] It was a world far removed from American social science, Woolf's Bloomsbury and Stalin's Comintern.

The word imperialism seldom appears in *The Round Table.* Since 1905 at least it had apparently stunk in the nostrils of British and colonial voters. It was associated with greed and grab and the debacle of the Boer War. The programme for which the movement stood — an imperial customs union, military strength and the orderly development of Britain's colonies — had therefore to go under another name.[4] Commonwealth, a robust Elizabethan word with overtones of democracy and shared riches, had the right sort of ring to it and soon became the standard shorthand expression for Round Table goals. The editor wrote in 1912 that 'there can be no doubt that Imperialism in its latest form' (strengthening the Empire to meet the threats posed by 'foreign fleets or hostile combinations') 'corresponds to a dominant ... instinct in the self-governing peoples of the British Empire'.[5] But this was unusual. Generally the word imperialism was used to refer to the designs of Britain's enemies. 'German imperialists' drove America into the World War, — a war of

3. Most articles which appealed in the journal were unsigned. They evince a generally coherent and consistent world view, because, as Kendle notes, 'nothing was published in the quarterly in those early years which met with the profound disapproval of any member' (Ibid 108).

4. *Round Table* I (1910-11) 1-2.

5. *Round Table* III (1912-13) 418-19.

free nations against 'the evils of a military imperialism'.[6] The peace of Brest-Litovsk 'placed the richest parts of Russia under the control of German Imperialists'; the Turks had 'imperialistic aspirations'; 'Japanese imperialism' had no justification.[7] The explanations offered by *Round Table* writers for the menacing activities of Britian's rivals often resemble the classic theories of imperialism concocted by Lenin, Schumpeter and others. Germany challenged British sea-power because in a world already divided up she could not otherwise 'extend beyond the narrow confines of Europe'. Russia and Japan 'each driven by the pressure of necessity claimed the right to expand and grow'. Wars arose from 'the pressure of national growth or development, which can only be satisfied at the expense of other nations'. 'The ruling classes in Germany', an 'oligarchic and aristocratic caste' sought 'the partition of the British Empire' and 'the hegemony of the world' in order 'to divert attention from domestic and external problems, to eclipse the hope of liberty at home with the glamour of ascendency abroad'. There was 'truth in the Bolshevik diagnosis ... of the German Government and the German people'. Prussian militarism rested on the Junkers' 'family tradition and the desire to maintain a grip on the land'.[8]

Round Table writers did not apply this sort of analysis to their own Empire. It was not class, caste or the pressure of economic necessity which had extended Britain's dominion. In the Round Table version of history, the foundations of the overseas empire were laid in the sixteenth and seventeenth centuries when 'England found that she could keep her freedom only by a long series of desperate struggles against the threatening might, first of Spain, and later of France ... To protect herself from subjection to the great continental

6. *Round Table* VII (1916-17) 513; VIII (1917-18) 10.

7. XVIII (1928) 266-67; X (1920) 516; VIII (1918) 740.

8. I (1910-11) 19-20, 116; III (1912-13) 24; II (1911-12) 237; IV (1913-14) 612-15; V (1914-15) 3, 6-7; VII (1916-17) 413-15; VIII (1917-18) 228-29; XII (1921-22) 20-21.

powers England had to keep command of the sea, and it was her sea power which, by enabling her citizens to conduct their enterprises safely all over the world, led to the acquisition of territory in Canada, Australia, South Africa and India'. From those foundations 'the Empire expanded almost of its own accord'. 'Every student of history knows how reluctant British ministries have been to extend the Empire they had to defend'. The reluctant imperialists agreed to further extensions for three recurring reasons. One reason was endemically turbulent frontiers: 'rapine and disorder on the frontier were inconsistent with peace and progress within British territory'; the government 'invariably found that it could prevent the recurrence of anarchy only by annexation'. Another reason was the need to protect strategic lines of communication: 'the only way of preventing hostile powers from occupying strategic positions threatening vital parts of the Empire was to annex them to the British crown'. The third reason was that private citizens, settlers, missionaries and traders who had pushed into new territories, 'found themselves engulfed by the anarchy or tyranny of native states appealed to the might of England to protect them from injustice and oppression'. The 'British Government found that if law and order were to be established it had no option but to step in'. The Empire was not maintained because of profit: 'from the purely material point of view the Empire is a burden rather than a source of gain'. Far from serving as 'a system of outdoor relief for the upper classes' as James Mill and Hobson had charged, 'the few civil service posts, reserved for men who are willing to pass their lives in savage and unhealthy parts' were 'not compensation for the enormous financial strain and the constant risk of war which the duty of preserving a world Empire entails'.[9]

Nevertheless, the Round-Table theorists argued that this empire which had been acquired reluctantly, defensively, and profitlessly could fulfill a great mission in the twentieth century — a mission summed up in the three words liberty,

9. I (1910-11) 12, 13, 43, 232-39, 411.

trusteeship and commonwealth. Round Table writers took for granted that the peculiar genius of the British form of government was the representative principle. The mission of the empire had been to spread that principle of liberty throughout the world. The Round Table did not share the fear of Cobden and Hobson that the extension of British rule to black and yellow peoples imperilled liberty by accustoming administrators to despotic methods of government. Autocratic rule today was but a prelude to self-government tomorrow or the day after. As 'backward' populations demonstrated progress and the capacity to manage their own affairs they would be directed along the path of liberty which Anglo-Saxons had trod before them. In the meantime Britain held their countries as a 'trust' for the benefit of all mankind. It would be irresponsible to give self-government to the Pacific island 'home of primitive barbarism', or to West Africa where 'over-indulgence in sexual thought... stops the full development of the brain', or central Africa where 'the intervention of civilized states' prevented the natives 'from being exploited by rampant capitalism, exploitation and aggression', or India where 'Gandhi and the Mohamedan extremists are seducing or terrorising those who stand for constitutional progress'. All those countries were 'in training to govern themselves' at some indefinite time in the future.[10] A *Round Table* review of Sydney Olivier's *Anatomy of African Misery* and Norman Ley's *Kenya* accused those socialists of introducing 'into the problem of race relations in Africa the terrible hatred and class war which the disciples of Karl Marx have managed to introduce into the problem of industrial relations'. It should be remembered that

> ... some of the noblest pages in the history of Great Britain are those which tell of the protection she has given to backward peoples. The development of the idea of trusteeship during the Warren Hastings trial, the abolition first of the slave trade and later of slavery itself, the establishment of methods of native rule, which had become the standard for the world ... are

10. IX (1918-19) 7, 28-29, 659; XVI (1925-26) 89, 457; XII (1921-22) 248-49.

achievements which ought not to be forgotten or disregarded.[11]

The concept of a Commonwealth not only solved the problem of reconciling liberty with autocracy, it also provided a means of developing the resources of the world for the benefit of all without threatening peace. Defending the gift of new territories to Britain by the Treaty which ended the first World War, the *Round Table* asked misguided 'pacifist propagandists' to consider the plight of 'vast areas of the world's surface devastated, depopulated and racked by misgovernment, crying out for the justice and freedom, the technical adminstrative skill and the material relief which civilised governments are alone in a position to give them'. Another version of the idea was embodied by the African administrator Frederick Lugard in his concept of 'the dual mandate for tropical Africa'. Europe owed Africa good government and development in the tradition of trusteeship.[12] Africa owed Europe a share of its wealth. Putting this idea in an historical perspective, an article on 'The African Labour Problem' pointed out that although the Victorian pioneers of British Africa had not possessed a conscious notion of developing resources, in 1928 'it is the generally accepted creed that the economic future of the Empire lies in the realisation of its untapped riches'.[13] In the past the British Empire had served the cause of peace by girdling the globe with her sea power. In the present the Commonwealth kept the peace of much of the world by reconciling the antagonisms of conflicting nationalisms in a single supra-national forum and maintaining a bulwark against despotic foreign powers. In the future, the *Round Table* argued in numerous articles, the Commonwealth would provide a model for a world 'league of Commonwealths' or

11. XVII (1926-27) 462-63. The weak solution to Kenya's problems offered by the reviewer was 'a gradual transfer of some measure of responsibility to local white communities under proper safeguards for the native, combined with a friendly and confident trusteeship by the Colonial Office'.

12. IX (1918-19) 96. Lugard, *The Dual Mandate in Tropical Africa* (London, 1922).

13. XVIII (1927-28) 498.

even a single world state.[14] Since the most basic cause of war was the division of the world into separate sovereign states, the *Round Table* confidently anticipated the gradual extinction of armed conflicts. A genuine association of nations could also solve the problems arising

> from the relations between advanced and backward, or strong and weak peoples. How are the backward and weak to be protected against exploitation? The answer is that once the nations begin to meet regularly together to discuss their common problems, a code will rapidly grow up, the nucleus of which already exists in the [League of Nations] mandate system. Eventually the question of whether intervention in Shanghai, or Nicaragua or Egypt or other places is legitimate or not will turn on whether such action is designed to establish the domination of one Power over another, or whether it is genuinely intended to protect reasonable rights, life and property, to restore order and so pave the way to a fair solution of the problems involved, and to independent and orderly self-government.[15]

It is easy to be cynical about the Round Table programme. The early left-wing theorists of imperialism would have had no trouble in giving it an economic interpretation. Hobson would note the South African gold and aristocratic backers which sustained the movement. Lenin would point to the emphasis on defense against would-be repartitioners of the globe. Kautsky would recognise the scheme for a league of commonwealths to decide when to intervene in Shanghai or Nicaragua as a project of 'ultra-imperialism'. From almost any point of view the programme appears deliberately calculated to advance the orderly development of twentieth-century capitalism in the face of challenges posed by nationalists and revolutionaries. But *Round Table* writers themselves denied that the promotion of capitalism was their aim. Perhaps because they realised at the very beginning that 'many associate imperialism with the projects of jingoes and capitalists', they were at pains to distance themselves from the profit motive.[16] *Round Table* writers displayed a unremitting hostility to

14. VIII (1917-18) 286; X (1919-20) 17-18; XVIII (1927-28) 498.

15. XVIII (1927-28) 471.

16. I (1910-11) 1-2.

economic interpretations of history. During World War I they argued against Norman Angell's case [as they misunderstood it] that war could be avoided by appealing to the economic self-interest of nations. After the Russian Revolution they cautioned against trying to understand communism as a rational programme instead of seeing it for what it was, 'a shrill reiterated clamour of irrational contradiction'. In the controversy over the colour bar in British Africa they condemned observers who attributed 'to malignant design on the part of individuals or to the ogre called "capitalism" what in the main was a natural outcome of the facts'.[17]

It could not be expected that people who regarded communism as a clamour of irrational contradictions would have much knowledge or understanding of socialist theories of imperialism. *Round Table* writers did, however, gradually become aware that such theories existed and that they could undermine the unfolding programme for the Commonwealth of the future — much as the charge that jingoes and capitalists provoked the Boer War had undermined the popularity of imperialism as a British political slogan after 1902. Round Table correspondents from around the English-speaking world reported the damage done to their cause by the socialists' 'doctrinaire attribution of the [World] war's outbreak to the universal dominion of capitalistic imperialism'. A search for clues to the motivation of the Bolshevik revolutionaries uncovered the thesis of a 1915 socialist conference at Zimmerwald, Switzerland 'that the war was simply a conflict between the capitalists and imperialists of the chief belligerent countries, that the big financiers had sent the proletariat to slaughter in order to grab territory and still further to enrich themselves, that Germany was not specially to blame for the war, no more to blame, at any rate, than England, and that the only way to end the war was for the proletariat of all lands to rise and overthrow its exploiters'.[18]

17. V (1914-15) 137; VIII (1917-18) 276; XVII, 462.

18. VIII (1917-18) 66, 834-35.

It did not occur to the Round Table writers that imperialism meant something different to the Zimmerwald left than it meant to the beneficiaries of the Rhodes Trust. They assumed that colonies and annexations were the sole issue. And when they stumbled across other uses of the word they complained. 'Economic imperialism' was 'a vague but dire phrase'. It was not helpful 'to use that invidious word' to characterise the policy of the United States in Central America. 'Imperialism was a wide and vague enough term to cover almost any programme ... and completely contradictory tendencies were covered by it'.[19]

These objections were not a scholar's quibble. They voiced a fear akin to the fear expressed by the secret policeman in India that communist agitators had invented a propaganda bomb that was getting into more and more of the wrong hands. The 'Bolshevik' theory of imperialism threatened the Round Table programme for a Commonwealth in four direct, practical ways. It threatened the programme of defence and customs union. Labour parties in the white Dominions and in Britain itself were becoming increasingly and vocally resentful of any economic burdens imposed in the name of empire. It threatened the moral underpining of the League of Nations' Mandates system by portraying mandates as selfish empire in a new guise. By extension it accused the concept of 'trusteeship' of serving as a hypocritical disguise for policies of economic exploitation which could no longer be openly justified by appeals to bald self-interest. Finally, the theory as generally expounded between the world wars threatened the orderly capitalist development of undeveloped colonies which was the pre-eminent economic justification of trusteeship. It was an axiom of the Round Table movement that the operations of a market economy would eventually assure the material progress of all the Empire's subject peoples, provided that wise colonial adminstration curbed the excesses of old-fashioned freewheeling laissez-faire capitalism. A theory

19. XVI (1925-26) 749; XVII (1926-27) 309; XVIII (1927-28) 714-15.

which charged that greed built and maintained colonial empires for the purpose of suppressing rather than uplifting native populations struck at the heart of Round Table ideology.

That ideology, if it must be given a label, was liberal, collectivist and capitalist. In its origins it owed much to the late-nineteenth century Cambridge philosopher T. H. Green. Many of its exponents at the turn of the century were happy to gather under the banner 'Liberal Imperialist'.[20] The ideology was, although its exponents never knew it, just the sort of ideology that the early theorists of imperialism — both on the left and right — had anticipated would characterise capitalism in the twentieth century. It accepted that economic individualism was a thing of the past and that the state must take a hand in social welfare.[21] It also accepted that state-supervised monopolies and cartels might be the best form of modern business organisation. It regarded the use of the state power beyond state frontiers to secure economic advantages as an inescapable necessity until effective supra-national institutions existed to regulate the world's political economy. But this was also an ideology which shyly veiled its commitment to capitalism as an economic system. Not for the Round Table the frank avowals of Joe Chamberlain or Rhodes or the Edwardian financial press, that state-regulated capitalism and imperialism were tools for fending off a socialist revolution. The Round Table view was that orderly capitalist development was a means to the goals of peace, freedom and prosperity; it was not a goal in itself. The Bolshevik belief that all great questions of politics could be reduced to conflicts of economic interests was held to be an error. In fact, all theories of economic determinism were said to be erroneous, including the economic theory of imperialism as it was understood in England by the early nineteen thirties.

20. Kendle, *The Round Table Movement,* passim.

21. See, for example, VII (1916-17) 480-81, 713-13; VIII (1917-18) 750-51); IX (1918-19) 114-34, 674; XI (1920-21) 55; XVI (1925-26) 252, 494.

The task of demonstrating with impeccable scholarship that the theory was not confirmed by the historical record was taken up enthusiastically by historians associated with the Round Table movement – old Rhodes Scholars, professors occupying posts named for Rhodes and Beit, academics who occupied the commanding heights of the historical profession on four continents. In 1902 Hobson had voiced the fear that 'Higher education', which 'has never been economically self-supporting' could be subtly corrupted by its 'parasitic' dependence, 'on the private munificence of wealthy persons'. While it would be wrong to charge that the first professional historians to write the history of the British Empire were in any sense 'bought' or 'owned' by the mining magnates and peers of the realm who endowed their universities and supported the Round Table movement, their historiography was directly descended from the ideas of the most powerful imperial enthusiasts of the turn of the century. They were themselves recruited from the ranks of imperial enthusiasts and they, in turn, attracted like-minded students who eventually succeeded to their positions in university life. Outside the academy they supported the ideal of a liberal, multi-racial British Commonwealth as part of a wider family of nations – an idea they vigorously defended against the illiberal alternatives of fascism and communism. The books they wrote retold the story of the growth of the British Empire in essentially the same way it had been told in volume I of *The Round Table*. The Empire was in the first instance the product of strategic necessity. From nodes of settlement planted for strategic reasons frontiers expanded, drawing imperial authority reluctantly after them. That authority was informed by maxims of liberty and trusteeship born in the eighteenth century. Economic development was the consequence rather than the motive for the growth of Empire.

The greatest champion of this version of imperial history against the conflicting versions being propagated by the associates of Leonard Woolf, M. N. Roy and George Padmore was William Keith Hancock. His career exemplifies the qualities of his generation of British imperial historians.[22] Son of an Australian vicar of formidable moral fibre, Hancock grew up with the Australian outback in his blood and the Empire in his house (in the shape of a Missionary Box which the children were supposed to fill several times a year to maintain a little brown boy in Papua). After much hesitation he determined that his own 'calling' was university life rather than Holy Orders and mobilised his rare academic talents as a scholar to win honours at Melbourne University and a Rhodes Scholarship. At Oxford in the early twenties he discovered that among his fellow Rhodes scholars were many other sons of earnest clergymen. He was thrilled to think that the path he had been following 'was little different from the paths they my contemporaries were following in the very different landscapes of Natal, Taranaki or British Columbia'.[23] And he took very seriously what he 'believed to be the intention of the Rhodes Scholarship — that men who were privileged to enjoy them should make an appropriate return of duty performed, each in his own country'.[24] His sense of duty, country and Commonwealth naturally attracted him to the Round Table. As a young Fellow of All Souls College he would frequently leave off his work on the Italian Risorgimento to go down to London for Round Table meetings with founder-member Lionel Curtis. After hours of talk on current politics he would go back to Curtis's flat in Chatham House, headquarters of the Institute of International Affairs which Curtis had helped to found after the World War.[25] In 1926 duty called him back to Australia as

22. See his autobiography, *Country and Calling* (London, 1954). Something of the academic atmosphere fostered by the Round Table is recalled in *Oxford and the Idea of Commonwealth* (London, 1982) edited by Frederick Madden and D. K. Fieldhouse. The essays by Colin Newbury and Deborah Lavin are particularly useful for showing how very gradual was the shift from the evangelical enthusiasm and political ideology exemplified by the early Rhodes Trustees and the first Beit lecturers to the more 'professional' approach characteristic of modern Commonwealth historians at Oxford.

23. Ibid 55.

24. Ibid 80.

25. Ibid 99-100.

Professor of History at the University of Adelaide, a notable nursery of historians. But the quality of his mind, his prodigious appetite for work and the influential friendships he had formed in England made it inevitable that he should one day return to the hub of Empire. In 1933 he accepted a Chair in History in The University of Birmingham. The next year he received a commission from Arnold Toynbee, Director of Studies at Chatham House, to write a general *Survey of British Commonwealth Affairs.*

Hancock entered into this enormous task fully conscious of his moral and intellectual intentions. While he shared the committment to a multi-national, multi-racial Commonwealth which animated most historians of the Round Table, he was concerned that the ideal was currently in danger.[26] Uneven rates of material progress in different parts of the Commonwealth were fueling racial, nationalist and ideological movements hostile to the British connection. 'A policy of economic development and social welfare', he believed 'might do a great deal to iron out the contrasts that impeded inter-racial partnership in the constitutional sphere and thereby frustrate the programme of the Commonwealth'.[27] Hancock's initial study surveyed the political dimensions of the problem but left him unsatisfied in his ambition of charting a course towards a brighter future. He decided to write a companion volume on the economics of the Commonwealth. Aside from the purpose of sorting out strategies for development which would meet the challenge of nationalist critics 'there was besides the challenge of Leninist and Stalinist doctrine; all I had hitherto done with it was to consider its political relevance; but since its basic postulates were economic — an equation of Empire with monopolistic, exploiting capitalism — I could hardly claim to have tested it seriously until I had studied the processes and policies of production and distribution within the area marked red on the

26. Ibid 151.

27. Ibid 163-64.

map'.[28] How much did Hancock know about Leninist and Stalinist doctrine? Not very much, it would appear from the cursory references in his published works. He did not know that the most vigorous early proponents of the theory of investment-powered imperialism had been capitalists. He did not know that the purpose of the first theorists of imperialism had been to predict the future rather than to explain the past. He did not know that the major concern of those theorists had been the causes of militarism and war in the twentieth century rather than the growth of the British Empire. For him the Leninist doctrine of imperialism was the pastiche of reasons for the growth of colonial empires that nationalist propagandists like George Padmore were offering in the nineteen thirties. Hancock *did* know that the word imperialism had been used to describe a bewildering variety of political and economic phenomena. But he regarded this as evidence that theorists of imperialism were woolly-minded, left-wing ideologues rather than serious seekers after the truth.

Hancock never cared for scholars who asserted the primacy of theory. He believed they were at war with life. 'The man who chooses theory may write a valuable monograph on monopolistic competition or the trade cycle in West Africa; but even if his statistics go back a hundred years he will write historical economics, not economic history. The man who chooses life will write history — with theory to support it, one may hope, and perhaps an adjective in front of it — but still history. Historical inquiry has its deepest impulse in the lust for life'.[29] Hancock therefore saw no need to investigate the origins of theories of imperialism. He knew instinctively that they must have been devised by ideologues who when confronted with contrary facts drawn from real life

28. Ibid 167. D. K. Fieldhouse's essay on 'Keith Hancock and Imperial Economic History' in *Oxford and the Idea of Commonwealth,* 144-63, acknowledges the 'normative' purpose of the *Survey* in its comments on African development but does not take up the question of Hancock's explicit challenge to Lenin and Stalin.

29. *Country and Calling,* 212-13.

would say, 'Bother all this life, it confuses my theory'. Hancock believed that he himself used theories as tools rather than dogmas. He did not admit that the theories he chose to employ reflected his own ideological aim of promoting regulated capitalist development to achieve the old Round Table dream of a liberal Commonwealth. To this extent he was less open than David Petrie the Indian secret policeman who banned the promulgation of communist pamphlets on imperialism because they threatened British power. Hancock's announced reason for pursuing 'the investigations to which Lenin and Stalin were goading me' was to set the record straight with impartial, objective scholarship. In the process he would expose the limitations of economic interpretations of history which were by now identified almost completely with the left. (The days when financial journals and capitalists proclaimed the historical necessity of predatory power politics in international relations were long past.)

The result of Hancock's labours is the grand historical overview of the growth of the British Empire which opens his volume on Commonwealth problems of economic policy.[30] It is a splendid piece, well worth reading forty years on. It elegantly expounds in economical, stylish prose, aspects of imperial history which lesser, later minds have belaboured in superfluous learned articles. After a preface in which Hancock proposes that Stalin's propositions about the Empire 'ought to be tested by investigations into fact', he launches a memorable attack on the word imperialism.

A dogmatic word challenges the investigator before he has even begun his work, and tells him to spare his pains. That word is *imperialism*. Many writers use the word as if it contained all the history and politics and economics of all the empires that are and have ever been ... Imperialism is no word for scholars. The emotional echoes which it arouses are too violent and too contradictory. It does not convey a precise meaning ...

The Marxist critics who have adopted this difficult word have managed to hammer it into some sort of consistency, so that it circulates within their

30. *Survey of British Commonwealth Affairs, II, Problems of Economic Policy, Part I* (London, 1940).

> restricted circle as coin which has at least its own definite ring ... They have ... postulated that the economic pressure is the basic thing in history. Imperialism therefore means to them the extension in space of a society whose action is determined by its economic and class structure; it is rooted in exploitation and grows by exploitation.[31]

For the edification of readers wishing to know more about Marxist theories Hancock appended a colleague's essay on what he insisted on calling 'Marxist theories of Empire'. The phrase is revealing. As far as Hancock was concerned, imperialism either meant empires with colonies or it meant nothing. He set out to show that the British Empire had grown through the expansion of a series of overlapping frontiers: a frontier of settlement, a political frontier, a missionary frontier, a frontier of trade, and so forth. Employing the recent research of imperial historians just reaching their prime (many of whom were associated with the Round Table), Hancock convincingly portrayed the growth of empire as far too complex a process to be summed up in a pat, one-cause theory.

As a reply to the recent polemics of dissident African and Indian Nationalists, Hancock's argument scored a few undoubted bullseyes. As a reply to the classic theories of imperialism, Lenin's included, it was almost totally beside the point. It was concerned with the nineteenth rather than the twentieth century. It did not address the question why did the era of free trade give way to an era of protectionism and militarism. It did not touch Schumpeter's problem of explaining the survival of predatory national policies on the Continent in the heyday of capitalism. Hancock did not realise the irony of his choice of Frederick Jackson Turner's concept of moving frontiers as a tool to oppose the theories of his enemies. (By asking what happens when there is no longer any room for frontiers to expand, Turner had helped to inspire the first capitalist theorists of imperialism in America.) When, in the course of discussing the development of the Empire in the twentieth century, Hancock did come across

31. Ibid 1-2.

examples of aggressive imperial thinking, he did not recognise their relevance to theories of imperialism. The report of The Dominions Royal Commission which sat from 1912 to 1917 sounded to Hancock like 'the menacing growl of the besiegers' of other economic blocs in the world economy. The post-war propaganda of the Empire Resources Development Committee which recommended using the wealth of subject colonies in Africa and Asia to pay off the British war debt struck Hancock as a 'farrago of cant and greed'. It 'represented popular economic superstition at its very worst'.[32] But it did not occur to Hancock to investigate to what extent such thinking was typical of British capitalists or to set it down as evidence on Lenin's side. Having convicted Lenin of being a bad historian of the nineteenth century Empire, Hancock set him aside as irrelevant. After the Second World War Hancock would tell students at Cambridge University that Lenin's use of twentieth-century material proved him to be either silly or dishonest:

> what really interests me is Lenin's manner of manoeuvre within the chronology of his own choice. He was faced with a dilemma. When he was discussing economic institutions, he had to choose a late opening date [1898] for the period of imperialism, for he could not put the dominance of industrial combinations earlier than the first decade of the twentieth century, and even this was too early for Great Britain, which, after all, possessed the largest empire in the world. But he had to choose an early opening date for the imperialist period when he was discussing the alleged political consequences of industrial and financial trustification; everybody knew, for example, that the partitioning of The New World was practically completed before the nineteenth century closed. Can the political consequences of an economic process precede the process itself? Lenin sought to escape his dilemma by shuffling his chronogical cards; he produced the early date or the late one in different parts of his book to suit the changing needs of his argument. Perhaps it is naive of me to explain this confusion by a crack in his logic; it may be merely a crack in his honesty.[33]

Here is the crux of the matter. Hancock doesn't trust

32. See also David Killingray, 'The Empire Resources Development Committee and West Africa 1916-20', *Journal of Commonwealth and Imperial History* X (Jan. 1982) 194-210.

33. *Wealth of Colonies* (Cambridge, 1950) 11-12.

Lenin. He doesn't trust him because he knows the Leninists to be the enemies of his own dream of a liberal Commonwealth. Because he doesn't trust him, he is incapable of taking Lenin's words at face value. Instead of seeing that Lenin had something else on his mind in 1917 than the history of the British Empire in the nineteenth century, Hancock chastises him for getting that history wrong. Examining the origins of theories of imperialism at the turn of the century would have spared Hancock much of his pains and revealed that he and Lenin had much in common in their analysis of nineteenth-century imperial expansion. But he was completely uninterested in that sort of research. Uninterested because he was a lover of life and an enemy of abstract theories. Exposing the pretensions of theorising left-wing ideologues was as much the aim of his work as setting the record straight. It was, in fact, a part of his own ideology which he concealed under his guise of objective researcher — the ideology he had absorbed as a Rhodes Scholar in the company of Lionel Curtis and the founders of the Round Table, the ideology of economic development and trusteeship in the service of a free, liberal, multi-national Commonwealth.

That ideology permeated not only his own works but the works of nearly all the imperial and commonwealth historians of his generation in the major universities of Britain and the Dominions. The accounts they gave of the nineteenth-century British Empire fleshed out but did not essentially challenge the story of Empire building which had been told without the apparatus of formal scholarship in early numbers of *The Round Table.* Lesser versions of Hancock's blast against 'Marxist theories of empire' appear explicitly or implicitly in their books and articles. With the rise of their school of historiography the stage was set for a misconceived debate on imperialism to be carried on all around the world.

On one side of the debate stood the straw man called the theory of economic imperialism (or sometimes, the economic theory of imperialism). It was not the theory of the American financial press in 1898-99 that the deployment of military strength overseas was necessary for further economic growth; it was not the theory of Lenin that attempts of developed economies to protect overseas outlets for goods and capital would see a series of twentieth-century wars for the repartition of the globe; it was not the theory of Karl Kautsky that the industrialised powers would settle their differences and combine for the purpose of maintaining an exploitative hegemony over agricultural hinterlands. Nor was it a reasonable facsimile of any of the other theories advanced between 1898 and 1920. It was instead an amalgamation of Leonard Woolf's account of the rise of colonial empires in Africa in the late nineteenth century and the hypothesis of investment capital in search of outlets which was first enunciated in the late eighteen nineties. It identified imperialism with empire building, placed the opening of the imperialist era in 1870, emphasised the centrality of the Scramble for Africa, and attributed the outbreak of World War I in some vague way to tensions over colonies. Around this stuffed effigy were clustered its real and supposed champions — a motley assortment of uneasy, unwitting allies: Bloomsbury socialists, American political scientists, Comintern agents continually restating theory to conform to Stalin's foreign policy, and a host of rebellious nationalists in Asia and Africa.

On the other side of the debate stood a much smaller, more select band of critics. Within the British Commonwealth they were mostly academic historians, many of whom had early contacts with the Round Table movement. They formed something of a self-perpetuating scholarly oligarchy, read the same books, contributed to the same journals, recruited the students who eventually succeeded them. Their studies basically confirmed the picture drawn before academic study of the British Empire had begun, a picture of empire spreading for a variety of reasons. They objected to what they understood to be the theory of economic imperialism for two reasons. First, they quite genuinely believed it to be wildly at variance with known facts. Second, they knew it to be propagated by ideologues opposed to the liberal values they themselves espoused. Belonging to an empirical tradition in historiography, they instinctively distrusted explicit theory and ideology. For this very reason they avoided the close study of development of theories of imperialism in the twentieth century which would have revealed to them that they had entered into a misconceived debate. Moreover, it is doubtful whether they would have welcomed that discovery. Men like W. K. Hancock relished a contest in which it could be decisively demonstrated that the devotees of 'isms' who spoke in the mumbo-jumbo jargon of the new social sciences had distorted reality to suit their political purposes. They wanted to make imperialism a word for scholars. They were delighted to defend the negative side in a debate on the proposition: resolved that European colonial empires were built in order to satisfy the vital needs of the capitalist system.

It would be a continuing source of frustration to the negative side that their opponents refused to come into the hall to debate. The two sides presented their arguments in totally different arenas. The historical indictment of empires and imperialism was shouted in the streets of Canton, Delhi and Jerusalem. It was reprinted in pamphlets put out by the activist agents of labour unions, socialist clubs and the Comintern. The opposing case was expounded in lecture halls and classrooms. Since there were no Leninists among the Rhodes or Beit professors of imperial history, the affirmative case had to be put rhetorically, as Hancock put it in his lectures: 'Here are the statements of Josef Stalin which we venture to test by investigations into fact'. It was a special source of pride to the negative side that they alone showed a willingness to consider all points of view before arriving at a reasoned conclusion. That was the liberal way. They were unaware that they had fixed the terms of debate in accordance with their own concealed ideology. Thus discussions of imperialism continued to be carried on, as they had been carried on since the eighteen nineties, from ideologically predetermined positions. In the heat of debate the participants failed to notice that their definitions and propositions had changed with the passage of time. World War II and the new order it brought to international relations would compound misconceptions and confusions.

CHAPTER 12
HOT WAR, COLD WAR AND DECOLONISATION

When war engulfed the world for the second time in a single generation, it came in a way that lent itself readily to explanation according to the classic Edwardian theories of imperialism. The Axis Powers proclaimed their aim of redrawing the pre-war map of the world which confined them to territories too small to nourish the future growth of their economies. Theirs was a frankly economic imperialism which they justified as a reaction to the economic imperialism of others. The socialist left could point to war as confirmation of long-standing predictions: Lenin's that the twentieth century would see a series of wars for the repartition of the globe; and Rosa Luxemburg's that the victory of the allies in World War I would 'lead to new feverish armaments in all nations – defeated Germany, of course at the head – and would introduce an era of undivided rule for militarism and reaction all over Europe, with a new war as its final goal'. On the eve of the war, Hobson's *Imperialism* appeared in a new edition, and H.N. Brailsford renewed his old argument with Norman Angell over the economic causes of militarism.[1] Taking another approach, the peculiar alliances between the bourgeoisie and militarist remnants of the old aristocracy which characterised the regimes of Germany, Italy and Japan could be held to show that, as Veblen and Schumpeter had suspected, the archaic element in some political economies had not yet entirely succumbed to the rationalising tendencies of modern capital and labour.

However, as the war progressed it became apparent that emerging from the conflagration would be a new world order bearing little resemblance to the projections of any previous theorist. Soviet Russia at first stayed out of the war on the Leninist ground that it was an inter-imperialist struggle, and on the Stalinist ground that the 1940 non-aggression pact with Hitler forestalled the long-feared attack on socialism in one

1. H. Brinton, ed., *Does Capitalism Cause War?* (London, 1935); H.N. Brailsford, *Why Capitalism Means War* (London, 1938).

country by the combined forces of fascism and bourgeois democracy. When Hitler attacked anyway, the Soviets struggled to a costly victory which put their armies in occupation of Eastern Europe where they fostered communist regimes to serve as buffers against any future attack from the West. Exhausted as they were, the Soviets appeared mighty in comparison to the prostrate victor nations of Western Europe. Only they could hope to challenge in any way the colossal power of the United States.

Socialism now existed in more than one country and reinforcements were confidently cxpected from eastern Asia where the war had exposed the fragility of Western colonial power. The success of Mao's Red Army in China suggested that the combination of anti-imperialist nationalism and socialism could stir up peasants better than any slogan since Lenin's 'land, bread, and peace'. In these new days of bi-polar superpower confrontation and Asian revolution there were good reasons to stress the anti-colonial, nationalist elements in Lenin's writings on imperialism and to neglect the older analysis of inter-capitalist competition tending towards perpetual war. This presented the possible danger of a future challenge to the 'leading role' of the Soviet Communist Party like the one which M.N. Roy had posed with his insistence on anti-colonial wars as a necessary pre-condition of world revolution. (Mao Tse-tung did eventually do just this). But for the moment the Soviets had no incentive to combat interpretations of Lenin's *Imperialism* which used imperialism as a synonym for capitalist domination of the undeveloped regions of Asia, Africa and Latin America.

This turn of events was very worrying for the old colonial powers who were struggling to keep a grip on their overseas possessions. Occupied France and Belgium had been cut off from their empires for much of the war. In the Far East the readiness with which some peoples collaborated with the Japanese invaders mocked the pretences of European rulers to be loved by their subjects. It would have been comforting in these circumstances to know that a staunchly anti-communist United States was prepared to stand by her 'traditional' European friends abroad as well as at home. However, at the beginning of the war American intentions were by no means clear. Before Pearl Harbor, the Americans stayed out of the war because a large part of the citizenry believed it to be Europe's quarrel. After the Japanese attack, they entered the war with slogans that recalled the preachy moralism of Woodrow Wilson. As W.K. Hancock characterised British amazement in 1941, John Bull woke one morning to read newspaper headlines which implied that Americans were 'making the liquidation of the British Empire one of their war aims'.[2] Hancock wrote two essentially propagandist wartime tracts intended to convince American doubters that the Commonwealth was really an instrument of freedom rather than oppression. Britain, he told them, had learned her lesson in the American Revolution and built her second empire on liberal principles that made further revolutions unnecessary.[3] Australia and Canada had trod a path which others were destined to follow in the fullness of time.

It is doubtful whether many Americans heard or heeded Hancock's argument, but the outcome of the war directed their thoughts along parallel if not identical lines. At last the self-appointed champions of capitalism and socialism stood face to face in Europe and Asia, towering hugely over the puny bodies of the former Great Powers. Each understood at once that their rivalry overshadowed every other conflict in international relations. As the Soviets moved to gird their flanks with eastern European and Asian satellites, the Americans looked for support to 'the Free World'. This did not mean that they overlooked the sins of European colonialism. Abandoning their pre-war isolationism, they entered into the United Nations with high sounding Wilsonian commitments to the rights of all nations to self-determination. American representatives on Trusteeship

2. W.K. Hancock, *The Modern Map* (Oxford, 1941) 3.

3. Ibid and *Argument of Empire* (Harmondsworth, 1943).

committees usually spoke up for early independence. On the other hand, the Americans increasingly perceived Soviet expansionism as the greatest single threat to national self-determination the world over. They were also aware that communist propaganda portrayed them as the leading exponent of 'capitalist imperialism'. The charge struck them as doubly unfair. In the first place, the Americans did not believe that they practised imperialism as the word was understood in their academies and in the press. They had given up or were in the process of giving up most of the territory they had acquired in the Spanish-American War; their occasional forays of 'dollar diplomacy' into Latin America were acknowledged mistakes which they hoped to correct with a 'good neighbour policy' and Pan-Americanism. In the second place, in view of the Iron Curtain which had descended over eastern Europe it seemed gross hypocrisy and damned villainy for the Soviets to maintain that imperialism was the 'highest stage of capitalism' and therefore something communists could not do.

American scholarship after 1945 reflected the fears and antagonisms of the Cold War. In 1948, E.M. Winslow published the first comprehensive attempt by an American to controvert the classic socialist theories of imperialism.[4] His principal target was the alleged link between capitalism and war, but he cast his net wide enough to include all the common meanings of imperialism. In the course of pursuing the intellectual origins of the left-wing theorists, he, like W.L. Langer before him, came across the first capitalist exponents of imperialism but refused to acknowledge their importance to his subject. He even made a convoluted, unconvincing attempt to show that the theories of the banking expert C.A. Conant had been influenced by Hobson.[5] Bent as he was on discrediting all Marxist and semi-Marxist theories of economic determinism, he was simply not prepared to consider that there might be a right-wing capitalist

4. *Pattern of Imperialism* (New York, 1948).

5. Ibid 104-05.

contribution to the theoretical discussion of imperialism. On the other hand, he lavished praise on Schumpeter for exposing the fallacy of blaming war on capitalism. In so doing Winslow contributed to a growing awareness of Schumpeter's theory among English-speaking scholars. Ignoring the inconvenient fact that Schumpeter wrote essentially within rather than outside the Marxist tradition, they seized triumphantly on his exoneration of capitalism from culpability in the crimes of imperialism.[6] Insofar as, like Winslow, they used Schumpeter as a weapon against socialist explanations of the World Wars, they were on firm ground. But when they attempted to employ his theory against propagandists who blamed capitalism for the growth of colonial empires in the nineteenth century, they made a huge mistake. Not only did Schumpeter pass in silence over the entire course of nineteenth-century colonialism, but he drew a pointed contrast between the anti-imperialist bourgeois democracies (including Britain, Belgium, Holland and the United States) and the pro-imperialist regimes of central and eastern Europe. Schumpeter's theory had nothing whatever to do with nineteenth-century empire building and could only appear to have something to do with it if his words were selectively quoted out of their original context.[7]

Selective quotation was unfortunately a widespread phenomenon in the lower levels of American university teaching in the decades after World War II. One of the most popular tools of instruction in introductory history subjects was 'the problem book' in which extracts from primary and secondary sources were reprinted to point up the salient features of celebrated historical controversies. A number of

6. See Paul Sweezy's introduction to Schumpeter's *Imperialism and Social Classes* (Oxford, 1951). An extreme example of misreadings of Schumpeter is D. G. Kruger, 'Hobson, Lenin and Schumpeter on Imperialism', *Journal of the History of Ideas* XVI (1955) 252-59.

7. Richard Koebner drew attention to Schumpeter's total 'neglect of colonial policy' when he reviewed English translations of *Imperialism* and Rosa Luxemburg's *Accumulation of Capital* for the *Economic History Review*, 2nd ser. IV (1951) 403-06. He thought both publications to be 'not only useless but definitely harmful and misleading.'

American publishers brought out books of this sort on 'the imperialism problem'.[8] All of them had a worthy liberal object. Out of the clash of opposing points of view the truth would emerge. But all the books on the 'imperialism problem' misconceived the issues, quoted documents out of context and led readers by the nose to the conclusion that Hancock had reached before the war: economic theories of imperialism did not fit the facts of nineteenth-century colonial expansion. By presenting a false dichotomy and selectively quoting the classic theorists of imperialism they did more to obscure than to reveal the truth. They misrepresented Schumpeter as an explanator of colonial expansion, Lenin as an historian, and Hobson as the author of the theory of investment-powered imperialism. They directed attention away from Rosa Luxemburg's problem of analysing the expansion of capitalism. Sometimes the ideological purpose was directly related to the Cold War. The preface to Louis L. Snyder's *Imperialism Reader* announces in advance the conclusions which students will reach.

> The great colonial empires of the West are shown as being reduced to a fraction of their former size as the great age of imperialism gradually comes to an end. The final section, Part 10, discusses the new Communist imperialism pouring into the vacuum left by the decline of Western imperialism. While Premier Nikita S. Khrushschev loudly condemns Western colonialism as 'disgraceful, barbarous and savage', and while the Soviet Union sets itself up as the sponsor of 'liberation movements' in Africa and Asia, the U.S.S.R. swallows up whole nations as it builds one of the largest empires in history. We see both the Soviet and Chinese Communist empires as the only major imperial systems which are not liquidating themselves, as others have done, but are still seeking to expand in all directions.[9]

While the Americans were discovering new affinities with the old empire builders, British students of empire were discovering more and more evidence confirming the conclusions Hancock had reached before the war. Richard

8. The earliest of the imperialism problems for students I have seen is in T.C. Mendenhall, B.D. Henning and A.S. Foord, eds., *Quest for a Principle of Authority in Europe 1715 - Present* (New York, 1948) 283-311.

9. (Princeton, 1962) ix.

Koebner, the distinguished Israeli historian, was disturbed by the failure of careful scholarship to combat the overwhelming weight of world opinion 'for which economic imperialism has become an accepted fact'.[10] Viewed from the perspective of his office at the Hebrew University of Jerusalem, the problem had a special urgency. Arab opponents of a Jewish State had taken up the slogans of anti-imperialism as weapons in their struggle. In these circumstances, the identification of 'capitalists' as the secret movers of British foreign policy smacked unmistakeably of anti-semitism. The Nazi holocaust had shown the extremes to which fanatics might be driven by the belief that 'Jewish capitalist conspirators' stood between them and their destiny. Koebner's scholarly contribution to combating this menace was an attempt to sort out the multifarious meanings of imperialism and to trace them to their ultimate origins.

His researches were dilligent but narrow. He assumed from the start that all the meanings of imperialism derived from British sources and that the concept of economic imperialism was established by Hobson. Looking into the speeches of politicians and articles in leading journals, he discovered that British enthusiasm for an aggressive foreign policy with avowed economic objectives flowered suddenly in the late eighteen nineties and wilted with equal suddenness a few years later. Koebner concluded that Hobson had erred by treating the excesses of a very short period as typical of British statesmanship over the course of many decades. These arguments, first published as an article on 'The Concept of Economic Imperialism' in 1949, came very close to placing Hobson in his proper historical context. Koebner was among the first to note that Hobson stood squarely within a radical tradition stemming from Richard Cobden.[11] On the other hand, because he did not read into economic and financial

10. 'The Concept of Economic Imperialism', *Economic History Review*, 2nd ser. II (1949) 5.

11. This is explored more throroughly in P.J. Cain, 'J.A. Hobson, Cobdenism and the Radical Theory of Economic Imperialism, 1898-1914', *Economic History Review*, 2nd ser. XXXI (1978) 565-84.

journals, Koebner underestimated the strength of the movement that Hobson opposed and missed seeing the international literature on the subject which Wilshire, Hilferding and Lenin discovered in other countries. His confident assumption that all theories of imperialism originated in Britain was wrong. And he failed to draw the proper conclusion from his study that historians attempting to test theories of imperialism should direct their attention to the behaviour of statesmen after, rather than before the late eighteen nineties. He therefore did nothing to discourage the younger historians who were eager to test the theories against the record of Victorian colonial expansion.

Restrictions on access to government records less than fifty years old had prevented scholars of the inter-war years from inspecting the official archives. When the doors were at last thrown open the most important historians to bury themselves in the British archives were John Gallagher and Ronald Robinson, researchers of comsummate dexterity whose published results were considered by the bulk of the historical profession as squashing for good the theory of economic imperialism.

It was not evident that this would be their mission when they first attracted widespread attention in 1953 with an article on 'The Imperialism of Free Trade'.[12] In that paper they challenged the notion of 1870 as a watershed in British imperial history. They identified industrialisation and commercial development as the underlying engines of British expansion. Victorian statesmen, they observed, regarded economic expansion with satisfaction and showed themselves willing on numerous occasions to use the power of the state to support it; hesitancy to undertake vast territorial annexations should not be taken as evidence that they opposed imperialism. The 'imperialism of free trade' used British power to support the growth of an 'informal empire' of British trade, investment and influence. This conclusion was, although Robinson and Gallagher did not seem to notice it,

12. *Economic History Review*, 2nd. ser. VI, 1-15.

remarkably similar to the conclusions reached fifty years earlier by Karl Kautsky and Rosa Luxemburg. But their further researches took them away from the analysis of the role of state action in the expansion of capitalism and back to Hancock's problem of the expansion of 'formal empire'.

In *Africa and the Victorians* they surveyed the archival record of British expansion in the last two decades of the nineteenth century and arrived at a categorical conclusion.

> The British colonies and protectorates in Africa had not been claimed originally because they were needed as colonial estates. Rather, they had been claimed for strategic reasons, and they had to be developed as colonial estates to pay the costs of their administration ... As an explanation of European rule in tropical Africa, the theory of economic imperialism puts the trade before the flag, the capital before the conquest, the cart before the horse.[13]

What exactly the theory of economic imperialism was they did not say (a footnote in an early chapter refers vaguely to Hobson, Lenin and Luxemburg). They assumed that readers knew what it was and that the appropriate place to meet and challenge it was in the archival records of the Scramble for Africa. What they met and defeated, however, was the straw-stuffed, stitched-up version developed during the inter-war years. Their failure to discover any important commercial or investment interest pushing for territorial annexations before 1895 does not undermine any of the conclusions reached by the Edwardian theorists of imperialism. The irrelevance of territorial ownership to the growth of trade had been one of their premises. No one had suggested surplus investment capital as a promoter of aggressive foreign policies before 1895. Furthermore, Robinson and Gallagher neglected to investigate the economic interests other than traders and investors which Hobson had singled out as the principal benefactors of empire building in the Victorian era: the army and navy, government contractors, railway builders, engineers, shippers, etc. (Hobson had refused to take statements of concern about strategic interests at face value. He suggested that the military

13. *Africa and the Victorians* (New York, 1961) 409.

and Foreign Office experts who delivered them had vested interests which tainted their judgment).

Nevertheless, Robinson and Gallagher's work was greeted enthusiastically by a large section of the academic community obviously eager for fresh evidence to discredit socialist critics of imperialism. Nearly as enthusiastic was the uncritical reception accorded to an article by D.K. Fieldhouse entitled 'Imperialism: An Historiographical Revision' which appeared in the prestigious *Economic History Review* in 1961. Revision was an odd word for Fieldhouse to choose. Beit Fellow in Commonwealth History at Oxford (he later became Beit Professor at Cambridge), he wrote in a tradition which stretched back to Lionel Curtis and the *Round Table*. The argument he proposed was a shortened version of the arguments W. K. Hancock had been making since the nineteen thirties. It represented orthodoxy rather than revision in British Universities. Fieldhouse put simply, even crudely that what he called 'the Hobson-Lenin thesis' did not fit the facts of imperial expansion. Ignoring the large differences between Hobson and Lenin as well as Lenin's clear statement that the era of imperialist began not earlier than 1898, Fieldhouse accused 'Hobson-Lenin' of 'sleight of hand' in attributing annexations occuring in the period 1870-1900 to monopoly capitalism and surplus investment capital which did not appear until the end of that period.[14] He pointed to the neglible percentage of British capital flowing to the new colonies, ignoring the fact that Hobson both knew and said that most investment went elsewhere. After disposing of 'Hobson-Lenin', Fieldhouse proposed his own explanation for late-Victorian colonialism. It was that after 1870 'Europe was again an armed camp' and competing military Powers strove irrationally to win points in the arms race by reaching for extra territory.

Nothing could be more ironic. Fieldhouse proposed as

14. Hancock's rehashers have not shown much imagination in their metaphors. Hancock accused Lenin of 'shuffling his chronological cards'. Fieldhouse accuses Lenin of 'sleight of hand'. L. Gann and P. Duignan accuse Hobson of 'intellectual jugglery', *Burden of Empire* (New York, 1967) 41.

an *explanation* of imperialism the very rising tide of militarism which Lenin (and Schumpeter and Luxemburg) had seen as the phenomenon which required explaining. It amounted to saying that capitalist states had embarked upon an arms race because they had become militaristic. But, because it said 'what oft was thought but ne'er so well expressed' in 1961, it soon found its way into the anthologies and 'problem books' on imperialism which the American academic publishing industry was producing at an unprecendented rate. American and British scholarship had moved much closer together since Hancock worried that the Americans were 'making the liquidation of the British Empire one of their war aims'. At the same time the English-speaking academics were making contact with francophone researchers working along similar lines. The researches of Jean Stengers on the origins of Belgian colonialism and Henri Brunschwig on the foundations of the French empire seemed particularly helpful.[15] (Brunschwig contended that the late nineteenth-century French enthusiasts who talked loudest about the economic prospects of empire were really motivated by a quest for prestige).

Although historians working in different countries differed on details, they were united in their rejection of the theory of economic imperialism — very much as the members of the Atlantic alliance stood united against communist attempts to gain ground in the newly independent 'Third World', however much they might differ on the Suez crisis or nuclear deterrents. They accepted all the postulates of Hancock except his insistence that 'imperialism is no word for scholars'. On the contrary, new categories of definition were elaborated to describe special historical situations. 'Informal imperialism' became entrenched as a phrase to describe domination, political or economic, without annexations or protectorates. 'Sub-imperialism' was used to describe

15. H. Brunschwig, *French Colonialism 1871-1914 : Myths and Realities* (New York, 1966), originally published as *Mythes et realites de l'imperialism francais 1871-1914* (Paris, 1960). J. Stengers, *Combien le Congo a-t-il coute a la Belgique?* (Brussels, 1957); *Belgique et Congo; l'elaboration de la charte Coloniale* (Brussels, 1963).

outward expansion from established colonies such as South Africa or Australia. 'Reactive imperialism' was coined to describe the picture painted by Robinson and Gallagher of Britain reluctantly expanding to cope with threats to strategic interests caused by rising nationalisms. These refinements of definition, which dealt exclusively with colonial and extra-European questions, signalled that the Edwardian use of imperialism to designate all foreign exercises of state power in pursuit of the presumed welfare of a single nation had been quite forgotten in the universities.

The appearance of neo-Marxist theories after World War II

While postwar liberal and conservative historians worked to impugn the classic theories of imperialism, there was a relative dearth of theorising on the radical left. As the great European colonial empires fell apart questions of imperialism temporarily lost interest for anti-colonial propagandists. In some quarters there were expectations similar to those harboured by M.N. Roy in the early twenties, that the end of empire would precipitate the downfall of capitalism by closing off sources of profit. There were also rosy predictions of better times for the impoverished masses of underdeveloped countries. One radical recalling those days of hope remembers that 'it was thought that all that was needful was the removal of the imperial yoke and all good things would follow. This was a plausible view, for Hobson and, following him, Lenin, had taught us that the imperial powers were drawing great wealth from their colonial empires. Once this process were ended, this wealth would surely be freed for the betterment of those from whose land and labours it was drawn'.[16] Whether Hobson and Lenin had really said such things was of little concern to the optimists. They awaited results.

Meanwhile, another group of Marxists employed concepts and theories of imperialism to explain the behaviour

16. Guy Routh. 'Development Paths in Tanzania', in Damachi, Routh and Ali Taha, *Development Paths in Africa and China* (London, 1976) 10.

of nations during the Cold War. Although they were few in number, in many ways they represented the purist line of descent from the Edwardian theorists. They were not narrowly concerned with colonies or territorial empires. They were concerned with why wars and armaments persisted, how the possessors of capital influenced the actions of governments, why some countries developed and others stagnated. Americans were surprisingly prominent in this endeavour at a time when hostility to Marxism in all its forms permeated the United States. Paul M. Sweezy, who had studied under Schumpeter at Harvard in the thirties and who managed a remarkable career as a Marxist scholar outside academia, produced a series of iconoclastic writings on American foreign policy. Sweezy's analysis prefigured (and in some cases inspired) many of the arguments popularised by 'anti-Vietnam' radicals in the late sixties. However, at the time he first expressed them, his opinions were so far outside the mainstream of American thought as to seem downright eccentric. While American conservatives were denouncing the Marshall Plan and Point Four programmes as 'pinko give-away schemes', Sweezy characterised all foreign aid as 'a support for American imperialism and a stimulant to its further development'. In his view, the object of aid to prostrate Europe was to preserve it within the capitalist system. The object of aid elsewhere was 'pretty clearly the encouragement and protection of American foreign investment, not the balanced development of backward countries'.

Sweezy was aware that his conception of imperialism differed greatly from the common understanding of the term. He explained that Hilferding and Lenin had broadened Hobson's notion of imperialism 'to take in the entire politico-economic system' of which colonialism 'was merely one part'. He then went on to adapt Lenin to current conditions. The aim of modern imperialism was not merely to ensure outlets. It was to turn 'the backward countries into economic appendages of the advanced countries, favouring the growth of those kinds of economic activity which complemented the advanced economies and blocking the growth of those kinds of activity which might compete with the advanced economies'.[17] This analysis shifted attention away from Lenin's explanation of struggles to repartition the globe. It pioneered a critique of American foreign aid and investment which would became increasingly popular during the next three decades. Sweezy received valuable support for his analysis in 1957 when his Monthly Review Press published *The Political Economy of Growth* by Paul A. Baran. An anti-Stalinist eastern-European scholar who migrated to the United States in 1939, Baran stuck close to Lenin's conceptual framework but moved away from Lenin in his treatment of the world's undeveloped economies. He was particularly concerned to show that the so-called backward countries were prevented from embarking on the road to balanced development by the workings of the capitalist system in advanced countries. From that time until his death in 1964, Baran collaborated so closely with Sweezy that their names became inextricably linked as the twin pillars of the American Marxist challenge to economic orthodoxy.[18]

In marked contrast to the mainstream economists who predicted that infusions of capital would eventually enable all underdeveloped countries to achieve self-sustaining growth, Sweezy and Baran argued that the effect of investment, particularly American investment, would be to ensure that underdeveloped countries stayed underdeveloped. This conception would later be called 'the development of

17. 'A Marxist View of Imperialism', *Monthly Review* (March, 1953).

18. Paul A. Baran, *The Political Economy of Growth* (New York, 1957). See also: P. M. Sweezy and L. Huberman, eds., *Paul Baran: A Collective Portrait* (New York, 1965), P. Baran and P. M. Sweezy, *Monopoly Capital* (New York, 1968); and P. Baran, *The Longer View* (New York, 1969). The hostility which greeted the publication of *The Political Economy of Growth* was typical of the time. One reviewer called it a 'straight Stalinist tract, unrelieved by humor, originality, new facts, close reasoning, ideological deviation or interest of any sort'. Another called it 'a predictable piece of Marxist orthodoxy, giving the characteristic impression of having been written under dictation from a public address system', quoted in the valuable introduction by R. B. Sutcliffe to the second edition (Harmondsworth, 1973).

underdevelopment'. Although, it claimed descent from Lenin, it actually deviated from Lenin's analysis in two vital respects. First, it postulated a form of imperialism which could exist without state assistance. Foreign aid programmes were state actions but private investment activities were not. The writings of Sweezy and his followers helped to spread the belief that economic imperialism constituted a special form of imperialism which did not require government help. In the second place, Sweezy and Baran deviated from early Marxist thought by de-emphasising the progressive, dynamising impact of capitalism in undeveloped parts of the world. The capitalist system is portrayed as an obstacle rather than an impetus to development. As Anthony Brewer cogently remarks, 'Marxists came to argue a position almost diametrically opposed to that of the classics. Where it had been argued that capitalist development had to come first to create the *possibility* of a socialist revolution, it was now argued that the absence of capitalist development made socialist revolution necessary'.[19]

Radical explanations of war derived from classic theories of imperialism also shifted ground to adjust to new circumstances. With the defeat of the Axis Powers in 1945, warfare among developed capitalist nation-states abruptly ended. The old quarrel between Lenin and Kautsky seemed to have been settled in Kautsky's favour. This result went largely unnoticed by the radical left, partly because the Nazis obliterated most of Kautsky's supporters and partly because it could be argued on Leninist lines that the aggressive energies of the capitalist nations had been deflected towards combating the menace of revolutionary socialist states. As Sweezy put it, at the end of World War II, 'the United States emerged as the undisputed economic and political leader — if not boss — of all the advanced and most of the backward countries outside the Sino-Soviet orbit'.[20] Her alleged aims were to fill the vacuum left by the retreating colonial powers, to resist all

19. *Marxist Theories of Imperialism* (London, 1980) 286.

20. 'A Marxist View of Imperialism'.

revolutionary movements aiming to withdraw areas of the world economy from the capitalist system, and to channel surplus capital into armaments rather than domestic reform. The driving force behind all these projects was said to be the old Adam of expansive capitalism. It followed that the United States was to blame for the Cold War.

This assertion seemed as astonishing in the nineteen fifties as the proposition that foreign aid was the tool of capitalist conspirators. The American right despised the statecraft of Roosevelt and Truman for failing to stop communist expansion. It was obsessed with ferreting out the State Department traitors who had 'lost' China and Eastern Europe. That American diplomacy had in reality been engaged in an anti-communist crusade on behalf of monopoly capital was quite unbelievable. Even more remarkable, the Marxist historian who set out to prove that case was a graduate of the United States Naval Academy at Annapolis. When William Appleman Williams and his talented group of students began to pursue this line of research at the University of Wisconsin they had the field virtually to themselves. So unique was their approach that they had something new to say about every aspect of American diplomatic history even when important archives (the recent American and the whole of the Soviet archives) lay beyond their reach. Their task was revision in the truest sense — looking again at well-known materials and showing them in a new light. In 1959, Williams brought together the results of his most creative period of research in a book, *The Tragedy of American Diplomacy.*[21] It stood twentieth-century American history on its head. The 'Open Door' was not portrayed as the characteristic expression of American anti-imperialism, it was seen as the imperialists' preferred weapon. As makers of foreign policy, Woodrow Wilson and F.D.R. were the capitalists' best friends. Senator Borah and other so-called 'isolationists' were not seen as small-minded reactionaries, but as misunderstood heroes who had struggled vainly to turn

21. (New York, 1959), especially, 15, 66, 79, 178-79.

the tide of open-door imperialism. And, it was asserted, throughout the period 1946-57 when the United States held a decisive advantage in military strength she stubbornly refused to negotiate with the Soviets, thereby throwing away a unique opportunity to set the world on the path towards peace and disarmament.

Some of these through-the-looking-glass inversions of recent American history remain unprovable because the archival record against which they might be tested is inaccessible. Some are salutory reminders of forgotten debates. One of Williams' students, Walter LaFeber, brought to light the influential fulminations of Brooks Adams and related them to the main currents of American thought at the turn of the century. Another student, Martin Sklar, rediscovered C.A. Conant and other American originators of the capitalist theory of imperialism and traced their influence on State Department policy making.[22] But the radical revisionists might well have remained an obscure tributary of the broad river of American historiography had not the Vietnam War suddenly turned it into a flash flood in the middle sixties. Under John F. Kennedy the confidence of America in her ability to intervene for good in the affairs of almost every other nation on earth reached an unprecedented height. A few short months of military escalation in 1965 converted a legion of idealist youth from belief in the righteousness of 'the imperial presidency' to a passionate belief in most of the uncomfortable tenets of the revisionist school of Cold War history.

The Vietnam War brought together two tendencies in radical thinking about imperialism which had been diverging since the first World War, i.e. explaining why war happens in the modern world, and explaining why tropical countries remain poor in relation to Europe and North America. Radicals proposed imperialism as a comprehensive explanation of why rich, developed America was making war

22. Sklar, whose energies were later diverted into active politics, still intends to put his conclusions into book form.

on poor, underdeveloped Vietnam. It is beyond the scope of this investigation to burrow through the mountain of anti-war literature generated by the conflict. Viewed from a distance it is clear that the critics represented broad tendencies analogous to the positions staked out by opponents of militarism before the first World War. Some resembled Norman Angell, regarding the Vietnam War as a mistake which could be corrected by a change of political leadership. Others resembled Brailsford, citing structural defects in the capitalist system as the fundamental causes of American aggression. Anti-war rallies and university 'teach-ins' gave the latter groups a public prominence which they had not enjoyed for decades. Sweezy's Monthly Review Press now found a vastly enlarged readership for publications such as Harry Magdoff's *The Age of Imperialism.*

Working within the basic framework established by Sweezy and Baran, Magdoff explained that since Lenin's day imperialism had developed several 'distinctly new features' which had not been anticipated by the classic Marxist theoreticians.[23] In place of struggles among capitalist nation-states for the repartition of the globe, there was 'a concerted effort by the U.S.-led Western bloc to reconquer that part of the world which had opted out of the imperialist system and to prevent others from leaving the imperialism network'. This struggle was partly concerned with preserving outlets for investment, but of much more immediate importance were markets for goods and sources of 'strategic raw materials'. American soldiers were said to be in southeast Asia for the dual purpose of halting the expansion of the socialist domain and preserving access to specific raw materials. Within the borders of the capitalist domain, Magdoff argued, domination of developed countries over undeveloped countries was no longer achieved through colonial rule. It was achieved through the instrumentality of gigantic trans-national firms (mostly run by Americans) which required little assistance from the armed state beyond

23. *The Age of Imperialism* (New York, 1969).

the provision of certain kinds of so-called 'foreign aid'. This kind of analysis served the immediate needs of a section of the American anti-war movement but it was bound to raise questions among the growing numbers of academics who were re-examining the concept of imperialism. What was the common denominator which could link Magdoff's analysis to Lenin's apocalyptic visions of capitalism in its final, dying stage or to the historians who continued to use imperialism as a synonym for colonial empires?

When the anti-war movement brought radical notions of imperialism into university classrooms, the left acquired an unprecedented awareness of conservative and liberal historiography on empire. Leonard Woolf, the Round Table historians, the Comintern, and the anti-colonial nationalists of the nineteen thirties had inhabited separate intellectual worlds which seldom impinged on each other. Academic radicals who were relearning the use of the word imperialism in the nineteen sixties soon became aware that one school of historians believed that 'the theory of economic imperialism' had been thoroughly discredited by decades of careful research. This discovery was made simultaneously on several continents because the radical upsurge of the late sixties was not just an American phenomenon. It was an international affair which went under a number of names : the New Left, the anti-war movement, the anti-Vietnam movement, the student movement, or simply The Movement. An interesting attempt to bring together diverse schools of thought on the subject of imperialism was made by Roger Owen and Bob Sutcliffe at an Oxford conference in 1969. One of the participants, Michael Barratt Brown, noted as a sign of the times that whereas in the early sixties only four social scientists had responded to an invitation to discuss current problems of imperialism, on this occasion more than a hundred gathered at Oxford.[24]

Ronald Robinson was there to speak up for orthodox historians of the British Empire. Harry Magdoff came from

24. M. Barratt Brown, *The Economics of Imperialism* (Harmondsworth, 1974) 17.

America to explain 'imperialism without colonies' in the nineteen sixties, Jean Stengers from Belgium to explain why Leopold acquired the Congo in the eighteen eighties. Tom Kemp stressed that, strictly speaking, Marxist theories of imperialism concerned the operations of world capitalism after 1900, but other Marxists insisted on talking about the nineteenth and even earlier centuries. Judging from the published results of the seminar, there was no meeting of the assembled minds.[25] One of the convenors concluded that in many ways 'it failed' because conflicting understandings of the word imperialism were not resolved by discussion. By and large the Marxists seem to have derived most benefit from the conference. Sutcliffe believed that it had served the useful purpose of separating theories of imperialism that concerned the workings of capitalism as a world system in the twentieth century from theories that were narrowly concerned with colonialism. But his division of theorists into these two camps is arbitrary and unsupported by references. Lenin, Hilferding and Luxemburg are placed in the first category; Hobson, Brailsford and Kautsky, in the second.[26] It is not difficult to see why this and other mistakes were made by participants in the seminar. Everyone treated theories as an abstract writings miraculously free from anchorages in space and time. No one tried to locate the classic theories in their concrete historical context. Attention was drawn to different meanings of the word imperialism but no effort was made to discover how these various meanings had originated. As a result, no one saw that the backdrop to socialist theories of imperialism was a set of capitalist theories of imperialism. Almost no one made the vital distinction between Marxist theories like Luxemburg's which sought to explain the process by which capitalism expanded as an economic system, and theories like Lenin's which sought to explain and to predict the political consequences of expansion. Both were lumped together as the

25. R. Owen and B. Sutcliffe, *Studies in the Theory of Imperialism* (London, 1972).

26. Ibid 313, 320-21. Sutcliffe does serious injustices to Hobson and Kautsky through his eagerness to defend Lenin.

Marxist theory of imperialism. No explanation of how Lenin came to distinguish twentieth-century imperialism from nineteenth-century colonialism was either given or attempted.

Yet even to read Lenin carefully enough to understand his subject represented a considerable step forward from the cavalier generalisations of the nineteen fifties. Sooner or later an imperial historian of the *Round Table* tradition was bound to do the same thing. Eric Stokes of Cambridge University appears to have been the first to do it. His article 'Late Nineteenth-Century Colonial Expansion and the Attack on the Theory of Economic Imperialism : A Case of Mistaken Identity?' appeared in 1969 and agreed in most essentials with the exposition of Lenin's theory which the Marxist Tom Kemp had written not long before.[27] Stokes took a close look at Hilferding, Bukharin and Lenin and found them to be basically unconcerned with Victorian colonial expansion. (He contrasted their arguments with those of Hobson, Kautsky and Luxemburg whom he wrongly believed had confined their attention to colonialism). Hancock, Fieldhouse and other earlier writers had, he concluded, mistakenly attributed to Lenin the argument that suplus capital in search of outlets was the driving force behind British and French empire building. Stokes' persuasive article ought to have caused all historians of the orthodox tradition to reconsider their rejection of Marxist theories for alleged failure to 'fit the facts'. But most of them ignored Stokes and doggedly

27. Stokes' article appears in *Historical Journal* XII (1969) 285-301. Tom Kemp's *Theories of Imperialism* (London, 1967) is not as clear in its restriction of Lenin's theory to twentieth-century conditions as his subsequent paper for Owen and Sutcliffe's symposium. But the book deserves an enduring place among treatises on theories of imperialism. It was the first Marxist work to protest against communist distortions of Lenin's theory, the first to rehabilitate Rosa Luxemburg, the first to notice Veblen and the first to engage historians of the Round Table tradition on their own ground. Like Barratt Brown's *Economics of Imperialism* and Brewer's *Marxist Theories of Imperialism*, it is written from the perspective of the economist rather than the historian and differs accordingly from the present work.

reiterated the hoary arguments.[28]

Marxist writers did not present a united front in the face of this continuing attack from the right. Some followed Kemp in regarding the attack as an ignorant misconstruing of Lenin's work. They advertised their intention of using the word to refer to 'the capitalist system as a whole' in the era of 'monopoly capitalism' which commences at the very end of the nineteenth century and persists to this day.[29] For them, imperialism was not a phenomenon to be explained but the setting in which the vital force of monopoly capitalism effected basic social, economic and political transformations. While paying fulsome tribute to Lenin as the pre-eminent Marxist theorist of imperialism, they ignored or played down the roles played by surplus capital, big banks, and intercapitalist warfare in Lenin's characterisation of the imperialist era. Other Marxists took quite a different tack and took up the challenge thrown down by establishment historians; they set out to prove that empire building after 1870 *did* occur because of economic pressures within European capitalism.[30] Still others defended themselves

28. Thus Benjamin Cohen wrote concerning 'Classical Imperialism' that 'the principal prize in the struggle was Africa', *The Question of Imperialism* (New York, 1974) 30; and A.J.P. Taylor wrote in 1979 that 'imperialism has disappeared without the social revolution that Lenin postulated', 'From Left to Right', *The Observer* 22 Jan. 1979.

29. Owen and Sutcliffe, *Studies* 22, 322. See also Ernest Mandel, 'The Driving Force of Imperialism in Our Era', in *Spheres of Influence in the Age of Imperialism*, Bertrand Russell Peace Foundation (Nottingham, 1972) especially 90-91.

30. See,for example, R.D. Wolff, *The Economics of Imperialism* (New Haven, 1974) 1-29, and Hans Ulrich Wehler, *Bismarck und der Imperialismus* (Cologne, 1969). It is important not to confuse this unpromising line of research with straight-forward studies of economic reasons for colonial expansion. The Edwardian theorists chose 1870 as a watershed because of its significance in German history, not because it represented any special divide in the expansion of colonial empires. It may be possible through dilligent research to show that 1870 was some sort of watershed for colonialism, but it must be recognised that this is a new hypothesis, quite distinct from classic theories of imperialism. Much valuable research of quite a different sort has recently been done on economic motives for colonial expansion in the Victorian era, beginning with D. C. M. Platt, 'Economic Factors in British Policy during the "New Imperialism"', *Past and Present* XXXIX (April, 1968) 120-38. The direction of recent British work is indicated by W.G. Hynes, *The Economics of Empire : Africa and and New Imperialism 1870-1895* (London, 1979) and P. J. Cain, *Economic Foundations of British Overseas Expansion* (London, 1980).

against the charge that they adherred to a 'monocausal' explanation of colonial expansion by denying that Lenin or any other important theorist had proposed such an explanation. Magdoff pointed out 'that even though Marxists stress the expansionist imperatives of capitalism, it does not follow that they hold to the theme that every instance of territorical aggrandisement is impelled by immediate economic interests'.[31] Walter Rodney, one of the very few genuine scholar-revolutionaries of the nineteen seventies, recognised that 'most bourgeois writers on the partition of Africa make snide remarks on the Leninist explanation of imperialism'. Because they had 'already established a near monopoly of what is written on the partition', Rodney undertook to dispel the 'common misconceptions'. He observed that Lenin was perfectly aware 'that the French are hung up on prestige', that 'changes take place in the so-called balance of power', that 'Western Europe invested far more in Eastern Europe, the United States, Latin America and Asia' than it did in Africa or other colonised areas of the tropics, and that racism 'as a part of the capitalist superstructure' impelled Europeans to make annexations of territories already enmeshed in the international capitalist system.[32]

Rodney was not willing, however, to follow Stokes and Kemp in limiting the application of Lenin's theory to twentieth-century international relations. He clung to the word imperialism as an umbrella term to cover all the ways in which Europe had dominated the development of other continents since the Renaissance. He viewed capitalism as a predatory system whose expansion had been a constant factor during the last four centuries but whose forms and techniques for extending its domain had changed many times. Rodney

31. Harry Magdoff, *Imperialism : From the Colonial Age to the Present* (New York, 1978) 7-9. He quotes Sweezy's important statement of 1942: 'Finally, we must not forget considerations of a strategic nature. An empire must be defensible from a military standpoint, and this broadly implies the need for well-placed land and sea bases, lines of communication and so forth.

32. 'The Imperialist Partition of Africa' in *Lenin Today*, ed., P.M. Sweezy and H. Magdoff (New York, 1970) 103-14.

was just one of a large number of scholars who were pursuing this approach in the early nineteen seventies. They were then commonly known as theorists of neo-colonialism or underdevelopment.

These popular new theories derived from two main sources. One was the concept of neo-colonialism which had been developed by continental Marxists to account for the disappointing failure of most newly independent countries to make socialist revolutions and to enter an era of dynamic, self-sustaining growth.[33] By the early sixties, neo-colonialism had been taken up as a catch-cry by leaders of new nations. It served both as a vent for their frustrations and as an excuse for their own failure to deliver to the mass of their fellow citizens the comforts which they enjoyed as successors to the departed colonialists. At the academic level, the concept of neo-colonialism particularly appealed to left-wing scholars who had misunderstood the classic theorists as postulating that political control over undeveloped countries was essential for the .continued functioning of developed capitalist economies. As a French Marxist observed, that notion had 'been put to severe trial recently. The huge colonial empires, which had taken centuries to build, broke up in a few years without proportionate violence and without any marked impoverishment of the great imperial parent states or any reduction in their capacity to exploit the rest of the world. The concepts of neo-colonialism and neo-imperialism ... were devised for argument's sake, in the face of an unexpected situation ... '[34]

Key premises of most concepts of neo-colonialism were : 1) that during the period of colonial rule the economies of underdeveloped countries had been 'locked into' the global

33. **Barratt Brown,** *Economics of Imperialism* 256; Ernest Mandel, 'After Imperialism', *New Left Review* XXV (1964) 17. Bill Warren in *Imperialism: Pioneer of Capitalism* (London, 1980) blames Lenin for first departing from orthodox Marxist views. Brewer in *Marxist Theories of Imperialism*, op. cit. 137-57, more correctly pinpoints Baran as the starting point for new explanations.

34. Arghiri Emmanuel, 'White-Settler Colonialism and the Myth of Investment Imperialism', *New Left Review* LXXIII (1972) 35.

capitalist system by bonds that made continued political control unnecessary and which could only be broken by the most strenuous efforts to leave the capitalist sphere; 2) that genuinely revolutionary leaders of ex-colonial countries had been displaced by a privileged strata of bureaucrats who mouthed socialist slogans while cooperating with capitalist agencies of aid, trade and investment; and 3) that a 'comprador class' of local capitalists had sprung up, acting as agents for large overseas firms who continued the profitable extraction of raw materials and cheap labour power.[35]

The idea that economic domination, once established, could be maintained automatically and indefinitely, was powerfully reinforced by the writing of Andre Gunder Frank, greatly influenced by Sweezy and Baran. His historical studies of Latin America popularised the notion that underdevelopment should be regarded as a process rather than a condition. Liberal economists of the fifties had proposed various nostrums for launching backward countries on the road to wealth-creating capitalist prosperity. When these economists used the word underdevelopment, they used it in a good sense : poor countries were not *un*developed, they were *under*developed, only needing sound policies and a helping hand from rich countries to set them on the road which Britain, Germany and the United States had travelled before them.

Marxists greeted this thesis — most famously expounded by W.W. Rostow in his 'non-communist manifesto', *The Stages of Economic Growth* — with profound scepticism. Frank's challenge to the thesis emphasised the dreary failures of development in Latin America since the fall of the Spanish empire in the early nineteeenth century.[36]

35. Examples of this analysis can be found all over the world. A particularly rich literature has come out of East African studies. I. Shivjis' *The Silent Class Struggle* (written 1970, published Dar Es Salaam 1973) fired an opening salvo in what has become an epic war of words. The main lines of battle are sketched by Paul Nursey-Bray, 'Tanzania : The Development Debate', *African Affairs* LXXXIX (1980) 55-78.

36. 'The Development of Underdevelopment', *Monthly Review* (September, 1966); *Capitalism and Underdevelopment in Latin America : Historical Studies of Chile and Brazil* (New York, 1969); *Latin America : Underdevelopment or Revolution* (New York, 1969).

Political independence had not brought economic growth and good government to the former colonies. Investment from Europe had made profits for capitalists but had done nothing to promote dynamic growth on the original British model. Instead of acquiring industries, Latin America nations continued to be what they had been under Spanish rule — mines and plantations producing raw materials for the rich nations of the North. Capitalism had created, not saved the impoverished peasantry. Frank used the word underdevelopment in a bad sense. Underdevelopment was the end result of a long historical process; it was the price the rural 'periphery' had paid for the enrichment of the urban metropolises of the worldwide capitalist system.

Much of the academic left eagerly embraced Frank's works as important contributions to the 'Marxist theory of Imperialism'. His article on 'the Development of Underdevelopment' appeared alongside articles on American militarism and neo-colonialism in a 1970 anthology significantly titled *Imperialism and Underdevelopment : a Reader.*[37] There were many reasons for Frank's celebrity. He provided historical case studies to counter the Rostow thesis. He gave ammunition to those who expected the worst from bourgeois decolonisation in Asia and Africa by delineating the results of an analogous process in nineteenth-century Latin America. And so long as the Vietnam War dragged on, the corollary of his thesis — that only a determined struggle to break free of the global system of capitalist production and exchange could cure the disease of underdevelopment — helped to explain why both sides were fighting. Scores of imitators set out energetically to apply Frank's thesis to other countries and continents.[38] Dubious additions to the English language such as 'peripheralisation' and 'peasantisation' were coined to epitomise aspects of the process of underdevelopment.

37. R.I. Rhodes, ed. (New York, 1970).

38. See, for example, Walter Rodney, *How Europe Underdeveloped Africa* (London, 1972).

Theorising about imperialism after Vietnam

The extraordinary period of radical ferment in the West that had opened with a 'free speech' movement at a California University in 1964, had been nourished by anti-war protests around the world in 1966, and had precipitated the fall of governments in 1968, began to wind down in the early seventies. It had reacquainted the man in the street with the word imperialism. For many radical activists of that time, anti-imperialism expressed the essence of The Movement. For the first time ever, Marxist and anti-Marxist notions of imperialism had confronted each other in academic circles. During that period new conceptions of imperialism had also developed on the left which had tenuous connections with each other and with older conceptions. One of these was the Sweezy-Magdoff explanation of capitalist war, another was the Continental/Afro-Asian theory of neo-colonialism, another was Frank's theory of underdevelopment. In addition there was the common conception of imperialism as direct or indirect political domination of distant territory. Vietnam did not compound these disparate elements into a single theory. It simply held them together in a cluster, rather as a chemical emulsion holds oil and vinegar together in temporary suspension. The communists were seen as 'anti-colonial' nationalists fighting to free their 'underdeveloped' land from its 'peripheral' position in the world economy. The Americans were seen as fighting alongside the 'neo-colonialist' Saigon regime to keep another domino from falling out of 'the capitalist sphere' and to justify the maintenance of a 'surplus-absorbing' military-industrial complex. Viewed from almost any position on the left, 'the war was about imperialism'.

Once this focus of attention was removed, Marxist research on historical problems of imperialism diverged in several directions. Study of the historical origins of the Cold War and the 'National Security State' has remained largely an American enterprise proceeding without much reference to the classic theories. The startling propositions of W.A.

Williams and other revisionists of the early fifties have been challenged and tested and reformulated.[39] Study of the old colonial empires and their economic policies has continued but has tended to be concentrated in the period between World War I and the onset of decolonisation. The passage of time has opened new archives to historians and revived interest in inter-war studies of colonial empires.[40] Workers in this field continue to misunderstand and misstate the original theories of imperialism.[41] But they generally show less interest in testing those theories against the archival record than in relating their studies to the hypotheses of neo-colonialism and under-development. Questions raised by these hypotheses became, in the nineteen seventies, the most vital branch of Marxist research concerned with relations between the rich and poor regions of the earth.

Though the word imperialism has often been employed by researchers in this field, the real subject of their investigation is not economically motivated state action but regional disparities in wealth and power arising from the expansion of the capitalist system. The real intellectual fountainhead of this type of study is not Lenin but Rosa Luxemburg. It was she who had first tried to show how capitalist expansion had extended its domination over rural hinterlands in the course of several centuries; it was she who had explained that this process went ahead sometimes with, sometimes without, and sometimes in spite of the intervention of the state. It had begun long before the

39. This research is indignantly reviewed by the old liberal Arthur M. Schlesinger, Jr. in *New York Review of Books* 25 Oct. 1979. A sweeping survey of different approaches to the problem of war in the twentieth century is attempted by K.L. Nelson and S.A. Olin, *Why War? Ideology, Theory and History* (Berkeley, 1979).

40. The effects on Marxist research of archival restrictions and ideological preconceptions are sensitively delineated by Terrence Ranger, 'Growing from the Roots : Reflections on Peasant Research in Central and Southern Africa', *Journal of Southern African Studies* V (1978) and A.D. Roberts, 'The Earlier Historiography of Colonial Africa', *History in Africa* V (1978) 153-67.

41. See, for example, G. Hull, 'The French Connection in Africa : Zaire and South Africa', *Journal of Southern African Studies* V (1979) 221.

mercantilist era, took new forms in the course of nineteenth-century colonial expansion, and contributed to the murderous rivalries of the imperialist era after 1895. Many neo-Marxists of the 1960s and 70s were engaged in precisely the same investigation as they attempted to show how capitalist domination of backward areas could continue after colonial rule and intercapitalist warfare had ended.[42]

By far the boldest attempt of this kind, and the one farthest removed from older conceptions of imperialism was Frank's underdevelopment theory. In his account, the European state as the primary agent of underdevelopment exits from the stage in the early nineteenth century. Yet somehow the dead limbs of the departed *hidalgos* continue to grip the neck of the Latin American peasantry throughout the twentieth century. To call this phenomenon imperialism is to completely abandon the distinction which all the classic theories had drawn between capitalist expansion under free trading, non-interventionist, laissez faire governments of the 19th century and capitalist expansion in the twentieth-century age of imperialist, interventionist states. It is also to abandon the notion of surplus investment capital as the principal engine of capitalist activity overseas. In Frank's scheme, imperialism becomes virtually synonymous with capitalist expansion over the last four hundred years; the system of exchange rather than the state or class domination is designated the principal oppressor of the impoverished peasants of the underdeveloped world. In the 1970s the historical study of capitalist expansion came to be acrimoniously divided between those who took up Frank's hypothesis and those who rejected it as wrong or un-Marxist.

An Africanist sociologist, Immanuel Wallerstein, has turned the hypothesis into a grandiose explanation of history

42. This literature is reviewed with unparalleled lucidity by Brewer in *Marxist Theories of Imperialism*, 158-257. He delineates the pioneering role of Rosa Luxemburg and shows precisely how the neo-Marxists of the post-war era abandoned work on the principal problems which concerned the 'classic' theorists. Brewer accepts with cheerful resignation that the new theorists use a definition of imperialism worlds removed from the definitions of Bukharin and Lenin.

since the Renaissance.[43] The French historian Arghiri Emmanuel has developed an overarching account of why rich nations are rich and poor nations poor which explicitly rejects key elements of classic Marxist theory.[44] He calls the hypothesis of investment-powered imperialism 'a myth' and Lenin's famous pamphlet 'a marginal work which never had any scientific pretensions'. It appears to him 'increasingly obvious that political domination, far from having been the condition or even the crowning of economic domination (or what I would call exploitation), really ran counter to it'. Without citing Hobson, he puts forward the very Hobsonian argument that a small number of particular vested interests were the principal generators and benefactors of colonial expansion. He accepts most of Robinson and Gallagher's explanation of British expansion in Africa but does not see that as an obstacle to a Marxist interpretation of history. He proposes that the essence of capitalist domination of the underdeveloped world is to be found in 'unequal exchange in international trade'. Goods produced by advanced, labour-saving technology in developed countries are exchanged for raw materials produced with labour-intensive technology. Thus 'surplus value' is extracted from the Third World and conveyed to the developed industrial countries. It follows that workers in rich countries are, in a technical sense, exploiting the workers of poor countries. Like Frank he prescribes withdrawal from the world capitalist system as a pre-condition for real development.

Such breath-taking departures from Marxist orthodoxy have provoked strong rejoinders. In 1971, Frank was independently taken to task by a Latin Americanist and an Africanist, who complained that he neglected Marx's emphasis on relations between classes in production. In his scheme, the market place of international exchanges displaces

43. Beginning with *The Modern World System : Capiatalist Agriculture and the Origins of the European World Economy in the Sixteenth Century* (New York, 1974).

44. *Unequal Exchange* (New York, 1972).

class struggle as the primary determinant of historical change.[45] Others have observed that Frank is simply wrong when he claims that countries which *have* developed since the industrial revolution have done so because they were not satellites of the world capitalist market at the time they began to develop. Emmanuel was attacked on similar grounds and especially berated for his division of the workers of the world into exploiters and exploited.[46] Nevertheless, most of the early Marxist critics of underdevelopment theory have been willing to grant that its exponents had brought a fresh perspective to problems of imperialism and that they provided a corrective to the classic theorists of imperialism who were more concerned with the effects of capitalist expansion on Europe than on the underdeveloped countries of 'the periphery'. They also tacitly accept that notwithstanding Lenin's formal designation of the twentieth century as the one and only era of imperialism, imperialism is an appropriate word to describe all the effects of the expansion of the capitalist system over several centuries. As Brewer has noted, in doing this they are throwing out the classical definitions of imperialism. They are using imperialism to describe the process of capitalist expansion which Rosa Luxemburg studied seventy years ago (but which she had never called imperialism). They are pushing to extremes the notion of economic imperialism without state assistance which had first cropped up between the world wars.

These tendencies are strongly apparent in Michael Barratt Brown's popular book *The Economics of Imperialism* (1974). The state does not figure in any of Barratt Brown's suggested definitions of imperialism.[47] He emphasises instead the role of the firm: 'Imperialism for the Marxists has to do with capitalist firms seeking for surpluses and seeking to use

45. E. Laclau, 'Feudalism and Capitalism in Latin America', *New Left Review* LXVII (1971) 19. See also Barratt Brown, 259-60.

46. Barratt Brown, 71-72, 254-55, 259. Critical comments by C. Bettelheim appear as an addendum to Emmanuel's *Unequal Exchange.*

47. Barratt Brown, 47, 57, 68, 255, 272, 320.

their surpluses wherever they can by incorporating new areas of the world economy into their system of accumulation'. (p. 68) Not one of the several time frames he uses to encompass the era of imperialism corresponds to the chronologies of the classic Marxist theorists. (He uses 1870 twice, 1750 once, the last two hundred years once and 'roughly the last four hundred years' once).[48] Colonialism and war are not subjects of his enquiry. The only states which feature as vital actors in his analysis are the regimes currently in charge of underdeveloped countries — the regimes which are bribed, bullied and cajoled by the large international firms which he singles out as the pre-eminent contemporary agents of imperialism. He does not bother to debate the anti-Marxist historians of colonialism. His aim is to reveal the underlying causes of the unequal distribution of material wealth within and between the nation-states of the modern world. He pursues this objective in a subtle series of dialogues with the competing explanations offered by Schumpeter and the Keynesians.[49] In the end, while criticising Frank and Emmanuel, he endorses their basic proposition that the impoverishment of the Third World was a necessary concomitant of the enrichment of the First World of industrial capitalism. This was achieved, in his opinion, not through the export of surplus capital (a notion he openly attacks) but through the operations of capitalist firms which created 'an artificial division of labour inside and between countries' (p. 126), assigning some regions to industrial production by well-paid workers and other regions to primary production by cheap labour (p.272).

By the time Barratt Brown's book appeared the terms neo-colonialism, underdevelopment and imperialism had already lost much of their popularity among radical scholars studying the malapportionment of wealth and poverty in the

48. Ibid 22, 66, 255.

49. Schumpeter is sensitively handled in most respects, but Barratt Brown totally misrepresents his theory of imperialism as an attempt to show that the *British* Empire was an atavistic survival.

world economy. Frank's later works rarely mention imperialism. Increasingly, the label 'dependency theory' was applied to all accounts which attributed unequal development in the world economy to the historic operations of the capitalist market place. And even as dependency theory was widening the circle of its admirers, it was being subjected to increasingly hostile criticism from within the Marxist camp. Added to the earlier charges that it ignores class conflict and dialectical processes are charges that it is a form of circular reasoning and that it is as extreme a variety of historical pessimism as had ever issued from radical pens. The argument is circular because it first identifies the victims of dependency by their poverty and then points to that poverty as proof of victimisation. The argument is pessimistic because it locates the ultimate origins of underdevelopment in the embryonic capitalist world economy of the sixteenth century, implying that once the process was set in motion it was an unstoppable juggernaut. This Calvinist scenario interprets all subsequent events as the more or less predetermined results of a diabolical first cause. One Marxist historian of early modern Europe calls the argument Neo-Smithian because it is the mirror image of the classical liberal account of development first propounded by Adam Smith. Whereas Smith had preached the comforting doctrine that the 'invisible hand' of capitalist competition would produce an indefinite increase of wealth among the nations, the dependency theorists propose that an invisible hand of unequal exchange relationships indefinitely holds the peasant masses in a state of backwardness.[50] Another Marxist charges that dependency theory is un-Marxist because it ignores Marx's emphasis on the progressive function of capitalism in energising the 'forces of production' throughout the world.[51]

50. R. Brenner, 'The Origins of Capitalist Development : A Critique of Neo-Smithian Marxism', *New Left Review* CIV 27-59, and 'Agrarian Class Struggles and Economic Development in Pre-Industrial Europe, *Past and Present* LXX (1976).

51. Warren, op. cit. Latin Americanists of the Marxist persuasion remain undecided on whether dependency theory is Marxian and whether it is synonymous with imperialism. See *Latin American Perspectives* VIII (1981) 1-179.

The pessimism of the early dependency theorists is unrelieved even by Leninist hopes of an ultimate world revolution. The dependent have to fight individually in a series of discrete struggles for escape from domination by overwhelmingly superior forces.

Critics of dependency theory offer the alternative views : that the development paths pursued by various nations depended on the outcome of conflict between antagonistic classes in particular nations; that dependency without poverty has been known in many countries; that industrialisation was no certain road to a more equal station; and that previous failure to industrialise is not a barrier to future industrialisation.[52] Arguments on all sides continue to this moment. As they have so far developed, they have maintained less and less connection with theories of imperialism and with other studies professedly concerned with imperialism. The editor of a recent attempt to present all varieties of contemporary Marxist theories of imperialism confesses that he can find no theoretical framework capable of comprehending both dependency theory and Cold War theory.[53] Another Marxist advocates dispensing entirely with earlier definitions. In his view modern Marxist theories of imperialism are concerned in the broadest sense with 'the development of the capitalist world economy'.[54] The distance which separates dependency theorists from Hilferding and Lenin is now enormous. The state, capitalist warfare, and partitions of territory have dropped out of sight. Even more remarkable, the concept of surplus capital seeking outlets — the idea which started people theorising about imperialism in the late eighteen nineties — is today ignored or rejected by most liberal and radical scholars outside the eastern

52. See, for example, Warren, op. cit. and P.J. O' Brien, 'A Critique of Latin American Theories of Dependency' in I. Oxaal et.al., *Beyond the Sociology of Development* (London, 1975).

53. Andrew Mack, David Plant and Ursula Doyle, *Imperialism, Intervention and Development* (London, 1979) 19.

54. Brewer, 210.

communist bloc. One reviewer calls this and similar concepts 'the tired old vent-for-surplus model, which is not what one expects from a Marxist'![55]

Thus the nineteen seventies, which opened with greatly renewed interest in the classic theories of imperialism and unprecedented efforts to inaugurate an academic dialogue between Marxist and non-Marxist concepts of imperialism, closed with the classic theories in eclipse and the chasms separating different concepts of imperialism yawning wider than ever. In communist countries the study of imperialism is moribund — straight-jacketed by the demands of Leninist hagiography, self-interested propaganda for consumption in the third world and a mud-slinging battle between China and the U.S.S.R. over the question of 'hegemonism'. Scholars of the Round Table tradition continue to use imperialism as a synonym for colonial empire-building and to denounce Edwardian theories for failing to conform to Victorian facts.

Marxist scholarship in the West has diverged into several schools. The most important of these schools studies the problem of unequal distribution of wealth in the modern world, honours Hilferding and Lenin as founding fathers but has abandoned their theories of imperialism. Many of its followers use the word imperialism as a synonym for the expansion of capitalism as an economic system without acknowledging debts to founding mother Rosa Luxemburg. In the newly independent nations of the third world, presidents-for-life and cabinet ministers cite imperialism and neo-colonialism as the source of all their ills. Meanwhile dissidents in their own countries and sympathetic scholars overseas denounce those same presidents and ministers as the bribed, 'comprador' agents of multi-national capitalist exploiters. It is both tempting and futile to revive the cry that imperialism is no word for scholars. We cannot purge the word. There is hope, however, that with the perspective of

55. Frederick Cooper, 'Peasants, Capitalists and Historians : A Review Article', *Journal of Southern African Studies VII* (1981) 244. He cites W.H. Freund and R.W. Shanton, 'Vent for Surplus Theory', *Savanna* VI (1977) 191-96.

this historical review, we can eliminate some misconceived debates and sharpen our researches into all the phenomena which have at one time or another been named imperialism.

CHAPTER 13
SORTING OUT HISTORICAL PROBLEMS OF IMPERIALISM

Summing Up

At the turn of the 20th century, statesmen, businessmen, economists, reformers and revolutionaries peered uneasily into the darkness of the unknowable future. The signs and portents around them were alarming. The accelerating growth of armaments, tariffs and monopolies suggested to many minds that a new era of world history had commenced. A slangy English phrase coined in the mid-eighteen nineties seemed an apt label for the transformations which were taking place : 'the New Imperialism'. It called to mind Caesars and Bonapartes who used the military and political tools of autocracy to pursue bigness in all things. At the same time, it suggested that there were novel elements in the unexpected recrudescence of Caesarism at the end of a century whose watchwords had been peace, freedom, laissez-faire and rationalism. The phrase 'theory of imperialism' was also first used at this time by people who were struggling to understand and survive the vast changes taking place around them.

Capitalists who feared for the survival of the prevailing economic order offered the theory that their salvation in the twentieth century required that their governments surround them with tariff walls and guarantee them access to raw materials, markets and outlets for 'surplus capital'. Reformers countered with the theory that militarism and economic nationalism were not necessary to the salvation of anyone except a minority of vested interests. Revolutionaries, on the other hand, agreed with the financiers that an alliance between big business and the armed state was a necessity for the capitalist system, but predicted that the fearsome rivalries of the Great Powers would eventually destroy rather than save that system. The theories devised by Marxists were the most complex and interesting because they attempted to place twentieth-century imperialism in a longer historical perspective. What the capitalists presented as a mere policy recommendation and the reformers presented as a mistaken idea which directly served the material interests of the privileged classes, the Marxists identified as a consequence of the centuries-long expansion of the capitalist system. They argued that the process of expansion required different political tools in different ages. In the seventeenth and eighteenth centuries, mercantilism and slavery had aided the first stage of capital accumulation. Free trade had served the needs of industrialists in the nineteenth century. Imperialism was the required policy of twentieth-century developed capitalist states.

Up to the conclusion of the First World War, the merits of conflicting theories of imperialism were not debated in the academy but in the realm of practical politics. However varied the interests of rival theorists, they generally agreed about the nature of their subject. They all understood imperialism to be the use of the state power, especially military power, for the purpose of winning economic advantages in the world at large. That was the phenomenon they were attempting to explain and whose future consequences they were trying to predict. Nevertheless, there were other meanings of the word imperialism current in the Edwardian era which would lead to confusion in decades to come. In contrast to Continental writers, who generally drew a distinction between colonialism and imperialism, British writers used the word imperialism ambiguously. Sometimes it simply meant empire-building — the annexation of colonies — in any era. Sometimes it referred specifically to the programme of Joseph Chamberlain which sought to defend Britain's position as a rich Power by consolidating the diverse territories of the British Empire into a centrally directed and military power : the sort of system the German Empire had developed after its creation in 1870. No one invented a theory of imperialism to explain empire-building in general. All the competing theories of imperialism were concerned with the politico-economic-military programmes promoted at the turn of the century by Chamberlain in Britain and like-minded statesmen in other countries.

Serious misunderstandings arose after the first World War had discredited those programmes in the minds of almost everyone except the leaders of fascist movements in Europe and the far east. In the nineteen twenties and thirties, the crusade against imperialism became identified with campaigns for reform and independence in colonised countries. Labour intellectuals in Britain, anti-colonial nationalists in Asia and Africa, and the enemies of American 'dollar diplomacy' in Latin America all singled out 'economic imperialism' as the Carthage which must be destroyed. The broader, pre-war meanings of imperialism were obscured by this special concentration on colonial problems. It was at this time that people began to misstate the theory of investment-powered imperialism. Its original appearance as the policy recommendation of certain capitalist writers was completely forgotten. Propagandists of the left began absurdly to attribute the annexation of colonial territories in Victorian times to the pressure of surplus capital. Under Stalin, the Comintern permitted this and other misunderstandings of Lenin's writings on imperialism to go uncorrected if they served the interests of Soviet foreign policy in Asia. Official guardians of the old colonial empires began to treat theoretical critiques of imperialism as aspects of a practical Bolshevik menace to the territories in their care. At about the same time, more idealistic champions of Empire who were busily sublimating the bellicose conceptions of the Edwardian era into ideals such as Commonwealth, *France Outre-mer* and Co-prosperity began to search for evidence that their projects were not built on an historical foundation of capitalist greed. Discussions of imperialism were further complicated when certain American writers began to use the phrase economic imperialism to describe relations of dominance/subservience between advanced and underdeveloped countries which resulted from the unaided actions of capitalist firms.

After World War II debates about imperialism reflected

the overarching importance of conflict between the United States and the Soviet Union. Socialist writers in America reworked the classic theories to support the thesis that the United States was to blame for the Cold War. More conservative Americans closed ranks with British and continental European historians who continued to pile up evidence that the classic theories did not 'fit the facts' of nineteenth-century colonial expansion. In the course of their work they invented new categories and sub-categories of imperialism to describe aspects of Victorian international relations. They also fed the mills of a minor academic industry which produced highly tendentious anthologies on 'the imperialism problem' for use in undergraduate classrooms. Serious misconceptions were perpetuated and spread by the selective quotation of bits and pieces of the original theories of imperialism in these anthologies.

Just when this flourishing academic industry appeared to have buried theories of imperialism for good, a resurgence of radical activism in the West caused them to be dug up and applied to new purposes. The debacle of Vietnam revived interest in capitalism as cause of war. Old conceptions of economic imperialism were transmuted into the new conceptions of neo-colonialism, underdevelopment and dependency. Exponents of these academic novelties stretched the original theories so far as to make them unrecognisable. Surplus investment capital, finance capital, militarism and state action were explicitly rejected or quietly ignored. The 'era of imperialism' was expanded by some authors to include the last four centuries. Never had the meanings and explanations of imperialism been so diverse as in the nineteen seventies. Never was there so great a need for historians to clarify their thinking about research into the multifarious phenomena which have been called by that name. Understanding the historical context of the original theories of imperialism lessens the difficulty of that task.

How to study historical problems of imperialism

It is too late now to revive W.K. Hancock's call for imperialism to be struck out of the scholar's lexicon. The best that can be done is to sort separate problems into separate categories. A primary task is to mark out chronological divisions roughly corresponding to the periodisation used by most of the original theorists of imperialism. Three periods which demand different treatment by historians are : 1) pre-1895; 2) 1895-1920; 3) post-1920. Within each of these periods it will also be helpful to distinguish between the actions of states and the effects of the expanding capitalist economic system.

Problems of expanding empires and capitalism before 1895

The first theorists of imperialism had very little to say about events before 1895 because most of them held that the era of imperialism only commenced at the close of the nineteenth century. Many subsequent writers, however, have used the word imperialism to refer to two distinct processes which were going on long before that date : 1) the growth of European colonial empires, and 2) the expansion of the capitalist system. There is a good case to be made for following the practice of early-twentieth century Continental writers who used the words colonialism or colonial policy rather than the word imperialism to denote the first of these processes. An enormous amount of confusion has been generated by using empire, colonialism, and imperialism as synonyms. Theories of imperialism were not theories of empire. Colonialism was only one aspect of imperialism as that term was understood in the Edwardian era. There are no general theories of colonial expansion. There is no special Marxist theory of colonialism. There are no 'mono-causal' explanations. Almost every historian who has ever written on the subject has acknowledged a mixture of causal agencies at work.

There are, however, tendencies in the historical interpretation of empire building which reflect the ideological and methodological predispositions of different sorts of historians including liberals, conservatives and radicals. These tendencies generate conflicting interpretations which stimulate thought as well as research. At one end of the spectrum stands Hobson with his cynical assertion that the ultimate begetters and beneficiaries of colonial expansion were cliques of identifiable vested interests — bureaucratic, military and business. At the other end of the spectrum stand the Round Table historians and their successors with their insistence that strategic interests, unstable conditions on the turbulent frontiers of empire, and idealistic considerations of 'trusteeship' were the primary factors which moved the great colonising powers to extend their dominion. Somewhere apart from both these tendencies in interpretation stand various kinds of Marxists who insist that the behaviour of all governments ultimately accommodates the requirements of the economic system which provides the material basis of their power. The most keen-witted early applications of this doctrine to the subject ol empire building are to be found in the works of Rosa Luxemburg and H.N. Brailsford which show how colonial annexations sometimes helped and sometimes hindered the expansion of the capitalist economic system.

There is still plenty of room for research into the motives of European empire builders before the twentieth century. The sheer bulk of the evidence and the inherent plausibility of the hypotheses offered by liberal, conservative and radical historiography make it unlikely that a consensus of interpretation will ever be reached. One great stumbling block stands in the path every historian who enters into this endlessly fascinating area of research. That obstacle is the widespread but utterly mistaken notion that the proper proving ground of twentieth-century theories of imperialism is colonial expansion in earlier centuries.

More than a decade after Eric Stokes and Tom Kemp

first called attention to the folly of this belief, it continues to be fostered at every level of the historical profession. It is fostered in introductory subjects at universities by little books on 'The imperialism problem' which contrast selective quotations from Hobson, Lenin and Schumpeter with sober historical appraisals of the 'real reasons' for Victorian empire building. It is fostered by professors who year after year repeat a set of lectures in which distorted versions of theories of imperialism are presented and then 'tested' against 'the facts' about the Scramble for Africa. It is fostered by Marxist graduate students who search for evidence that Victorian investors wanted colonies and by non-Marxist graduate students who search for evidence that they did not want them. All these activities should cease. The misconceived 'problem books' should be removed from reading lists and not replaced. The professors should write new lectures. The graduate students should stop chasing wild geese. There are more fruitful ways to study the dual problems of empire building and capitalist expansion before the turn of the twentieth century.

First it must be recognised that the two problems differ vastly in quantity and quality. Expanding capitalism involved agents of every trading nation and touched nearly every society on earth. Colonial expansion was the work of a handful of nations of which Britain and France were by far the most important. Except for Germany and Italy all the colonising nations of the Victorian era built on the foundations of pre-existing overseas possessions. It is therefore doubtful whether any general theory is required to explain their expansion. It is also doubtful whether anyone has gone very far beyond Hobson in suggesting reasons for it. His list of commercial, bureaucratic, military and 'philanthropic' agents of expansion is as comprehensive as any ever compiled. Many of them have received surprisingly little attention from historians.

In their misplaced endeavours to prove or disprove the alleged theory that colonies were required to serve the needs of the highest stage of capitalism, historians have concentrated on the *motives* of the officials who did the annexing. Robinson and Gallagher, for example, say a great deal about how 'official minds' worked and almost nothing about how official bodies were recruited, fed, clothed and sheltered. The historical sociology of colonial bureacracies merits careful scrutiny. More needs to be known about the links between personnel of government departments concerned with foreign and colonial affairs and the outside agencies who directly profitted from expansionist policies. Hobson placed special emphasis on engineering firms, shipping companies, railway promoters and other government contractors. Study of their activities have been neglected in comparison to the activities of traders and financiers whose interests were less intimately bound up with the work of government departments.[1]

The role of the military in colonial affairs also deserves more study than it has received. Hobson denied the existence of strategic interests as a disembodied motive for annexations. Not only did 'officers with an itch for glory' stir up trouble on distant frontiers; their superiors stirred up trouble at home. When governments wanted advice on what interests were strategic and how they should be defended, they turned to generals and admirals who had a vested interest in promoting 'forward policies'. Attention also needs to be paid to dogs that didn't bark in the night. Most developing, industrialising, trading countries did not acquire colonies. Why not? Anyone who proposes an overarching explanation of colonialism must include an answer to this question.

This applies especially to those who wish to apply Marxist theory to the study of colonial expansion. If one begins, as they do, with the assumption that the actions of states generally reflect the perceived material interests of the

1. Special credit is due to John S. Galbraith not only for his work in following up the early Round Table notion of turbulent frontiers but also for his pioneering studies of business and empire in North America and Africa. Since 1970 such studies have proliferated enormously.

dominant classes within the state, it is vital to explain why some dominant classes promoted colonial expansion and others did not. Rosa Luxemburg's partial answer to this question was that Britain's free trading empire served the interests of the German bourgeoisie very well but that the aristocratic, autocratic top layer of the German state perceived special advantages to be gained from the pursuit of an aggressive colonial policy. An historian of nineteenth-century Portuguese colonialism has argued in a similar vein that a policy which was ruinous for the nation as a whole was a source of considerable profit to 'precise classes or fractions of classes'.[2] A more complicated problem for Marxists is weighing the relative importance of metropolitan and peripheral promoters of expansion. The anti-Marxist historians who have stressed the reluctance of the empire-builders to extend their colonial responsibilities offer overwhelming evidence to support their case. Marxists can live with that evidence, provided that they give up the quixotic attempt to prove that expanding capitalism needed colonialism. They start with the advantage of being able to point to the fact of empires — reluctant or not, they did expand. They may also note that a policy which benefited particular classes or 'fractions of classes' was best presented to the rest of the nation as a course of action which was undertaken with the greatest reluctance. Future Marxist historians should devote some time to showing how and why small-time entrepreneurs on the fringes of empires sometimes could and sometimes could not contrive annexations to serve their local interests. There is no reason why Marxist writers on colonial expansion should not produce explanations as rich, varied and 'multi-causal' as those served up by non-Marxists. After all, they have the immense advantage of viewing this peculiar phenomenon against the panoramic background of the expansion of the capitalist economic system.

2. W.G. Clarence-Smith, 'The Myth of Uneconomic Imperialism : the Portuguese in Africa, 1836-1926', *Journal of Southern African Studies* V (1979) 165-67.

Historians cannot help anyone to determine whether the expansion of capitalism was necessary because necessity is a subject which lies outside their realm of competence. They can, however, tell us much about how capitalism grew from its European homeland into a global network of production and exchange. This work will be done better once the simplistic model is abandoned which envisages capitalism spreading primarily through the agency of formal and informal empire. The most enduring legacy of the boom in Marxist historiography which occured during the nineteen sixties and seventies may well be its decisive smashing of nationalist versions of nineteenth century history which portrayed Asian and African societies as classless, contented communities unanimously and heroically resisting the onslaught of 'Western imperialism'. A host of studies have shown that many of those societies had ruling classes, exploited peasantries, subjugated females and slaves. By exploding the myths of Merrie Africa, spiritual Asia and other Rousseauistic fantasies these studies have made the cardboard 'victims of imperialism' into human beings of flesh and blood. They implicitly challenge the self-serving propaganda of ruling elites in many parts of the world who find it highly convenient to attribute all the ills of their people to the legacy of colonialism.

The expansion of capitalism can now be seen as a process which generally took place with the active cooperation of elements of the societies absorbed into it. Trading, migratory labour and production for the world markets were phenomena which occured apart from, and often in advance of colonial expansion. Countries such as Thailand, Turkey, Ethiopia and Liberia which escaped incorporation into European empires, did not escape incorporation into the capitalist system. With incorporation these societies were stratified along new lines. Colonial rule, on the other hand, often consciously strove to *inhibit* the growth of indigenous capitalism. In extreme cases such as Kenya and South Africa, the full power of the State was employed in attempts to crush successful black farmers and traders.[3] In the study of capitalist expansion there is a possibility of a real convergence of Marxist and non-Marxist studies. There is not much difference between the conclusions reached by Rosa Luxemburg and H.N. Brailsford seventy-five years ago and the conclusions reached by Robinson and Gallagher in their epochal study of *Africa and the Victorians.* Both approaches emphasise the decisive importance of Victorian capitalism as a disrupting force in non-European societies.

Problems of the period 1895-1920

This ought to be the primary testing ground for all the classic theories of imperialism, for it was the period in which they were expounded. It was the era which invented the concept of 'the new imperialism' and made the phrase a household word. This was the period when financiers and economists recommended that nation states should make the expansion of capitalism a matter of conscious planning. This was the period in which adventurous politicians argued that unless they employed the full force of the armed state to maintain avenues for future expansion their nations would perish in war or revolution. This was the period when socialists first pointed to that doctrine as proof that capitalism was in deep trouble. It is therefore surprising that the connections between economic pressures and state policies in this era have been relatively neglected by historians. The reason for the neglect is almost certainly the misguided choice

3. The most fruitful of recent Marxist studies of colonial situations are those which seek to explain the diversity of third world experiences with development in terms of the 'articulation' of the 'capitalist mode of production' with various sorts of 'pre-capitalist' modes. The subject bristles with difficulties and is often presented in almost impenetrable jargon. Nevertheless, these investigations illuminate previously neglected phenomena. At their most basic level they postulate that the kinds of political economies which arise during the incorporation of new societies into the world market are not determined solely by the needs of invading capitalism. They are also determined by the nature of the pre-existing political economies and the way they are fitted into (or 'articulated with') the expanding capitalist system of production. An excellent introduction to the subject appears in Brewer's *Marxist Theories of Imperialism* 182-207 and 261-73.

of the late nineteenth century as the proving ground for the classic theories.

An exception to the general pattern of neglect has been the controversy surrounding the work of the German historian Fritz Fischer.[4] His account of Germany's objectives in World War I squares with the hypothesis of Edwardian theorists that the full force of the armed capitalist state would be employed to secure the outlets for investment capital and sources of raw materials which were thought to be necessary for survival in the twentieth century. This implication has tended to get lost in the heat of battle over Fischer's contention that Hitler's war aims in the second World War were fundamentally the same as the Kaiser's aims in the first. Because only Germany had Hitler, the controversy has been treated as a uniquely German affair. There is no reason, however, why the war aims of all the combatants should not be subjected to the same close scrutiny.

To what extent did statesmen in other countries subscribe to the doctrine that imperialism was a necessity? One need not adhere to Marxist notions of 'economic imperatives' in order to recognise that *belief* as a potential source of international conflict. Even Norman Angell and Joseph Schumpeter who challenged the rationality of that belief recognised its widespread appeal. Ample evidence exists in the public statements of European leaders before the war, in the provisions of the secret treaties drawn up by the Allied powers during the war, and in provisions of the Versailles settlement after the war, to justify a deeper search into the archives. This research must not proceed on the assumptions that imperialism = colonialism and that therefore the radical theories of imperialism attributed World War I to a competition for overseas colonies. Historians have rightly poured scorn on that thesis (as Rosa Luxemburg poured scorn on it in 1916) but that is not what the radicals

4. Fischer's *Griff nach der Weltmacht* (Dusseldorf, 1961) began the controversy. At the end of the 1960's he replied to his critics in *Weltmacht oder Niedergang* which has since appeared in English as *World Power or Decline, The Controversy Over Germany's Aims in the First World War* (London, 1975).

said. The importance of doctrines of imperialism in goading nations into world war cannot be finally determined until all the archives have been examined. To what extent were foreign offices in countries other than Germany influenced by the conventional wisdom of bankers, economists and investment counselors? Was Schumpeter correct in his assertions that imperialism was discredited in Britain by the fall of Chamberlain, and in America by the failure of Theodore Roosevelt's Bull Moose campaign? His theory has been as neglected in debates about the causes of the World War I as it has been emphasised in debates about the expansion of colonial empires.

Obviously the expansion of capitalism was closely connected to the policies of states and empires in an era when politicians openly proclaimed that continued expansion was required to keep nations healthy. But just because people said so does not mean it was so. Nor does it mean that the study of high politics and high finance can answer all the historian's questions about the operations of the economy in the period when the phrases 'world economy' and 'weltwirtschaft' were first coined. Not every economist subscribed to the proposition that competition among nation-based capitalisms was the predominant feature of economic life. Many agreed with Hobson that capital was international and that its vaunted patriotism was but a mask to be donned when it suited fractional interests. The merits of this case can best be studied by rigorously maintaining a distinction between the expansion of states and the expansion of the capitalist system of production and exchange.

Problems of the period 1920-present

With respect to our last period, a good case could be made for ignoring theories of imperialism altogether. The capitalist and socialist writers who expounded them were mere mortals no more endowed with supernatural prescience than the rest of us. What they said about the future was star-gazing which does not deserve to be elevated to the level of ironclad laws of history. That is not to say that what the Edwardians had to say about the future is not very interesting. Part II of Hobson's book — the part most people never read — is full of fascinating projections. One is that future investors might plant industrial enterprises in other continents whose access to cheap labour and technological innovation would eventually ruin industry in Britain. Another is that Asian governments might break free of their thrall to Europe, impose tariff defenses as Germany and America had done before and embark upon their own aggressive schemes for economic and military aggrandisement. Rosa Luxemburg predicted that victory by the allies in World War I would be followed first by their open or veiled seizure of territories formerly dominated by the Central Powers, and second by a feverish burst of rearmament by the defeated nations, 'Germany, of course, at the head'. Both Hobson and Karl Kautsky mused that the capitalist countries might eventually find a way to regulate their mutual relations so as to avoid war. All these predictions can be said to have been uncannily confirmed by some subsequent events. The predictions of Lenin and Schumpeter are less impressively borne out. Schumpeter failed to see the complex of forces that would plunge the United States into a series of wars and an upward spiral of expenditure on the tools of war. Lenin did not foresee the international consequences of a limited success by his own revolutionary movement. But the history of the last six decades can be written very satisfactorily without reference to any of this stargazing.

The importance of theories of imperialism in the modern period lies mainly in the way they have influenced writing on the radical left. Liberal and conservative historians rarely mention the theories except occasionally to notice that colonies, chartered companies and African development schemes did not generate the profits for foreign investors which had been predicted at the dawn of this century. (This, incidentally, is less of a blow to the original theories than is usually claimed. Most of them recognised that imperialism was a perilous, self-defeating policy that did not pay. Only Bukharin and Lenin, grasping for any weapon with which to bash the hated Kautsky, ascribed the progress of revisionism in western European socialist movements to the 'bribery' of the workers' leaders made possible by the booty of imperialism.) For many scholars further to the left, however, imperialism remains a concept of central importance. Some elementary mistakes have been made in its employment which have led researchers into blind alleys.

Foremost among these is the mistake of first confusing imperialism with possession of colonies, and then attempting to show the continuing 'necessity' for European control of colonised lands. When Arghiri Emmanuel realised that 'the concepts of neo-colonialism and neo-imperialism were devised for argument's sake, in the face of an unexpected situation', he concluded that the original theorists were wrong; there was no necessity for investment-powered imperialism.[5] This attack on the classic theory was misdirected. The original hypothesis was not that colonies were a *sine qua non* of trade and investment, but that in a world divided up between competing economic blocs, there would be a perpetual general pressure from business for aggressive foreign policies including competition for control of territory. When inter-capitalist military rivalry came to a sudden halt after World War II, there was no longer any pressing national interest, real or apparent, to be served by hanging on to expensive colonies troubled by rising nationalisms. Trade and investment could go merrily on provided only that newly independent countries maintained an open door for foreign capital. This, of course, is a big proviso. Neo-colonialism is the term coined to describe dominating political and economic pressures brought to bear on decolonised countries which force them to serve the interests of foreigners.

5. Above, p.250.

There are good reasons for dropping the term from the scholar's vocabulary. When open or covert pressures are exerted by the agents of one state which infringe the independence of another, those pressures are best described by the good old-fashioned term imperialism. That is what Hobson, Lenin, Brailsford and the other Edwardian writers understood imperialism to be : the use of the state power against foreign countries, for the purpose of winning economic advantage. That is what Robinson and Gallagher understood 'the imperialism of free trade' to be. When agents of the American government worked to bring down the Diem government in Vietnam or the Allende government in Chile they were behaving as classic imperialists. Other forms of domination, achieved without invoking the assistance of the state, are best described by other terms. Three forms of alleged domination have been the subject of vigorous discussion during the last decade: (l) the domination of individual third-world states by multi-national companies; (2) the 'development of under-development'; and (3) structured 'dependency'. The appearance of the first of these forms was actually predicted by Hobson eighty years ago. A foreign company can turn an independent nation's tariff barriers to its own advantage by setting up *inside* them and claiming the privileges of a local concern. Whether this situation, which cannot be contrived without the active connivance of the local government, constitutes domination is a matter of controversy. This policy has often been undertaken by governments with the conscious intent of escaping domination. Calling it imperialism confuses rather than clarifies matters. Corporate pressure on governments to serve their private purposes has been a fact of life in all capitalist countries for centuries. The concept of imperialism is only usefully invoked when corporate pressure is accompanied by the pressure of a foreign state.

There are equally good reasons for not using the term in connection with the theory of underdevelopment popularised by Andre Gunder Frank, which proposes to explain the impoverishment of the Third World as a necessary consequence of the development of capitalism as a world system. Frank's conception strongly resembles the picture developed by Rosa Luxemburg in *The Accumulation of Capital*, according to which capitalism battens upon and sometimes prolongs the existence of pre-capitalist modes of production in agricultural hinterlands. Rosa Luxemburg did not call that process imperialism or colonialism and there is no reason for any modern scholar to do so. Regional disparities in wealth and power exist in every country on earth. Why should the contrast between the poverty of West Virginia and the wealth of New York City, or between the misery of Clydeside and the affluence of Southwest England be explained by a different theory than is used to explain the poverty of Malawi relative to the wealth of France? Using the words imperialism or colonialism in connection with 'the development of underdevelopment' implies a causal connection between political control and immiseration which obscures the deeper reasons for 'uneven development' within the world economy.

The same objection can be made to those who treat 'structured dependency' as a type of imperialism or colonialism. This approach to questions of development became popular when serious problems were discovered in both the reasoning and the empirical evidence employed by Frank and his school. There *was* an obvious circularity in argumentation.[6] In addition, Frank's thesis did not offer convincing reasons why some countries which had once been satellites of distant European economies had managed to break free and others had not. Moreover, recent developments indicated that dependent economies on the periphery of the global economy need not be condemned to perpetual primary production or mining. Industrialisation could occur without weakening bonds of dependence. The new wave of post-Frankian scholarship concentrated attention on the development, over long periods of time, of economic and social structures which tend to ensure that basic decisions

6. Above, p.259.

about development fall into line with the plans of the great controllers of capital in Europe and North America. In particular, the theorists of structured dependency have studied the way in which the allegedly 'bureaucratic-bourgeois' ruling groups in Third World countries have tied themselves to the leading strings of foreign masters. Whether or not this theory adequately accounts for the behaviour of Third World states since decolonisation is a question beyond the scope of this book. It is, however, clear that the use of the words imperialism and colonialism to characterise the relations between the allegedly dependent and their supposed masters is inappropriate. Neither the interference of a foreign state nor a period of colonial rule is necessary for the dependent relationship to arise.

Historians and theory

Much of this book has been devoted to exposing the reasons why historians have misread and misapplied the classic theories of imperialism. Although particular attention has been paid to the confusing effects of ideological special pleading and the multifarious meanings of imperialism, there is more to be learned from this study than the trite lesson that historians ought to define their terms and acknowledge their biases. There is a warning that theory, like imperialism, is a word with many meanings. It needs to be marked 'Handle With Care'. When the first capitalist proponents of imperialism spoke of a theory of imperialism they used that phrase to signify a rational and coherent justification for a proposed course of action. Their theory underpinned their policy recommendation. One theory of this sort claimed that imperialism was justified by the need to maintain outlets for surplus investment capital. Others were that imperialism was justified by a civilising mission or by the struggle for life among nations.

When socialists, especially Marxist socialists, spoke of a

theory of imperialism they meant something quite different. They meant the application of a particular set of beliefs about causation in history to the study of international aggression. According to Marx's theory of causation states generally act in the economic interests of the dominant classes within them. So when Wilshire, Hilferding and Lenin saw the capitalist financial press justifying imperialism and saw capitalist powers behaving aggressively, they assumed a causal link between the two phenomena. That is how they turned a policy recommendation into an account of history. Schumpeter's work on imperialism is a theory in the same sense. It postulates that the behaviour of states reflects the interests not only of the presently dominant classes but also formerly dominant ones. Applying this belief about causation in history to the question of who was to blame for the First World War led Schumpeter to indict dying autocracy rather than monopoly capitalism.

When non-Marxist historians, writing some years later, spoke of theories of imperialism, they meant something different again. They used the phrase to denote explanations of the growth of colonial empires which emphasised the importance of one particular factor. Hence they spoke of the theory of economic imperialism, the theory of capitalist imperialism, the theory of strategic imperialism, etc. In so doing, they not only misunderstood socialist theories, they stacked the deck against them. Once they had reduced theories to discrete causes it was easy to win support for the proposition that explanations which pointed to many causes were more comprehensive, sophisticated, scholarly and convincing than explanations which emphasised only one cause. However, the triumph thus achieved is apparent rather than real. There is no reason why a theory of imperialism in the Marxian sense cannot offer multi-causal explanations of colonialism, war or any other historical phenomena. At the same time, it must be said that many Marxists have been as sinful in this respect as their opponents. They have assumed that their theory is nothing more than an explanation of colonialism cast in terms of the single factor of capital exports. They therefore deserve all the abuse they have received from the enemies they are prone to call 'mindless empiricists'.

Before tackling any problem of theory and history, historians must carefully distinguish among the three quite separate meanings of theory set out above. Otherwise they may easily fall into the errors of those who have tried unsuccessfully to thread their way through the minefield of imperialism. It is as wrong to speak in the same breath of Conant's theory of imperialism (a justification for a recommended policy), Lenin's theory of imperialism (the application of a theory of history to the study of a particular phenomenon), and Fieldhouse's theory of imperialism (an explanation of the scramble for Africa based on national rivalries) as it is to add up apples, pears and oranges.[7] Another aid to avoiding such mistakes is to locate theories precisely in their original historical context before proceeding to test them. Hancock and his successors erred by assuming that Marxist theories of imperialism originated in the imaginations of radical ideologues. Marxists of the same period erred by treating the theories as something written in the sky with no anchors in earthly time and space. The debate between these schools was falsely cast in the form of theoreticians (or mere theoreticians) versus factfinders (or mindless empiricists).

And yet, for all the misunderstandings and false dichotomies and deliberate distortions that have afflicted their

7. Errors of just this sort have been made by historians who perceive strong similarities between 'Hobson's theory of imperialism' and the theory put forward by the early nineteenth-century British colonial reformer Edward Gibbon Wakefield. (See for example Bernard Semmel's *The Rise of Free Trade Imperialism* [Cambridge, 1970] passim.) Wakefield justified his scheme for 'systematic colonisation' on the ground that there were 'surpluses' of population and capital in Britain which required overseas outlets. This 'theory' *is* similar to the justification given by the *U. S. Investor* in 1898 for its policy recommendation that the American government should join the arms race. It is not similar to Hobson's 'theory' that investors with surplus cash had pushed the British government into adopting dangerous foreign policies. Wakefield and the *U.S. Investor* were advocating courses of action they thought 'necessary' to secure the national welfare. Hobson was conjecturing that a certain chain of past events had been causally connected to the perceived needs of investors.

study, it is not yet time to shelve theories of imperialism. At the close of the twentieth century, we find ourselves still embroiled in controversies stirred up at its dawning. This is partly because the ideological struggles of that era persist in this one. But it is also because the classic theories of imperialism retain a rare power to carry us up to the mountain top where we seem to see meaningful patterns formed by the incessant to-ings and fro-ings of iniquitous mankind on the plain below. Some have given up the search for patterns conforming to the sketches of the Edwardian theorists because they think they have been conclusively proved to be mirages. This is not so. Locating the theories in their original provenance helps to clear up longstanding confusions. Distinguishing what the theories had to say about empire-building from what they had to say about the expansion of capitalism and the unexpected appearance of ferocious military rivalries among nation states at the end of the nineteenth century heightens our appreciation of their insights. Separating into distinct categories their comments on past, present and future events gives us a better measure of the progress we have made in testing them against the historical record.

Index

Index

Index

Index